Homo Novus

A Brief His-story of Tomorrow

HOMO NOVUS
A BRIEF HIS-STORY OF TOMORROW
Amakiri Welekwe

Forerunner
Press

Homo Novus

Copyright © 2023 by Amakiri Welekwe
This first edition is published in Nigeria by Forerunner Press
Printed in the United States of America for worldwide distribution

Hardback Edition © 2023: ISBN 978-978-798-797-1
Paperback Edition © 2023: ISBN 978-978-798-796-4
ePub Edition © 2023: ISBN 978-978-798-798-8
Kindle Edition © 2023: ISBN 978-978-798-799-5

Any internet addresses (websites, blogs, etc.) in this book are offered as part of bibliographic citations. They are not intended in any way to be or imply an endorsement by the author, nor does the author vouch for the content of these sites for the life of this book.

All Scripture quotations, unless otherwise indicated, are taken from the Holy Bible, New Living Translation (NLT), copyright © 1996, 2004, 2015 by Tyndale House Foundation. Used by permission of Tyndale House Publishers, Inc., Carol Stream, Illinois 60188. All rights reserved.

Scripture quotations marked AMPC are taken from the Amplified® Bible. Copyright © 1954, 1958, 1962, 1964, 1965, 1987 by The Lockman Foundation. Used by permission.

Scripture quotations marked AMP are taken from the Amplified® Bible. Copyright © 2015, by The Lockman Foundation. Used by permission.

Scripture quotations marked CSB are taken from the Christian Standard Bible. Copyright © 2017 by Holman Bible Publishers. Used by permission.

Scripture quotations marked ERV are taken from the Easy-to-Read Version. Copyright © 2006 by Bible League International. Used by permission.

Scripture quotations marked GNT are taken from the Good New Translation in Today's English Version—Second Edition. Copyright 1992 American Bible Society. Used by permission.

Scripture quotations marked MSG are taken from the Message. Copyright © 1993, 2002, 2018 by Eugene H. Peterson. Used by permission of NavPress. All rights reserved. Represented by Tyndale House Publishers, a division of Tyndale House Ministries.

Scripture quotations marked NKJV are taken from the New King James Version®. Copyright © 1982 by Thomas Nelson. Used by permission. All rights reserved.

Scripture quotations marked KJV are taken from the King James Version. Public domain.

Please note that the name satan and related names are deliberately not capitalized in this book.

Cover design: Colibrian
Interior design: Spiro Books
Author headshot: Photoville Studios

DEDICATION

To the Homo novus species—all loyal citizens of God's kingdom—in the hope that it will inspire them to remain steadfast in their faith even in the face of hostile technology and severe persecution until the very end.

CONTENTS

INTRODUCTION

As one who has spent many years in the information technology sector, I am personally amazed at the rapid developments taking place within the industry, and the significant impact it has had on the world. I still remember sitting in my office in Victoria Island, Lagos, Nigeria, way back in July 2005, and reading on the Internet about the purchase of a seemingly unknown startup called Android by Google. Today, Android and smartphones have become an integral part of our daily lives. Also during this period, one of the earliest social networking sites called MySpace, was purchased by News Corporation. And while I was still trying to figure out MySpace and others like Hi5, Facebook came on the scene!

Today social networking sites have become an indispensable part of life. The same applies to technologies such as cloud computing and many others. How the world got comfortable with the idea of cloud computing to the point of giving over control of personal and corporate data to someone else is still a shocker to me. I still stand amazed as the Digital Revolution with its advances in artificial intelligence is threatening to take over control of human power and our personal freedoms. What is even frightening is that whole generations are oblivious to the sweeping changes happening in society as they blissfully tap away at their smartphones.

Humanity is at a crossroads. We are at a critical moment in history and this book addresses that. The decisions we make both individually and collectively will have a far reaching impact on our future and the future of our species as a whole. If you have lived long enough in this world, you would know that something isn't quite right here. You know it deep in your heart. What you know you can't really explain; but you feel it. This feeling has probably been with you for as long as you can remember, like a bothersome noise in your head that won't go away. It's possible that this feeling and the desire for answers have led you to this book. My mission is to assist you in uncovering the truth.

I'm sure you'll agree that the most glaring trend in recent years is globalization. Nations have become increasingly interdependent and interconnected—which is not a bad thing in itself. However, with globalization, do you get that stifling sense of being watched and controlled by unseen hands that seem to govern your choices, your privacy and mobility? As you watch the news on TV, do you have a looming sense of dread? Climate change and the potential for catastrophic environmental damage, the threat of nuclear war, the fear of alien invasion, the possibility of an asteroid colliding with earth—you name it—are upon us every day. The uncontrolled proliferation of new technologies, the risk of artificial intelligence becoming dominant, and the specter of human extinction all hang like a dark cloud over us. The prevailing narrative is one of anxiety about the direction we are heading. And so we comfort ourselves with the Sports channel, social media, and other mindless entertainment.

Many scholars and historians have presented a range of theories regarding the trajectory of history and its potential outcomes. The first is the cyclical viewpoint. It sees history as a series of repeating cycles, rather than a linear progression, marked by recurring patterns of growth, decline, and rebirth. The second is the sinusoidal viewpoint. It sees history as sinusoidal, a series of ups and downs like a sine wave pattern. Whether it will culminate in a "happy" or "sad" ending is anyone's guess. The third viewpoint is of human decline. The underlying assumption is that our species is inherently flawed and prone to corruption with little hope of long-term improvement. It views the human race as continuously moving down an escalator that may be slowed but cannot be stopped. This suggests that the world will deteriorate until existence is no longer sustainable. The fourth is the human progress viewpoint. This view emphasizes the belief that the world is getting better and better and will continue to get better. Proponents of this view are confident that through reason, scientific knowledge, and technological innovation, humanity can achieve greater levels of prosperity, freedom, and happiness. In other words, the human race is on an ascending escalator towards the state of bliss. This is the dominant 21st century view.

And, finally, there's the theistic viewpoint. This perspective interprets history as a story with a divine purpose or plan. It holds that God is actively involved in human affairs, shaping the course of history according to His divine plan and directing it towards a beautiful ending. The theistic viewpoint sees history as a progression towards the ultimate fulfillment of God's purpose, with the ultimate goal being the establishment of a perfect Kingdom of God on earth. From this perspective, the events of history are seen as part of a larger narrative that leads to a final resolution of all things in accordance with God's will. It combines the human decline and human progress viewpoint in a way that paints a picture of a world that is steadily getting worse; then suddenly (because of divine intervention) changes to be better than it has ever been—and stays that way forever. This view has been prevalent throughout history and remains a powerful motivator for uncovering the truth.

A few years ago, while reading Gates Notes—a blog maintained by Bill Gates, I came across a book titled *Sapiens: A Brief History of Humankind* and another title *Homo Deus: A Brief History of Tomorrow*. The books were written by an Israeli scholar named

Yuval Noah Harari. The book's positive reviews from Bill Gates and Barack Obama caught my eye, so I grabbed a copy and decided to read them. The first book, *Sapiens*, explores the past and tries to explain how our species came to dominate the earth. The second, *Homo Deus*, was even more intriguing. It explores the future of humanity and paints a vivid picture of where history is headed and the nightmares that come along with it. According to Harari, the new human agenda is the pursuit of bliss, immortality, and divinity. He argues that, as technology continues to advance, it will fundamentally alter our understanding of what it means to be human. We are, in fact, on the verge of the next stage of evolution characterized by the creation of a godlike human species in which the traditional categories of "human" and "God" may be obsolete.

It was obvious that Harari's view of history was anchored on the human progress viewpoint (but with an unusual mix of utopia and dystopia). No doubt the book was a masterpiece. He was spot on in his analysis about the development of new technologies that could potentially challenge our understanding of what it means to be human. But his naturalistic and atheistic worldview had a significant influence on his interpretation of where history is headed and the future of our species. He writes and sounds like a harbinger who foretells the coming of somebody or something. He says he is not a prophet and that his book is not prophetic; yet he writes and sounds like a prophet—albeit a false one, for his words betray him. His persuasive rhetoric ultimately reveals where his true loyalty lies. His obvious rejection and open mockery of God, and his view of history that completely disregards God raises eyebrows. All this came through the subtle tinge of deception and seductive falsehood in some of his assertions, predictions and conclusions about our species and its future.

It was at that point that I had an overwhelming compulsion to offer an alternative perspective into what is going on. So I set out on a project to write this book. I had one singular motive in mind: to help humanity see history from a completely different perspective—God's own perspective, the theistic view of history—and to invite them to partner with God and be part of what He is doing in history. Although I have a keen interest in history, I am no historian or scholar like Harari, neither am I a religious leader. I am just an ordinary man. But I understood the assignment and was well equipped for the task. I knew it wasn't going to be easy, but God's investment in my life over the years prepared me well enough for the task ahead.

I can still clearly remember a dream I had during my last year as an undergraduate. An angel visited me and conveyed a message from the Lord, stating "I will make you a harbinger …" This was followed by similar encounters over the years. Throughout my journey, I have been equipped by God for this assignment through His word and the work of the Holy Spirit in my life as a believer, Bible teacher, and evangelist. Although this is my first attempt at writing a book, I am certainly not new to writing. I frequently write articles at the intersection of technology and people. Having spent all my working life in the information technology sector, I am also fully aware of ongoing developments in the technology industry and its implications for our species.

So here is *Homo Novus: A Brief His-story of Tomorrow*. What you hold in your hands has the potential to not just impact your understanding of history, but to also transform your life. The book takes a look at history from God's perspective for your consideration, so as to empower you to make a more informed choice. It explores the past and tries to explain how our species came to dominate the earth. It also projects into the future and explores how it will all pan out in the end. It attempts to answer some important life questions such as who we are, why we are here, why the world is in such a mess, where history is headed, and the role of technology in all of it. In my propositions, I make it clear that the future of humanity is not in Harari's Homo deus. It is in God's Homo novus.[1]

The book is divided into three Parts. The first Part explores the origin story of the cosmos and humanity, and how God appointed humans as His chosen partners to rule over the world in His name, and advance His will for the entirety of creation. The second Part explores how humanity fails woefully in fulfilling this task. It examines the tread of civilization as humans choose to forge their own path, often with tragic outcomes, and how God provides a means of rescuing us from our failures and their outcomes. It also deals extensively on the subject of free will. In the third and final Part, the focus shifts to the potential risk of the extinction of our species and the emergence of a new human species that will replace the current one and become dominant. It further investigates the supremacy of God over earthly kingdoms and dominant global powers, as well as His mission to replace them with His Own Kingdom. This leads to a conflict. A conflict between the forces of good versus the forces of evil through their various actors and agents. This is a battle that is being waged on all fronts: political, economic, religious, and powered by our current digital technology. It is now at our doorsteps. Who will win this battle and what will be our stance as we watch the opposing forces gain ground? Will God's redemptive endeavor culminate in humanity's renewal of partnership with God, and the eventual fulfillment of God's will for the whole creation?

I appreciate that not all of my viewpoints may align with yours, but please bear with me. My allegiance is solely to God and His truth, not to any specific religious denomination. I've done my best to conduct thorough research and present a logical and factual set of arguments based on the Word of God. While I do not profess to have all the answers, I do possess sufficient wisdom to offer many sound answers grounded on the Word. And, although some of the insights I share may initially seem like impossible fiction, I encourage you to approach them with an open mind and pray for understanding from God. If you truly find anything that is contradictory to the Word, I urge you to follow the Word of God instead.

So here we are at the most crucial moment in history. God is once again opening our eyes to what is coming so that we can be prepared to stand firm, resist evil, and endure the persecution that comes with it. History doesn't just tell us something about the past; it also points to the future. We cannot change the past, but history helps us avoid costly mistakes and change our path for our tomorrow. I sincerely hope that my effort will aid you in comprehending history from God's lens and enable you to partner with Him in carrying out His will for all of creation. So, without delay, I urge you to delve into its pages and uncover the truth for yourself. May the truth make us all free!

PART I

HUMANITY PARTNERS WITH GOD

Where did the universe and humans come from?
Who or what brought them into existence and why?
What does it mean to be human?

CHAPTER ONE

IN THE BEGINNING

Where did the universe come from? Who or what brought it into existence? And most importantly, why does it exist? These are important questions but certainly not easy to answer. Throughout history, countless myths together with scientific hypotheses and theories have attempted to explain the origin of the universe. Virtually every culture or nationality across the world has one narrative or the other about how the universe began and how humans first came to inhabit it.

In the ancient world, for example, the Mesopotamian creation story (popular among Sumerians and Babylonians) claims that the heavens and the earth (including humans) were created from the remains of a dead god. As it goes in the *Enuma Elish* epic, a god named Marduk created the heavens (skies) and the earth from the remains of another god named Tiamat, whom he killed in battle.[1] The newly created heavens and the earth became the new home of Marduk. Following his great victory and work of creation, Marduk consults with another god named Enki (the god of wisdom) and decides to create human beings from the blood of the remains of another god named Quingu, who was also killed in battle. The first man created was named Lullu, and he was to be a helper to the gods in their eternal task of maintaining order and keeping chaos at bay.

The ancient Egyptian creation myth, on the other hand, had several versions of how the world unfolded out of darkness and raging chaos. Different myths attributed the creation to different gods. One of the popular versions claims that the world was created by a god named Atum and his two offspring, Shu and Tefnut.[2] Their union, in turn, gave birth to Geb (the earth) and Nut (the skies or heavens). The earth was seen as a sacred landscape and provided the first solid dry land for the sun god, Ra, to rest. Despite the numerous versions of the Egyptian creation myth, there is one view they all held in common: that the world had arisen out of an infinite expanse of chaotic darkness and purposeless waters, named Nu.

Today, the Big History Project (now OER Project) spearheaded by historian David Christian and Bill Gates has captured modern global thinking about the origin of the universe based on their naturalistic Darwinian worldview. The project articulates a unified history of the cosmos, earth, life and humanity, which it makes freely available to educational institutions around the world for the global teaching of this origin viewpoint.

FOUR ORIGIN THEORIES

So what do we make of all the numerous origin stories out there from ancient times to the modern era? If all of humanity shared a unified origin story of the cosmos, what would it be? Let me put to you four widely held explanations of the origin of the universe:

Steady-state theory

The first explanation says that the universe has no beginning and perhaps no end, that it has always been there and will always be there. But it does not tell us why it is there. This "no beginning" and "no end" view of the universe is based on what scientists call the "steady-state theory." According to this view, there was never a time when matter did not exist. This was a widely held view among ancient Greek philosophers and some 20th century intellectuals such as Thomas Gold and Hermann Bondi. For example, Aristotle, among the prominent Greek philosophers, believed the universe had existed forever.

In their landmark studies, Gold and Bondi stated that despite the expansion of the universe, its appearance remains constant and unchanged over time, and that it has no beginning and no end.[3] The famous British astronomer, Fred Hoyle, also subscribed to this view, and found the idea that the universe had a beginning to be pseudoscientific and motivated by arguments for a creator. The argument about whether or not the universe had a beginning persisted right up to the end of the 20th century and early 21st century. But evidence from modern scientific research makes it an increasingly difficult position to defend.

Holographic universe theory
The second explanation is that the universe is a gigantic and wonderfully detailed holographic illusion. Holograms, as you may already know, are three-dimensional images encoded in two-dimensional surfaces. When viewed, the two-dimensional surface appears to have a third dimension, thereby giving the illusion of having depth. The concept of a holographic universe is based on what scientists call the "holographic principle."

According to this theory, matter is not as solid as we would suppose. What we have in reality are energy fields, which are decoded by our brains into a 3D solid picture to give the illusion of a physical world. However, when you tear matter apart, all you find are molecules which are made up of atoms. When you tear atoms apart, all you find are electrons, protons and neutrons, and when you drill further down, all you find are energy fields. So what we refer to as the material world is basically energy fields. This theory does not tell us who made this holographic universe, what brought it into existence, and why it exists. As bizarre as this idea may sound, it has been gaining ground in recent times following advances in quantum physics.

Big Bang theory

The third explanation is that the universe is a product of chance with no definite purpose. In the beginning, there was nothing. And then all of a sudden, from a single point, all the energy in the universe burst forth. It started out as just a single point (gravitational singularity) and expanded (and continues to expand) to get to its present size. The Big Bang theory is the predominant modern scientific explanation of the origin of the universe.

The Big Bang theory acknowledges that the universe had a beginning. It gives details about how and when it was formed. But it leaves several major questions unanswered, one of which is that it does not tell us the original cause of the big bang itself, and why it happened. All it says is that the universe was a result of random, impersonal chance without any purpose. As with any scientific theory, however, more observations and experiments are needed to establish and consolidate its credibility.

There are many on-going efforts to further explore this theory and gain a better understanding of the universe. Some well-funded initiatives are the European Union Large Hadron Collider (LHC) experiment at CERN, and the United States SPHEREx (Spectro-Photometer for the History of the Universe, Epoch of Reionization, and Ices Explorer) NASA space mission.

Intelligent Creator

The fourth explanation is that the universe was created by an "eternal being" possessing an intelligence far greater than the universe itself. That "eternal being" is the person to whom we ascribe the title "God." This idea postulates that the universe was created for a purpose. It tells us who made it, and why it was made. It does not give details about how and when it was created, other than God speaking it into existence. He gave the word and the universe came into being. He not only created the universe, He also controls and sustains all the moving bodies and elements that function within it.

This narrative is documented in an ancient book called Genesis found in the Bible. The Book of Genesis opens with the words: "In the beginning God created the heavens and the earth. The earth was formless and empty, and darkness covered the deep waters. And the Spirit of God was hovering over the surface of the waters" (Genesis 1:1-2). Make no mistake, the word "heavens" in this context isn't referring to some invisible supernatural realm as most people wrongly assume. The word "heavens" comes from the Hebrew word *shamayim* which literally means "skies." It is not something that exists intangibly in the supernatural realm, but rather is a part of the material universe.

Furthermore, the word "earth" in its original context primarily refers to the whole dry land, or the land of the living. The word "earth" comes from the Hebrew word *erets* which literally means "land." So the expression "heaven and earth" encompasses everything God has created from the celestial to the terrestrial realm. The opening sentence in Genesis 1:1 announces in summary fashion that "In the beginning God created the heavens and the earth." This is followed by a description of this event in a "seven-day" sequence starting from Genesis 1:2 down to its completion in Genesis 2:1 where it concludes with the statement "So the creation of the heavens and the earth and everything in them was completed." God made it function for us by bringing out form, fullness, and light out of its formless, empty, and dark state, and making out of it a world full of order and beauty and goodness where life can flourish.

The Genesis narrative stands in complete contrast to other ancient creation stories of the time, such as the Mesopotamian and Egyptian polytheistic narratives we just read about, which ascribes it to their numerous gods. Genesis is in fact an utter refutation of the then prevailing ancient origin stories of the universe. It also stands in complete contrast with our modern conception of the origin of the universe which completely takes the Creator out of the equation.

Underlying the Genesis account is the rather bold denial that the universe was either a product of the creative ingenuity of the gods of the then leading superpowers—Babylon and Egypt, or the product of chance as put forward by the intelligentsia of today's leading superpowers. It simply asserts that God Almighty did it. One important take-away from the Genesis narrative is that it shows us the universe did have a beginning, something that virtually everyone in the science community has come round to agreeing with. But it took science a long time to arrive at this point. Long before Aristotle, Fred Hoyle, Thomas Gold, and other proponents of the steady-state theory and Big Bang theory existed, Genesis showed us that this well-organized universe had a beginning.

The Genesis narrative has generated a lot of controversy and skepticism among scientific minds. Its credibility has been called into question especially among modern readers who due to their faith in scientific theories naturally dismiss it as ancient mythology or fairy tales. So in light of the numerous origin stories out there, which one do we regard as the most credible? What is the true origin story of the universe? On what ground can one claim that this being we call God is the creator? In short, is the Genesis narrative a product of human imagination or divine inspiration?

Well, suppose you were exploring outer space with four friends, and you stumbled upon a well-planned beautiful mini planet with a magnificent palace and a courtyard in its center.[4] Each of your friends offers an explanation for its existence. The first one says "It has always been there." "There was never a time it was not there." The second one says, "It doesn't really exist, it's only a holographic illusion"—even after he has seen and touched the concrete walls. The third one says, "It put itself there by a remarkable process of chance." Lastly, the fourth one who happens to be a veteran space explorer says, "It was built by a famous king. The palace and courtyard were designed to be the official residence and workplace of the king and his regents—I know because I had a chance to meet him myself." Which of those explanations would you find the most plausible?

THE TRUE ORIGIN STORY OF THE COSMOS

Can I propose that the Genesis creation narrative is the true origin story of the cosmos? As you will later find out as you read this book, this origin story which was once shared by humanity got corrupted or lost at some point as various ancient nations sought to ascribe it to their gods in order to elevate them above the others. And that explains the apparent similarity between the Genesis creation story and all the other ancient Middle Eastern creation stories, particularly the Babylonian and Egyptian versions.

The Genesis account of the origin of the universe is one that was inspired by God Himself through chosen human communicators. The authority of the text which guarantees its credibility comes directly from the Creator God, bestowed on these writers who acted as His agents.[5] God has revealed Himself through those texts, and the texts represent His authority. As noted by the professor of the Old Testament, John Walton, these writers are our access to God's authority.

But how do we know the Genesis account was truly inspired by God? We know this because no human observer was present during the creation of the world. Therefore, the author could not have composed the creation account without inspiration from the one who was there when it all began—the one directly responsible for it. The result of the divine inspiration of scripture is that it remains forever infallible. The Creator Himself, who holds the entire universe in balance, had His hand on the writing in such a way that we can accept the entire account as trustworthy.

But, even if there were no God-inspired Genesis accounts to reference, God did not leave Himself without a witness. The reality and glory of the invisible God is plain enough in the visible world. Just open your eyes: take a look at the wonders of nature in the world, and gaze into the heavens, and you will see it. The universe abounds with more than enough evidence to support the existence of an infinitely intelligent mastermind behind it. "The heavens proclaim the glory of God. The skies display his craftsmanship. Day after day they continue to speak; night after night they make Him known. They speak without a sound or word; their voice is never heard. Yet their message has gone throughout the earth, and their words to all the world," declares Psalm 19:1-4.

The mind-blowing awesomeness of the observable universe and its unfathomable expanse is enough to convince any fair inquirer. None can match the impressive beauty and splendor of one starry night. Experts generally agree that the actual size of the entire universe is unknown, and might be infinite in extent, but astronomers estimate the observable universe to be approximately 93 billion light-years in diameter.[6] They also estimate that there could be anywhere from 100 to 400 billion stars in our own galaxy—the Milky Way galaxy.[7] And most of those stars are bigger than the Earth. If you travel at the speed of light, which of course is impossible, it will take you roughly 4.24 light years to get to the nearest star.[8] That is an incredibly large distance. But that's just in the Milky Way galaxy—our own backyard in space. Data from NASA's New Horizons space probe reveals an estimated 200 billion or more galaxies in the observable universe.[9] Indeed, the constellations declare the glory of God and His handiwork, and give us a clear testimony of God's existence. By taking a thoughtful look at the universe, you will be able to see what your eyes as such can't see: the infinite intelligence and power of its Architect and Maker.

But how can you be sure that the conclusion you arrive at by taking a thoughtful look at the universe corresponds to reality and is not merely a figment of your imagination? Well, that is why you have a two-witness testimony: nature (God's world) and scripture (God's word), so that you can use the one to validate the other. God has revealed the truth about Himself in scriptures as much as He has in nature, so that no one will be left in doubt. This is a double advantage. The only reason you don't see Him is because your inner world might be clouded with things that prevent clear perception. When you get your inner world—your mind and heart—recalibrated, you will see God in the external world. Genesis gives us a clear picture of the nature and attributes of this creator God. So what does the picture tell us?

Firstly, it tells us that God is an eternal being who has always been there—He is the timeless one. He alone is eternal. There has never been a time when God was not. He existed before anything else came into being. He was, He is, and He will always be. He is the God always. Occasionally, questions such as "who created God?" arise. I recall my six-year-old son asking me this very question a while back. And I simply told him that God is not a created being like us, and that He has always been there. He found it difficult to comprehend. Indeed, it can be difficult for our finite minds to comprehend an infinite God. The finite cannot contain the infinite. Only an infinite mind, one that is imbued with the Spirit of God, can comprehend every aspect of infinite reality. So questions about who created God are pointless because they wrongly assume that God is a created being.

Secondly, God is a good and perfect God. God's goodness is not just what He does: it's who He is. He embodies the very essence of benevolence. Because God is perfectly good, everything He does is bound to be good and right. From the creation story in Genesis 1 and 2 alone, we can clearly see God's goodness in action. After each day of creation, He said that it was good. God's goodness sets the standard for all goodness. He alone defines what is good and what is not good. There is no reason to look elsewhere. He is the ultimate moral authority. The God who created heaven and earth is just, dependable, trustworthy, generous, compassionate, merciful, and filled with unfailing love and faithfulness. He is simply in a class by Himself. God created the world to reflect and display His good nature. And, in its original design, creation measured up to God's standard of goodness.

Thirdly, God is all-powerful. He is the omnipotent one. God's ability to speak things into being by His word is a clear demonstration of His omnipotence. Being all-powerful doesn't mean that He does whatever He fancies (like some ruling despot), but it does mean that He can do anything He sees fit to do. In other words, despite being infinitely powerful and able to do anything He sees fit to do, He is never corrupted by it.

Fourthly, God is all-knowing. He is the omniscient God. He knows all the science that is not yet known. He knows all hidden thoughts and secret things. He knows the past, the present, and the future. But His foreknowledge of evil does not necessarily mean that He predestined it. Predestination and foreknowledge are two separate things. All that foreknowledge guarantees are that something is foreknown. Unlike others, God does not use His foreknowledge of the future to manipulate and control; rather, He uses it for good.

Lastly, God is everywhere. He is the omnipresent God. He has the ability to be present everywhere at the same time. There is no place that isn't visible to God's all-seeing eye. He can dwell in the midst of an entire nation or in the heart of an individual, and cannot be limited to any one locality. Neither is He tied to a space-time continuum. He is simply unbounded and ubiquitous. His presence fills creation.

Since God is eternal, perfect in goodness, all-powerful, all-knowing, and everywhere, it is only right to acknowledge our limitations and say, "God, I may not understand all things, but I trust You, and I submit to Your infinite power and wisdom." When you accept the truth that God exists and is responsible for creating the universe and all life, new possibilities open up as a result of that trust. This implies that there would be no space in your life for worldviews such as atheism, agnosticism, polytheism, deism, animism, existentialism, humanism, and others.

Now, let us examine some of the claims of the Book of Genesis in relation to the origin of the universe:

> In the beginning God created the heavens and the earth.
>
> Now the earth was formless and empty, darkness covered the surface of the watery depths, and the Spirit of God was hovering over the surface of the waters. Then God said, "Let there be light," and there was light. God saw that the light *was good*, and God separated the light from the darkness. God called the light "day," and the darkness he called "night." There was an evening, and there was a morning: one day.
>
> Then God said, "Let there be an expanse between the waters, separating water from water." So God made the expanse and separated the water under the expanse from the water above the expanse. And it was so. God called the expanse "sky." Evening came and then morning: the second day.
>
> Then God said, "Let the water under the sky be gathered into one place, and let the dry land appear." And it was so. God called the dry land "earth," and the gathering of the water he called "seas." And God saw that it *was good*. Then God said, "Let the earth produce vegetation: seed-bearing plants and fruit trees on the earth bearing fruit with seed in it according to their kinds." And it was so. The earth produced vegetation: seed-bearing plants according to their kinds and trees bearing fruit with seed in it according to their kinds. And God saw that it *was good*. Evening came and then morning: the third day.
>
> Then God said, "Let there be lights in the expanse of the sky to separate the day from the night. They will serve as signs for seasons[c] and for days and years. They will be lights in the expanse of the sky

to provide light on the earth.» And it was so. God made the two great lights—the greater light to rule over the day and the lesser light to rule over the night—as well as the stars. God placed them in the expanse of the sky to provide light on the earth, to rule the day and the night, and to separate light from darkness. And God saw that it *was good*. Evening came and then morning: the fourth day.

Then God said, "Let the water swarm with living creatures, and let birds fly above the earth across the expanse of the sky." So God created the large sea-creatures and every living creature that moves and swarms in the water, according to their kinds. He also created every winged creature according to its kind. And God saw that it *was good*. God blessed them: "Be fruitful, multiply, and fill the waters of the seas, and let the birds multiply on the earth." Evening came and then morning: the fifth day.

Then God said, "Let the earth produce living creatures according to their kinds: livestock, creatures that crawl, and the wildlife of the earth according to their kinds." And it was so. So God made the wildlife of the earth according to their kinds, the livestock according to their kinds, and all the creatures that crawl on the ground according to their kinds. And God saw that it *was good*.

Then God said, "Let us make man in our image, according to our likeness. They will rule the fish of the sea, the birds of the sky, the livestock, the whole earth, and the creatures that crawl on the earth."

So God created man in his own image; he created him in the image of God; he created them male and female.

God blessed them, and God said to them, "Be fruitful, multiply, fill the earth, and subdue it. Rule the fish of the sea, the birds of the sky, and every creature that crawls on the earth." God also said, "Look, I have given you every seed-bearing plant on the surface of the entire earth and every tree

whose fruit contains seed. This will be food for
you, for all the wildlife of the earth, for every bird
of the sky, and for every creature that crawls on the
earth—everything having the breath of life in it—I
have given every green plant for food." And it was
so. God saw all that he had made, and it *was very
good* indeed. Evening came and then morning: the
sixth day.

So the heavens and the earth and everything in
them were completed. On the seventh day God had
completed his work that he had done, and he rested
on the seventh day from all his work that he had
done. God blessed the seventh day and declared it
holy, for on it he rested from all his work of creation
(Genesis 1:1-31; 2:1-3 CSB, emphasis added).

So according to the above text, God within a period of six
days creates a beautiful and well-ordered world out of nothing
but the word of His mouth. We will see in a bit how He forms
man differently because he is unique. But for now let's focus
on the universe. So, on the seventh day, He stops working. He
rests. To a modern reader armed with advanced knowledge of
the structure of the cosmos, this origin account may be a difficult
and confusing concept to grasp. But asking the right kind of
questions may help us unravel the confusion.

First off, what did the author of Genesis, in his own ancient
cultural context, mean by describing the origins of the universe
in a seven-day sequence? How did the very first set of readers
of the seven-day creation story of Genesis understand this
narrative?

As John Walton explains, the initial audience of this narrative
would not have engaged in a discussion about whether the story
was literal or symbolic. Rather, they would have readily recognized that the story of the seven-day creation served as the inauguration of the world as God's cosmic temple or place of hab-
itation (Leviticus 8:33; 1 Kings 8:65).[10] Now, on the surface, that

may not seem obvious. The Genesis text doesn't use the term "cosmic temple," and it doesn't explicitly say creation is God's dwelling place. Yes, it didn't explicitly say it; but the whole story shows it. And if we look deep below the surface by reading the text in the context of the entire Old Testament scriptures as well as in the cultural context of the original readers, we can uncover the deeper meaning of the text, which becomes unmistakably evident and as clear as day.

When we put all that together, the conclusion is pretty hard to miss. It presents God's creation of the world as the building of a temple where God can dwell. The assertion that "God rested on the seventh day" provides ample confirmation. An ancient reader would immediately recognize it as the inauguration of a temple where God rests or settles in to rule. But it is not just God's dwelling place; it is also to be the dwelling place of a special kind of being called humans that God wants to dwell with. And that leads us to the origin story of humans.

ORIGIN STORY OF HUMANS

We have established that God created the world, especially earth as His cosmic home, and made it a place where life can flourish. All this was in preparation for the arrival of a special kind of being—distinct from animal life—called "human being." As soon as God got everything ready, this "special being" appeared on the scene. Now wait a minute, "appeared on the scene" from where? Where did humans come from?

There is certainly more controversy today over the origin of humans than there is over the origin of the universe. There are competing worldviews about *how* humans came into existence. Some argue that humans are simply a product of random permutations of mindless matter without any ultimate significance, while others are of the view that humans are a product of an intelligent mind with an ultimate purpose.

In his book, *On the Origin of Species* published in 1859, Charles Darwin presented the scientific theory that animal populations evolve over the course of generations through a process he called natural selection—generally termed the theory of evolution. Today, Darwin's theory of evolution has become the predominant scientific theory of the origin of humans and also the unifying theory of the life sciences. The popular Israeli historian, Yuval Harari, upholds this view when he says, "Like it or not, we are members of a large and particularly noisy family called the great apes. Our closest living relatives include chimpanzees, gorillas and orangutans. The chimpanzees are the closest. Just 6 million years ago, a single female ape had two daughters. One became the ancestor of all chimpanzees; the other is our own grandmother."[11] You may have seen (in books or on the internet) one of the numerous versions the famous but fallacious "March of Progress" image, which depicts ape-like creatures gradually evolving into an upright human form.

So what do we make of Darwin's revolutionary findings in light of the Genesis account? Has it rendered the scriptures obsolete? Did we really descend from apes?

Well, first and foremost, let me make it clear that science and scripture address different sorts of questions. Science is more focused on unraveling the process (the how) that brought life into existence, while scripture is more focused on unraveling the purpose (the why) of life. God has revealed Himself in both nature and scripture. God's revelation in nature is not something anyone should overlook. It needs to be considered alongside His revelation in scripture, and science is the tool that helps us make the wonderful discoveries in nature. We don't have to compromise our intellectual integrity in order to maintain a belief in God and His revelation in scriptures. But just as it is important that we face the findings of science with an open mind, it is equally important that we learn to recognize when a naturalistic worldview is masquerading as science.

The Genesis creation account presents us with a clear description of human origin: humanity is simply an invention of God. God made a deliberate personal decision to create humans in His own image; and He put them in charge of all other animals. But humans are not the only beings that God created. God also created "supernatural beings" to serve His purposes. They are what most people usually refer to as angelic beings. They are far superior to humans in terms of intelligence, beauty and power. But God made humans to be in charge of the physical world. This is the Genesis account of human origin:

> Then God said, "Let us make human beings in our image, to be like us. They will reign over the fish in the sea, the birds in the sky, the livestock, all the wild animals on the earth, and the small animals that scurry along the ground." So God created human beings in his own image. In the image of God, he created them; male and female he created them (Genesis 1:26-27).

> Then the Lord God formed the man from the dust of the ground. He breathed the breath of life into the man's nostrils, and the man became a living person (Genesis 2:7).

From our knowledge of science, we know that human beings and other animals are made of similar materials (chemical elements from the earth), but there is something about the creation of humans that makes them different from other animals. The Genesis account doesn't say that God commanded the ground to bring forth humans as He did with plants and animals. It also doesn't say that God took an existing animal such as ape and made human beings out of it. According to Genesis, God took the dust of the earth and made human beings directly from it. But that's not all. God breathed into his nostrils the breath of life; and the man became a living being. Man did not become a living being until he received the breath of life from God. God breathes life into humanity in a way that distinguishes us from animals.

Genesis describes this breath-giving act by God only in relation to humans.

The characteristic Hebrew word used to describe God's activity in the creation of humans is the word *bara* and *yatsar*. The word *bara* is often used in contexts involving God or a deity, either as the explicit or implied subject. The term conveys the idea of bringing something into existence from nothing or creating it. On the other hand, *yatsar* is often used in contexts where a potter is crafting a vessel from clay. The term conveys the idea of fashioning or molding something into a specific form. God breathes His own life force or spirit into the "earthen vessel," and it becomes what is described in Hebrew language as *nephesh*, which means "a living breathing physical being." This is often translated as a "living soul" in English. "Soul" in this context refers to the whole human as a living physical organism. Man is a living breathing being because he has access to God's life through the spirit or breath of God in him.

While the scripture distinguishes between body and spirit, the idea of dualism, which sees body and soul as two separate parts of the person, is a Greek idea that has no root in the Genesis creation narrative. In the Genesis creation narrative, a soul is not something you have. It is not something distinct from the body. It is a living breathing body. God did not put a soul into the body of clay that He had made; rather the clay became a living soul. God's idea of life is one that is lived in the material world as a living breathing being—fully energized and animated by the spirit of God. Anything outside this falls short of the ideal.

Now, there are those who claim that their rationality led them to the conclusion that they came into existence through a natural, mindless, unguided process. But do they realize that this very thinking undermines the foundations and reliability of the very rationality they claim to have used in arriving at that conclusion. In the words of John Lennox, the Oxford Emeritus Professor of Mathematics, "Either human intelligence ultimately owes its origin to mindless matter or there is a creator. It is strange that some people claim that it is their intelligence that leads them to prefer the first to the second."[12] Genesis clearly points us in the direction of the second.

We all know that behind every intelligent computer we use and trust today, is an intelligent human mastermind. Now, imagine for a second "if that computer was the end product of mindless unguided processes, would you trust it?"[13] Or put differently, imagine if the airplane you are about to board was the end product of mindless unguided processes; would you trust your life with it?

The Bible doesn't give us the full scientific details of how human beings originated. What is important for us to know is that God made a deliberate personal decision to create humans, and He did it with a purpose and vision in mind.

GOD'S VISION FOR THE COSMOS AND HUMANITY

After reading the first chapter of Genesis, you immediately get the impression that the sequence of events was leading to something. What was it leading to?

Firstly, on the sixth day, God creates a certain kind of being which we've come to know as humans. They alone are said to exclusively bear the image of creator God. God created all the beautiful things in preparation for the arrival of this wonderful being. They represent the pinnacle of God's creation to the extent that God even prepared their home and made provision for their sustenance long before they arrived. It's similar to how an expectant mother prepares for the arrival of her baby. She goes shopping, buys befitting clothes, makes a comfy bed and sets the home ready for the arrival of the baby. God prepared this world for us, to be our home. In fact, it's actually His home, not ours. He's made it accommodating to us because He wants to be here in a relationship with us, so that where we are, there He will also be. Or rather, where He is, there we will also be.

Indeed, any careful observer of the planet Earth would be led to rightly conclude that it was intentionally designed to be accommodating to human life. Do you remember that popular children's story *Goldilocks and the Three Bears*? A young girl named Goldilocks tastes three different bowls of porridge and finds she prefers porridge that is neither too hot nor too cold, but has just the right temperature. Like Goldilocks' preferred porridge, the universe appears to be "just right" for life. Light had to be separated from darkness, dry land from the ocean, visible lights in the sky, plants for food—in order for life to flourish.

But that's not all. Modern science has observed that certain physical parameters of the universe such as gravity and electromagnetism seem perfectly fine-tuned for life to exist, so that if any of them were only slightly different, the universe would not likely be conducive to life. In his book *A Brief History of Time*, renowned physicist Stephen Hawking noted that "The laws of science, as we know them at present, contain many fundamental numbers, like the size of the electric charge of the electron and the ratio of the masses of the proton and the electron. The remarkable fact is that the values of these numbers seem to have been very finely adjusted to make possible the development of life."[14]

In the core of the Sun, for example, hydrogen is constantly being converted into helium at inconceivable temperatures in a process called nuclear fusion. But somebody set the "thermostat" to regulate the heat of the sun that gets to the earth, so that our little planet in space never gets too hot or too cold. It stays at just the right temperature range to sustain life as we know it on this planet. A very narrow range of temperature does all the magic. If it got much hotter for much longer, the whole planet would become an arid desert, too hot and dry to support life. If it got much colder for much longer, the whole planet would become a frozen arctic, too cold to support life. It doesn't do either one or the other; it just stays at the right temperature to sustain life. Who else could have set this cosmic thermostat? All these lend credence to the idea that God intentionally designed the universe, and in particular planet earth, as a very special place for life to flourish.

Secondly, on the seventh day, creation is brought to its completion, and God rested. Curiously, the phrase, "There was evening and there was morning," does not appear on day seven. It is like a day with no end. Again, if we put aside our modern notions about the cosmos and ask what the seventh day rest meant to the ancient readers, a whole new understanding opens up. How did the original readers understand the concept of the seventh day rest?

The word "seven" is connected to the idea of fullness or completeness. "Rest" in this context isn't quite the literal dictionary meaning of the word as we know it, as in the sense of vacation or relaxation. God's rest was not a withdrawal from the world and its operations. It was not a leave of absence or a break—an omnipotent God does not get tired (Isaiah 40:28). Rather, it was the point at which **God's presence fills creation** as He takes up His rest and rule. God settled in and took up residence with humanity to begin the business of governance, or running His kingdom. Now God's home or dwelling is now with humanity. He will live with them, and they will be His people. God Himself shall personally be with them and be their God. As the creator, He alone has the absolute right to rule over creation and the universe. And so it is only right for humanity to accept His authority as King, and ally and align with Him.

We see this pattern of "seven" and "rest" on display throughout the Old Testament scripture in a way that is analogous to the Genesis creation narrative. For example, the consecration ceremony of the tabernacle constructed by Moses took a period of seven days. Solomon's temple was also constructed within a period of seven years, and the consecration ceremony, just like the Genesis creation story, took a period of seven days. In both cases, on the seventh day of the consecration ceremony, which is a day of rest (Sabbath day), **the presence of God** filled the completed building, that is to say, God rested or settled in. This is what the Lord Himself says in Isaiah chapter 66:

> Heaven is my throne, and the earth is my footstool.
> Could you build me a temple as good as that?
> Could you build me such a resting place?
> My hands have made both heaven and earth;
> they and everything in them are mine.
> I, the LORD, have spoken! (Isaiah 66:1-2a)

In this text, God reminds a group of religious folks that they are mistaken if they think that His only dwelling place is a temple made by hands. No temple built by human hands is befitting enough to be a place of rest for the almighty God because He has already made something more befitting for Himself—the heavens and the earth. No man-made temple can ever match the majestic grandeur of the universe that God Himself made. "God, who made the world and everything in it, is Lord of heaven and earth and does not live in temples made by human hands" (Acts 17:24 GNT). Little did they know that the so–called temple made for God to dwell in was just a microcosm or miniature version that points to what He intends all of creation to be. The whole creation is His resting place, and from there He directs its affairs.

The skies or heavens are a perfect metaphor for the glory and transcendence of God beyond normal limits or boundaries. The throne of God is an image that conveys God's majesty and glory, but it also conveys powerful regal control and authority. The one who sits on the throne is the one who is in charge because it is the seat of power. Since God sits on the throne, He has complete regal authority and the right to reign and rule. He is the highest authority, and all other authority is subject to Him. God's sovereign control of the heavens is such that it is as if they were His very seat of power, and His sovereign control over the earth is such that it is as if it were merely the place where He rests His feet.

God's desire is to sit in the seat of authority in your life, living and acting through you. He is the only one who can claim the highest place up in the heavens and in your hearts too. Yet, despite being all-powerful, He doesn't force Himself on us. How awesome it is for God to be contained by the heavens, yet living and acting through us as we willingly yield to His rule and authority! In other words, the "seventh day rest" ushers in the Kingdom of God and its blessings. The implication of God's rule is that the land overflows with the goodness of life and provides for all of God's creatures, including humans.

The important point to grasp here is this: it's not so much how we were made or what we are made of as **who** made us and **for what purpose** we are made. Human beings are created by God to fulfill His purpose and vision. We are the very pinnacle of creation, the only creature that bears the image of God, and that makes us very special. We are not just mere animals. We are a special kind of being that stands out among the animal kingdom. The reason is simple: we are made in the image of God. This describes our calling as God's appointed representative rulers on earth. God gave us a special role in the world. We are the caretakers of God's world.

Humanity was created first to relate to God, and secondly to relate to one another and the environment. God's vision for humanity is for us to live in harmony with Him forever, in the material world that He created for us, reflecting His will and character. God wants humanity to live with Him and enjoy His perfect world in that unending "seventh day," sharing in His "rest," which results in abundant life, goodness, peace, joy, order, stability, and much more.

That is God's ultimate vision for humanity, and indeed for the whole cosmos. A perfect picture of the good life— life as it was intended to be, the opposite of which is unrest, chaos, injustice, lack, pain, sadness, suffering, sickness, and death. Science is incapable of deducing or substantiating our divine calling or spiritual dimensions, so there is really no contradiction between science and divine revelation. For some of us, I know all I have said may come as a big shock to us. So, before you proceed to the next section, please take a break and let it all sink in.

SCIENCE AND THE GENESIS NARRATIVE

But in today's world, isn't it science, rather than God, that holds the key to answering life's deepest questions? Haven't new scientific and technological breakthroughs rendered the Genesis narrative out-of-date?

Science, and the technologies it has spawned, has given so much to the world: improved food production; better healthcare; better quality of life, ease of communication and locomotion, etc. Our era is characterized by swift advancements in science and technology, which have the potential to offer solutions to many of the challenges humanity confronts. These developments have been so significant that some individuals question the necessity or relevance of God and belief systems that attempt to clarify the mysteries of our universe and the fundamental principles of existence. For them, science has provided all the answers. Some even go as far as advocating for a complete rejection of the use of the term "cause and effect," simply because they are uncomfortable with the idea that if you trace the chain of cause and effect backward far enough, you would eventually reach an uncaused cause and thereby prove the existence of God. Rather than say "there's a cause or a reason why," they prefer to say "they just obey mathematical equations" or in layman's language "they follow the science."

According to them, since science and God don't go together, you either accept one or the other, but not both. This idea has in recent times been promoted by many scientists and intellectuals. According to John Lennox, the impression being created is that "belief in God is obsolete and belongs to the days when people didn't really understand the universe, and just took the lazy way out and said that 'God did it;'" and that to be an accomplished scientist or intellectual, you have to embrace an atheistic worldview.[15] This is obviously false.

The English chemist Robert Boyle (1627-1691) was an outstanding example of a scientist whose belief in God interacted fundamentally with his science. His faith in God shaped the ways in which he conducted his scientific life; and he strove to demonstrate ways in which science and religion were mutually supportive.[16] Michael Faraday (1791-1867) was another outstanding example of a scientist whose belief in God coexisted with his science. "He conceived his role in the scientific community as a natural extension of his religious values;" and "his science was directed to ascertaining the way God had created the universe."[17]

The same can be said of James Clerk-Maxwell, George Stokes, John Charlton Polkinghorne, and a host of other great scientists. Even the originator of the Big Bang theory, Georges Lemaitre, was himself a Catholic priest. Lemaître viewed his theory as neutral with neither a connection nor a contradiction of his faith in God, and held that science and God were not in conflict.[18] And even today, there are a good number of God believers active in the academic and scientific community. Examples include Owen Gingerich, Fred Brooks, Don Page, Rosalind Picard, Allister McGrath, Hugh Ross, Francis Collins, Ben Carson, John Lennox, among others. The point is that you don't have to embrace atheistic worldviews in order to be a successful scientist or intellectual.

Of course, the Book of Genesis was not written in a scientific language. Imagine if it describes the statement "In the beginning

God created the heavens and the earth" in terms of the general theory of relativity and quantum mechanics with humongous complex mathematical equations like the one below:

$$W = \int_{k<\Lambda} [Dg][DA][D\psi][D\Phi] \exp\left\{ i \int d^4x \sqrt{-g} \left[\frac{m_p^2}{2} R \right. \right.$$

$$\left. \left. -\frac{1}{4} F_{\mu\nu}^a F^{a\mu\nu} + i\bar{\psi}^i \gamma^\mu D_\mu \psi^i + \left(\bar{\psi}_L^i V_{ij} \Phi \psi_R^j + \text{h.c.} \right) - |D_\mu \Phi|^2 - V(\Phi) \right] \right\}$$

quantum mechanics · spacetime · gravity · other forces · matter · Higgs

Figure 1.0 | The core theory equation.[19]

Only a few would be able to understand it even in our modern age. The author had no vocabulary for accurately describing in detail the complex processes that took place during creation, and even if he had, the people of his time would have no appreciation of the complex physics, organic chemistry and thermodynamics involved. Neither would we for that matter. So he described it as simply as he could in their cultural context, hoping to make the story as intelligible as possible to a relatively "nonscientific" audience. God wanted the story of creation to reach everyone irrespective of their background. Besides, we know there is more to heaven and earth than a bunch of mathematical formulae.

Imagine how you would describe the process of building a palace for a king in seven steps in a book intended for laymen. You want to be as clear as possible while avoiding all the detailed complexities involved in building construction in order not to confuse the non-specialist. God chose the home story instead of a building construction (house) story. The home story is God preparing not just a house with nobody living in it but a home for us, functioning for us and God living there with us.[20] God's intent was not to provide detailed scientific processes that took place during creation. Rather He wanted a narrative that gives an orderly account of what took place, who was behind it and why so that everyone can appreciate it irrespective of your culture, level of education, or the era you live in. Science can perhaps fill out the rest of the details for us as new discoveries emerge.

Indeed, both science and scripture don't explain everything—rather they should be viewed as complementary. One should not approach the Book of Genesis as an exhaustive record. It is more interested in *who* was behind the process that brought the universe and life into existence and *why* (the purpose). In fact, the first chapter of Genesis is more about who was behind creation than about creation itself. In just 31 verses, the word "God" appears 35 times.

On the other hand, science is more interested in the process that brought the universe and life into existence, and when it occurred. It asks "when?" and "how?" and will answer these questions empirically. Science excels at describing matter and physical laws but it cannot tell us why this matter exists and why they obey these laws. For instance, science can describe gravity and thermodynamics and how the atmosphere formed, but it cannot say why it all exists. It's also worth noting that scientific views are themselves evolving, given that scientific knowledge is continually expanding. Even the original concept of the Big Bang theory has changed over the years. What science thinks is true today may not be seen to be true tomorrow as new discoveries emerge.

In fact, there's still a huge gap in our scientific knowledge of the universe called the "chasm of ignorance." Scientists generally admit that all of our physics only really describes 5 percent of what we know about the universe. The remaining 95 percent is still a mystery. Often, when scientists speak about the origin of the universe, they do not solely rely on scientific evidence and are not completely certain in their assertions. Instead, they are offering their opinions and philosophical viewpoints. They are not saying this is what we know. They are saying this is what we think, and if they are sincere, they will admit that what they are thinking today is probably not what they were thinking yesterday. And what they are thinking today probably won't be what they will be thinking tomorrow.[21] There's therefore no need to be dogmatic about our scientific views, knowing that they are subject to change.

The only way one can speak authoritatively concerning the origin of the universe is if someone who was there when it happened or the one directly responsible for it makes it known to you. This kind of information is not derived by a process of reasoning but by a process of revelation.[22] God knows every law that is known to scientists. He knows every law that scientists acknowledge as being beyond their knowledge and understanding. He also knows every law that scientists are unaware of— laws that they do not even know of their existence. He knows these laws not because He investigated and discovered them, but because He invented them.[23]

The table below highlights some of the key differences in the approach of science and the Genesis account of creation:

SCIENCE	GENESIS
Answers the question *how* and *when*	Answers the question *who* and *why*
Speaks to the intellect	Speaks to the heart
Appeals to our quest for knowledge	Appeals to our quest for meaning
Fact based	Values based
Changing views	Enduring text

Table 1.0 | Science vs. Genesis

The truth is some scientific evidence agrees with the Genesis narrative. For example, the scientific concept of fine-tuning points to a creator. In genetics, the "Y-Chromosomal Adam" and "Mitochondrial Eve" confirm that all humans do share a single man and single woman as common ancestors. The scientific account of our origins also generally agrees with the order of creation in the Genesis account. The heavens existed before the earth appeared, plant life existed before animal life, creatures existed in the sea and air before they appeared on the land and animal life existed long before humans appeared. Humans happen to be the most recent creature to show up on the planet. Interestingly, we are also the most influential. How late comers like us can be this significant in the context of the universe is something very remarkable. There are also some who view the science of evolution as somewhat compatible with their view of the Genesis account in what is termed "theistic evolution."[24] But even at that, they still acknowledge that God does something special at some point to transform whatever it was into a human made in the image of God.

Notwithstanding all these points of confluence, the theory of evolution isn't merely a scientific theory or an academic exercise. It has far reaching socio-economic and political implications. Some have attempted to extend and apply the idea of natural selection to competition between nation states and human ethnicities even to the point of justifying military aggression, imperialism and totalitarianism. This justifies the withdrawal of government intervention, and unethical business practices, all in the name of natural selection.

In fact, the concept of the survival of the fittest when applied to human beings has arguably caused more suffering than any other idea since the advent of the theory of evolution. How we each understand our origins has a profound effect on how we view and treat mankind as a whole. The table below compares and contrasts the implications of the concept of evolution versus creation.

EVOLUTION	CREATION
Sees the universe as a building construction story	Sees the universe as a home story
The universe is the result of a random, impersonal chance	The universe is the result of a deliberate personal choice
Random pattern without a purpose	Intelligent design with a purpose
Coincidence (everything is by luck and chance)	Providence (God provides for His creation)
Humanity looks up to Mother Nature	Humanity looks up to Father God
Humanity is autonomous	Humanity is under divine authority
Humanity is independent of God	Humanity is dependent on God
Humanity is rising and progressing	Humanity is fallen and retrogressing
Created god is malevolent	Creator God is benevolent
Good and evil defined by humanity	Good and evil defined by God
Rights and wrong are relative	Rights and wrong are absolute standards
Demands and rights	Duty and responsibility
Survival of the fittest (strong)	Salvation for the weak
Might is right	Right is might
Leads to indulgence	Leads to obedience
Leads to war and confrontation	Leads to peace and harmony

Table 2.0 | Evolution vs. Creation[25]

In conclusion, I believe true science ultimately points us in the direction of God, not the opposite. The books of nature and scripture beautifully reveal the intelligence, power, and the glory of God. Yes, there may be conflicting views in certain areas, but certainly not the historical "conflict thesis" put out there (premised largely on two historical episodes involving Galileo and Darwin) that suggests that there is an intrinsic intellectual conflict between belief in God and science. But once you grasp the idea that science and the Bible are addressing different kinds of questions, the so-called conflict naturally dissolves.

The main source of conflict lies in the worldview of those who fund and conduct scientific research and their tendency to impose their viewpoint. As noted by Yuval Harari, most scientific studies are funded by persons or groups of persons in pursuit of a certain ideological, political or economic goal. Their ideology or worldview "influences the scientific agenda and determines what to do with the discoveries."[26] This nuanced worldview of scientists and their sponsors determines the direction of the interpretation of the evidence which science provides. We should be more concerned with the ideological forces that influence and motivate individuals engaged in scientific pursuits and directing them towards a specific path. That is where the real conflict lies. It is therefore imperative that we consciously think through our worldview which we may have unconsciously picked up from society and influences around us, and weed off where necessary any ideas, beliefs and presuppositions that negatively control our response to life's most important questions.

In the next chapter, we will explore what it means to be truly human, and how God's vision for humanity and the whole cosmos unfolds.

CHAPTER TWO

THE DIVINE MANDATE

Who am I? Why am I here? What does it mean to be human? These are important questions that we all ask ourselves at various intervals in our lives. It is stirred by our quest for identity, purpose and meaning. By not knowing the answer to those questions, you or the world around you will keep inventing new identities of yourself, leading you farther and farther away from your true self. Most people have at some point in their lives experienced uncertainty about who they really are and their proper role in life. This uncertainty or confusion is what the neo-Freudian developmental psychologist Erik Erikson describes as an identity crisis.

As social beings, identity is an essential part of our psyche and well-being. In fact, it is arguably the key to solving many of today's societal problems. Someone once said that a meaningful life is impossible unless you understand your true identity. We all want to feel important and appreciated. We all want to belong somewhere and be worthwhile, so we try to identify ourselves with associations, fraternities, secret societies, professional societies, street gangs, religious groups, and political ideologies that may provide these securities. Some have even narrowed their identity to their personality type, social network, skill level, marital status, family heritage, animals and mythical creatures, among other options.

There has been a growing trend of people identifying as "otherkin," a subculture made up of individuals who view themselves as partially non-human. Some now view themselves either as animals or mythical beings such as angels, aliens, demons, dragons, elves, hobbits, or mermaids, both socially and spiritually. When you don't know who you are, and you embrace a worldview that is anchored on falsehood and shifting foundations, then you will inevitably base your identity on a constantly changing subjective reality instead of objective truth. The psychiatric condition known as Therianthropy, wherein a person has a delusional belief of being an animal, is now gaining recognition as a personal identity.

The identity question has generated much philosophical and scientific speculation throughout history. But guess what? Philosophers don't have the answers. They can only speculate and postulate but it's all a product of human conjecture. None of them was there either to observe or record the creator's intentions.

Scientists certainly don't have the answers either. They may provide some details about the *how* but certainly not the *why*. According to John Lennox, "True science is not embarrassed by its inability at this point—it simply recognizes that it is not equipped to answer such questions. Therefore, it would be a serious logical error in methodology to look only within the ingredients of the universe—its material, structures, and processes—to find out what its purpose is and why we are here. The ultimate answer, if there is one, will have to come from outside the universe."[1] It has to come from the one who was there when it all began, indeed the one who was responsible for it: God.

OUR TRUE IDENTITY

So what does God say about our true identity? To answer the question, we turn once again to the Book of Genesis where God said, "'Let us make mankind in our image, in our likeness, so that they may rule over the fish in the sea and the birds in the sky, over the livestock and all the wild animals, and over all the creatures that move along the ground.' So God created mankind in his own image, in the image of God he created them; male and female he created them" (Genesis 1:26-27). The Book of Genesis tells us that God made humankind in His "image" and after His "likeness." If we understand the Hebraic style of one word reinforcing the other, they are essentially the same thing. This is our defining **identity.** It's usually referred to as the "image of God." And the stated **purpose** for why God makes humankind in His image is "**so that they may rule over creation.**"

So what exactly does the phrase "image of God" mean? Let's begin by defining the term "image." According to Dictionary.com, an image is a physical likeness or representation of a person, animal, or thing. Oxford dictionary defines image as a person or thing that closely resembles another. In Hebrew, the term "image" as noted by John Walton, "is a representative in physical form, not a representation of physical appearance."[2] Next is the phrase "image of God." Since God is Spirit, we can more properly define the "image of God" as a person whose character closely mirrors what we know of God in terms of His nature, attributes and virtues. So in a nutshell, humans are the living representatives of God on earth. They are the visible expression of the invisible God.

In order to deepen our understanding of what it means for humans to be made in the image of God, let's examine how kings were viewed in the ancient world. In ancient kingdoms, people lived under the rule of a king who claimed to be a representative of the gods. Rightly so, because they claimed the gods imputed "something" in them that enabled them to act as a representative of the deity in the physical world. The empowered king would then refer to themselves as the "image of god," meaning they had authority to tell people what to do—the authority to define good and evil. They would often make statues or images of themselves throughout their kingdom as an indication of their presence.

Another popular kind of image in the ancient world is an idol, a physical object that represents a god in the temple or shrine. Idols were not considered gods themselves. They were statues that signaled that gods were present. These statues or images invoked in some mysterious sense an atmosphere of "being ever-present" for the gods.

The Book of Genesis employs the use of this imagery, but with a marked difference designed to make a contrast. It makes a bold claim that all humans are living images of God on the earth. They are representatives of God in the physical realm, including His authority and character. And so this task of representing God and ruling creation, that once belonged only to elite kings as it were, is according to Genesis, the task of every human being. The role of royal image-bearer was conferred not only on a line of kings but also on all humans. This was a groundbreaking statement in its day because it called for all humans to take part in governing and contributing to the collective human endeavor, and carry out God's will for the whole creation.[3] This is our divine calling and purpose and the very source of our significance that markedly distinguishes us from other animals.

Just as the gods imputed "something" into ancient kings, God almighty imputed "something" of Himself into man. Genesis calls this the "breath of life." With that breath of life, God also endowed us with outstanding ontological properties like consciousness, higher cognitive abilities, freewill, language, morality, awareness of self and God, and the ability to have a relationship with God. These immaterial properties were requisite to function as God's image. They enable us to represent Him in the physical world. These qualify us to effectively function as living images of God on the earth. Therefore, we are not to make any images of God because God has already made images of Himself—humans.[4]

Another way to understand the concept of the image of God is via image reflections on the mirror. The reflections you observe in a mirror rely entirely on the object that produces them. They exist only as long as the object maintains the right physical relationship to the mirror and cannot exist independently.[5] Although they can reflect, they lack self-sufficiency. Certain exclusive qualities that you have as a human being made in the image of God will survive as long as you do. Qualities such as intelligence, freewill, language, morality, self-consciousness, God-consciousness, and others as earlier described. But there is also an 'image' which you can lose, one that wholly depends on your being in a face-to-face relationship with God.

In other words, God alone is King, He rules over creation and He defines what is good and what is not good. But then surprisingly, in an attempt to extend His kingdom to the earthly realm, He makes humans in His image and after His likeness, to reflect His will and character just like the moon reflects the light from the sun to the earth. He gives them the authority to rule the earth and bring the government of heaven down to it. The word "rule" in Hebrew, *radah*, can be translated as "to rule," "to reign," or "have dominion." It is a call to actively partner with God in taking the world forward. Their success in this vocation is highly dependent on their continuous connection to the source of life Himself.

What could this look like in daily life? It means living consciously as God's representatives and stewards of creation, protecting and bringing order to God's beautiful creation, reflecting God's nature and wisdom, encouraging a friend, supporting the weak, upholding justice and fairness, mentoring our young, or even starting a business that adds value to humanity and brings out more of God's goodness to the world.[6]

Living consciously as though our lives represent God and further His kingdom would radically change the way we approach each day. Each day and activity is an opportunity to partner with God in moving His story forward. When we see ourselves as God's agents and allies, and consecrate our legitimate work to Him, it becomes a holy vocation to the Lord; bringing blessings and God's goodness to fellow humans. It means our routine 9 to 5 jobs, and the decisions we make each day matter. God doesn't view people in ministry or any religious service for that matter as more special because of their job descriptions. The work of an evangelist, pastor, rabbi, imam, or Buddhist monk is not more important to God than the work of an engineer, architect, lawyer, or politician. What God cares about is how each of us represents Him where we are as religious leaders, journalists, taxi drivers, traders, doctors, teachers, or police officers. We either sweep away the darkness by reflecting the light of God to the world, or we are submerged in that darkness.

Your identity is not your profession or race. You are not an animal of no significance; you are not a naked ape; you are not a mere biochemical machine. Don't fall for those reductionist imaginations of the human identity. You are the image of God—that's your true identity. You are here to represent God, bringing out the God-colors in the world. You are here to rule over creation in partnership with God, bringing out the God-flavors of the earth. That is what it means to be human. This is the central goal of humanity. Once you miss this goal, you fail to be truly human. The American Christian band, Salvador, captures it well enough in their song titled *Shine:*[7]

> Lord, let me shine, shine like the moon
> A reflection of You in all that I do
> Lord, let me be, a light for Your truth
> Light of the world, I wanna be used to
> shine for You

So, there you have it. Today, Humankind dominates the world because God appointed them as His representative rulers on the earth. God made them male and female: and He blessed them and charged them to be fruitful and multiply. He planted a beautiful garden and put the humans there. They were to cooperate with God to bring His will to it to make it a place where life could flourish even more.

GOD AND HUMANITY UNITED IN PARADISE

Then the Lord God planted a garden in Eden in the east, and there he placed the man he had made. The Lord God made all sorts of trees grow up from the ground—trees that were beautiful and that produced delicious fruit. In the middle of the garden he placed the tree of life and the tree of the knowledge of good and evil. A river flowed from the land of Eden, watering the garden and then dividing into four branches (Genesis 2:8-10).

The tradition of creating lush and beautiful gardens for both enjoyment and religious purposes was prevalent among ancient civilizations. Temples served as sacred spaces where people could connect with supernatural entities, and many had attached gardens featuring aromatic and fruit-bearing trees that symbolized their vision of paradise. The renowned Hanging Gardens of Babylon, a part of the Seven Wonders of the Ancient World, epitomized this concept. From the towering ziggurats of ancient Babylon in Iraq to the pyramids in Egypt and the grand Mayan temples in Mexico, these architectural marvels were some of the most impressive structures in the ancient world.[9] They were regarded as holy places that blurred the line between the physical and spiritual realms and were considered as portals to the supernatural (thought to be the demonic realm). The entrances to some of these temples were often guarded by an imposing hybrid statue known as sphinx, much like the idea of a guardian cherub.

The Book of Genesis employs similar garden-temple imagery. But, surprisingly, God didn't create a sacred physical temple for Himself in the beginning, as it were. In fact, the entire creation is His temple, and the fullness of His presence is everywhere.

Long before the Babylonians, Egyptians, Mayans, and other ancient civilizations existed, God planted the very first garden—the Garden of Eden. It was the most magnificent garden of all time. What makes this garden particularly remarkable was that it was not planted by any man. It was the handiwork of God Himself. It was called the garden of God, the holy mountain of God. Which means that it played host to God's throne where He directed the affairs of the universe. Tim Mackie and Jon Collins of BibleProject perfectly capture the very essence of the garden by describing its core as "the hotspot of God's presence, beaming and filling the entire creation."[8]

The Garden of Eden was a place where God and humans rested together. God creates humans and places them in the garden, to tend and watch over it (Genesis 2:15). The characteristic Hebrew word used here is *nuakh*, which literally means "to rest" or "settle in." God "rests them" or "settles them" in the garden with Him where they enjoy the fullness of God's goodness. God Himself is in the garden, walking and talking with humans (Genesis 3:8a). God and humanity lived together in harmony without anything separating them. We are used to thinking of heaven as God's exclusive domain and earth as ours. However, these domains are not always mutually exclusive. In fact, God's ultimate intention is for heaven and earth to merge (Matthew 6:10). The Garden of Eden was a place where God's domain and humanity's domain completely merged. It was a place where God's space and our space are one and the same, a perfect environment where humankind can partner with God in building a beautiful flourishing world.[10]

Unlike other gardens, the Garden of Eden was not a sort of resort for people to visit once in a while, but a place for humans to live and work in union with God. The name Eden means "delight" or "land of happiness." This delight does not mean "happiness" as we normally use the term, but it describes the kind of joy that comes through being intimately connected with

God. Humans had full access to God, and God had full access to humans—no blazing angelic bouncers standing in the way.

The garden was reminiscent of a temple not only because God's presence was there, but also because He placed images of Himself there—humankind. Mackie and Collins puts it this way: "Instead of setting a statue in one specific place in the garden to symbolize His reign, He commissioned the living, breathing humans to be the figures that represented His rule."[11] The command, "be fruitful and multiply" shows that there's an expansion project in view. As the humans worked and kept the garden, and as they were fruitful and multiplied, Eden would grow beyond its current boundaries, and the glory of humanity's royal rule and by extension, God's rule, would increase.

We see therefore a picture of God's Kingdom: God's people (humanity), living in God's place (the Garden of Eden), under God's rule. And as a result, they enjoy God's blessing.[12] Humanity lived in unity with God, and this resulted in unity with each other, and unity with nature. As humanity yields to God's rule and authority, nature in response yields to humanity's rule as they exercise the authority God gave them over the created order. Living in union with God inside the garden results in abundant life because humans are connected to the very source of life. God's plan was to make the whole earth like Eden, and humans are His chosen partners to carry this vision forward, spreading His good rule and the order and beauty of the garden into the rest of creation. This is our divine mandate, and that makes us special.

AN ANIMAL OF NO SIGNIFICANCE?

The strategic position of humans in the created order has been called many names in the secular world: human exceptionalism, human supremacism, human superiority, anthropocentrism, humanocentrism, speciesism, and so on. It should be obvious to everyone that there are powerful forces out there who don't want humans to be in this unique position. These forces are determined to knock humans off the pedestal of exceptionalism in order to erase the ultimate vestige of God from humanity. They have totally dedicated themselves for various reasons to convincing us that we really aren't all that significant. It is therefore not surprising the ferocious efforts being made to blur the lines between humans and animals, on the one hand, and between humans and machines on the other hand with the intent of reducing us to nothing but physics, chemistry and algorithms.

Yuval Harari, who writes from a purely naturalistic standpoint, wastes no time in tearing down human exceptionalism by portraying humans as having no greater importance than animals such as apes, pigs, and chickens. According to Harari, "Homo sapiens long preferred to view itself as set apart from animals, an orphan bereft of family, lacking siblings or cousins, and most importantly, without parents. But that's just not the case … Our lack of brothers and sisters makes it easier to imagine that we are the epitome of creation, and that a chasm separates us from the rest of the animal kingdom."[13]

Such efforts are driven in part by the desire to enthrone Darwinism and its notion that humans are just another creature along the animal chain that is not qualitatively any different from other animals. As noted by Wesley J. Smith, a Senior Fellow at the Discovery Institute's Center on Human Exceptionalism, the unrelenting assault against human exceptionalism of which many remain unaware is being mounted on many fronts. One of such is the idea of extending legal personhood (the status of being a person) to animals. For years, animal rights advocates have sponsored so-called "animal-welfare" laws to pave the way for the legal consideration of animals as persons, a position solely enjoyed by humans.[14] These laws would inevitably give your cow or your chicken the right to bring a lawsuit against you or anyone who tramples on their rights, of course not by themselves directly, but via human proxies.

Let me clarify that I am not justifying any form of animal abuse or cruelty. Although animals are given to serve humankind, that does not grant us permission to inflict harm or to make them extinct. It's our obligation as humans to treat animals humanely. That's in fact an intrinsic part of human exceptionalism. This is an important point to grasp in today's world where more value seems to be placed on the protection of animals than on upholding the sanctity of human life. However, to the surprise of many, the concept of animal personhood has garnered endorsement from several renowned legal experts affiliated with Ivy League institutions.

Some even claim that granting legal personhood to animals is not even enough; they are now actively calling for personhood and legal rights for individual plants and Mother Nature.[15] As bizarre as these ideas may seem to some people, it has transitioned from being solely within the confines of academic institutions to being implemented in public policy in Europe and other parts of the world.

And now, a new front appears to have been opened in an effort to blur the lines between man and machines. This new front sees human beings as just biochemical algorithms and data processing systems just like machines (computer algorithms), and questions the continued assignment of special value to human life. It sees members of the species Homo sapiens as completely losing their economic value because of the rise of intelligent machines. According to the proponents of these ideologies, it is just a matter of time before computer algorithms outperform biochemical algorithms in terms of intelligence. If that happens, would the machines rule over humans and treat them as a lower class of beings?

But are humans just biochemical algorithms lacking in free will? David Hodgson, a legal expert, counters this claim by stating that it is the combination of our consciousness and a type of reasoning that is not accessible to non-conscious AI, that gives us libertarian free will.[16] Humans can operate algorithmically, but this is not the only way that humans operate. According to Hodgson, there are two types of reasoning that humans can perform: algorithmic reasoning and plausible reasoning.[17] Hodgson further noted that our ability to engage in plausible reasoning is a vital component of human rationality, allowing us to evaluate and determine what actions or beliefs to adopt.[18] This according to Hodgson is a unique capability of human consciousness that non-conscious intelligent machines lack, and it plays an essential role in our ability to make moral judgments.[19] Plausible reasoning occurs when individuals are faced with the challenge of weighing incommensurable options about "what to believe" or "what to do." For instance, when you are torn between honoring a request to help a person in need (an act of love) and accepting an invitation to dine with someone (not your spouse) you have a romantic interest in (pursuit of lust), both of which require your physical presence at the same time.

We have the capacity to make decisions that are not wholly determined by the way we are or the way the laws of nature work. We are not merely biochemical algorithms and algorithmic choosers. We are not just a brain. We are the thing that has the brain. If we are just a brain, we cannot have free will. We would just be a complex physical machine. So, what we have here, therefore, are two different types of things: an immaterial mind and the material brain. Yet, there are many who believe that physical matter is all that exists; and that everything can be explained in terms of physics, chemistry and biology. Those who hold this view believe that we're no more than robots, and that free will is just a fable.

Accepting an algorithmic account of humanity is the sort of reductionist position that typically leads to the conclusion that humankind is no different from machines and therefore should not be accorded any special position. Much is at stake. It's apparent that there are some who are bent on "liberating" society's general embrace of human exceptionalism. This poses a great risk to the survival of humankind, and would inevitably set the stage for totalitarianism. A complete opposite of what God envisioned for humanity.

The first part of this book began by exploring how God created the cosmos, and humans as His chosen partners to carry forward His will for the whole creation. In the second part, we will look at how humanity failed woefully in this task, and how God made a way to redeem humankind.

PART II

HUMANITY BREAKS PARTNERSHIP WITH GOD

Why is the world in such a mess?

Who bears the responsibility for this mess?

Is it possible for this mess to be resolved?

CHAPTER THREE

REBELLION IN PARADISE

In the earlier chapters, we saw how God created a world full of beauty and goodness, teaming with life. He goes on to fashion the apex of His creation: humans. He created them with a purpose and set them apart by giving them a specific purpose, appointing them as His sole representative to rule the world on His behalf. God had planted a garden and placed the man He created in it. The garden was intended to serve as a starting point for building the new world in partnership with Him, a launching pad for extending God's Kingdom to the rest of creation. God's intention is to work through human beings in such a way that it becomes difficult to distinguish between the actions of the human and those of God.

But as exciting as God's intention for humanity was, what we see in the real world is a far cry from God's vision. We are far below the mark. Life in our world—and indeed our reality—does not conform to the original blueprint. It is filled with evil, suffering, and injustice. Think about it yourself. Are you truly representing God and reflecting His will and character in your daily life? Does your life here on earth epitomize God's rule? If not, who or what is responsible for the abysmal failure? As we look at the world around us, it is obvious that something has gone terribly wrong. The world is in a big mess. What is the explanation for the mess?

FROM PARADISE TO EXILE

The Bible's perspective on the human condition usually sounds strange to modern people. It is often ignored or treated as primitive mythology, having nothing to do with reality and the progress of civilization. But surprisingly, in this very perspective (the biblical one) lies the explanation of the mess we're in. Humans opted for independence from God, and redefined their own purpose and will in the world. It all began when God decided to share His attributes (qualities and abilities) with the humans and the supernatural (angelic) beings He created. He endowed humans with certain qualities similar to His, to enable us function as His representatives here on earth.

One of such qualities is free will. Without genuine freedom to make real decisions we simply would not resemble God. Without free will, we could not genuinely love or obey Him. If decisions were pre-encoded, how could they be considered authentic? For decisions like love and obedience to be authentic, they must be made against a truly possible alternative. I believe the basic reason why God gave us this kind of freedom was that His heart is for voluntary partners, men and women who would choose Him of their own accord, men and women who would be keen to partner with Him because they wanted to. Such a union would produce a far stronger and more authentic relationship than forced or programmed obedience ever could.

God created all things for His pleasure and He derives tremendous satisfaction from other living things (plants and animals), and nonliving things such as the moon, stars, the winds, mountains, the oceans, the waves. They are ever ready and pre-set to do His will. But God knows that He could never get the same pleasure from creatures that were programmed to be His subjects as He would have from those who voluntarily submitted to His Lordship. So God gave humans and the angelic beings He created the freedom to either stick with Him or reject Him.

Let's review the story of the garden in Genesis chapter 3:

> ...The LORD God planted a garden in Eden in the east, and there he placed the man he had made. The LORD God made all sorts of trees grow up from the ground—trees that were beautiful and that produced delicious fruit. In the middle of the garden he placed the tree of life and the tree of the knowledge of good and evil.
>
> The LORD God placed the man in the Garden of Eden to tend and watch over it. But the LORD God warned him, "You may freely eat the fruit of every tree in the garden—except the tree of the knowledge of good and evil. If you eat its fruit, you are sure to die" (Genesis 2:8-9, 15-17).

God has served as the moral authority since the beginning of time. From the very beginning, God defined what was good and what was not good for the newly created humans. You'll find hints of it scattered all over the early chapters of Genesis, such as "and God saw that it was good," and "it is not good for man to be alone." God's moral authority refers to His ultimate and unchanging standard of right and wrong or good and evil that serves as the foundation for ethical and moral behavior. But humans also have a choice about how they're going to go about building this world. God gave them dignity, sound reasoning, and the freedom of choice.

The big question is: were they going to trust God's definition of good and evil or were they going to seize the opportunity and define good and evil for themselves? Second, were they going to use their authority for their own selfish gain? That in a nutshell is what the Tree of the Knowledge of Good and Evil in the garden represents. It is not the tree of knowledge, and it is also not the tree of the knowledge of everything as some people wrongly assume. God is not attempting to prevent humanity from gaining knowledge. In fact, in the Garden of Eden, there was a wealth of knowledge which they were at liberty to obtain.

The knowledge of good and evil is the power of determining for yourself what is good and what is evil and of acting accordingly. I am not referring to free will—they already had that. In fact, as free-will beings, Adam and Eve were not pre-programmed to only obey God. They were already capable of disobedience. This power is a privilege which God reserves for Himself, but which humanity, through disobedience to God, will seize.

The Tree of the Knowledge of Good and Evil gives them the opportunity to experience evil first hand and decide for themselves whether it is good or not good. There exist two contrasting approaches to moral experience: One involves surrendering oneself to God's authority and accepting and adhering to His definition of good and evil without any personal experimentation. The other approach involves rejecting God's authority and choosing to independently experience and evaluate what is good or evil for oneself. Would Adam and Eve submit to God's Lordship and not eat of the tree or would they try to become their own lords by deciding what was good or what was not themselves? The stakes were really high. Their decision— knowingly or unknowingly—had the capacity to shape the future of humanity and the fate of their offspring.

Rebelling against God or going against His will is equivalent to accepting death because you're turning away from the very source of life Himself. This is represented by the Tree of Life right there in the garden. God's message was clear: "I am your source and the sovereign one; you are My appointed representatives, I retain the right to define what is good and evil. You should not rely solely on our own experiences to make such decisions." That's God's sovereignty in action. But then again, as free-will beings, humans have a choice in how they want to go about building the brand new world before them. Would they trust God enough to partner with Him in this journey or would they want to run the show without Him?

The Tree of the Knowledge of Good and Evil was put in the Garden of Eden to give them a choice. A choice to vote themselves out of God's Kingdom and become independent. A choice to either remain as tenants in God's Paradise or to become their own landlord. A choice to say, "Yes, Lord! I accept Your sovereignty!" Or, a choice to say, "No! I will define good and evil on my own terms!" Unfortunately, the human race by their actions preferred the latter to the former. They chose to define good and evil on their own terms. How did this happen?

We read in Genesis 3 about a new player in the field:

> The serpent was the shrewdest of all the wild animals the LORD God had made. One day he asked the woman, "Did God really say you must not eat the fruit from any of the trees in the garden?" "Of course we may eat fruit from the trees in the garden," the woman replied. "It's only the fruit from the tree in the middle of the garden that we are not allowed to eat. God said, 'You must not eat it or even touch it; if you do, you will die.'" "God knows that your eyes will be opened as soon as you eat it, and you will be like God, knowing both good and evil." The woman was convinced. She saw that the tree was beautiful and its fruit looked delicious, and she wanted the wisdom it would give her. So she took some of the fruit and ate it. Then she gave some to her husband, who was with her, and he ate it, too. At that moment their eyes were opened, and they suddenly felt shame at their nakedness. So they sewed fig leaves together to cover themselves (Genesis 3:1-6).

So here was this mysterious entity—a serpent that could talk (yes, you read that right, a talking serpent) on the scene. Remember, this event took place in God's Paradise (the Garden of Eden). The Garden of Eden was not merely a place the first humans called home, but also the abode of God with humankind. The idea of a talking serpent in the garden has puzzled a lot of modern readers. The Genesis account does not provide any information regarding the serpent's origin. However, it is clear that the serpent mentioned is not an ordinary member of the animal kingdom, but a supernatural creature (Old Testament Bible scholar, Michael Heiser, explains this in detail in his book *The Unseen Realm: Recovering the Supernatural Worldview of the Bible*). We learn from other biblical sources that it was one of the supernatural creatures which was responsible for guarding God's throne in the garden—a guarding cherub. This guarding cherub is undoubtedly in rebellion against God. Take a look at Ezekiel 28:13-15:

> You were in Eden, the garden of God. Your clothing was adorned with every precious stone— red carnelian, pale-green peridot, white moonstone, blue-green beryl, onyx, green jasper, blue lapis lazuli, turquoise, and emerald— all beautifully crafted for you and set in the finest gold. They were given to you on the day you were created. I ordained and anointed you as the mighty angelic guardian. You had access to the holy mountain of God and walked among the stones of fire.
>
> "You were blameless in all you did from the day you were created until the day evil was found in you.

Cherubim function as guardians of God's throne. For example, on the "mercy seat" of the Ark of the Covenant, which symbolizes God's throne, two cherubim are described as surrounding the Ark and defining a space for God's presence to be revealed. So God is ultimately responsible for their existence. Yet this cherub is undoubtedly opposed to God's plan to have humanity in charge of creation.

The serpent is depicted in Genesis as a dissenting voice and a deceiver. It promotes what has been prohibited by God and demonstrates exceptional cunning in its ability to convince. This fallen cherub was apparently unhappy about the position of humans in the created order. Why were humans given dominion over creation when angels exceeded them in might and power and could have done a better job? The psalmist asked the same question and provides the answer:

> …what is man that you are mindful of him, and the son of man that you care for him?
>
> Yet you have made him a little lower than the heavenly beings and crowned him with glory and honor (Psalm 8:4-5 ESV).

That is the prerogative of the supreme God, but we see here His desire to raise humankind above the angels and make them His crowning glory. Could this be the reason for satan's intense hatred towards humankind?

The enemy therefore decided to persuade Eve to dishonor her Creator by going against His command, probably hoping God would immediately destroy her and her husband Adam— and, by extension, the entire human race. The Bible refers to this deceiver as "satan" or "the devil," which means "the adversary" or "opponent" (Revelation 12:9). He comes to Eve and tells a twisted story about the forbidden fruit, claiming that eating the fruit is actually the way to "enlightenment" and becoming like God (*Elohim*). "God knows that your eyes will be opened as soon as you eat it, and you will be like God, knowing both good and evil" (Genesis 3:5). This essentially means having the ability to define good and evil on their own terms just like God. But you see, ironically, we know that humans are already like God. Were they not made "in the likeness of God"?

However, when Eve took the bait and listened to the adversary's beguiling words, "you will be like God," her craving for the perceived wisdom that the fruit would give her overshadowed her ability to judge wisely. Already the couple's trust in God's goodness towards them, and integrity in His word have become shaky. They have been blinded and overcome by the ambition to become like God. Enlightenment and independence beckon: they have to get it. Just a bite of the forbidden fruit was all they needed to experience enlightenment and independence, and "become like God" as the deceiver suggests.

The deceiver's ability to mislead people is legendary as he continues to lure unsuspecting humans down a path of **false enlightenment**. Thousands of people have been lured deep into the occult and new age belief systems in the name of gaining "secret knowledge" and spiritual enlightenment, only to be drowned in darkness and devoured. What the deceiver did not say was that walking in this experience would damage Adam and Eve's relationship with God and pervert their notion of good and evil. Before eating the fruit of this tree, they were under God's rule; they lived by God's definition of good and evil. However, they knew good but did not know evil. Prior to knowing good and evil, Adam and Eve had never made a conscious decision to disobey God; neither had they seen an act of disobedience. They were innocent. But by choosing to eat from the tree, they usurped God's prerogative to define good and evil and chose to define it in their own terms. When they chose to experientially gain the knowledge of evil, they had effectively lost their innocence and were now "Homo sapiens" ("wise man" or "knowing man").

As a father, watching my little boys grow up was quite an interesting experience. As kids they were unaware of what was good and what was bad, and it was up to me as their dad to decide for them. I would tell them, "Don't touch that connected electric iron; if you do, it will burn you. Don't take someone else's toy without their permission; if you do, it may hurt your relationship with that person." The power to decide what was right and what was not basically lay with me as their father. However, as they grow up into adulthood, they are becoming independent and acquiring the sense of judging the good and bad of things for themselves. By this point, they possess the ability to establish their own standard for determining what is good and evil, and act accordingly. It is now up to them to trust my definition of right and wrong or go with theirs.

So when Adam and Eve rebelled against God, they lost their innocence or dependence on God as their Father to decide for them what was right or wrong. They established their own standards of good and evil. They no longer accepted God to determine what was right or wrong for them; they were going to decide for themselves, what to do with their lives apart from God. Vaughan Roberts accurately portrayed the true meaning of the "knowledge of good and evil" by stating that:

> The 'knowledge of good and evil' refers not simply to knowing what is right and wrong, but rather to deciding what is right and wrong. Their sin is that of law-making, not just law-breaking. They were saying, 'From now on, God, we want to be the law-makers in the world, setting the standards by which we will live.' It was a bid to be like God, but not in any noble sense. They were usurping his authority and establishing their independence. That has been the nature of sin ever since.[1]

In doing so, they inadvertently landed in enemy territory, fraught with its snares and traps. They were out of their depth, in the hands of a malevolent and far more intelligent foe. This one decision brought misery and death to themselves and humankind.

Indeed, God could have decided not to have a human family knowing that they may ultimately ditch Him. But He took the chance. You did the same when you decided to have children. There was absolutely no guarantee that the children you brought into the world would turn out to be responsible citizens and bring honor to you as their father. But you still took the chance, hoping something in you would rub off on them, or at least that some of them would make you proud.

Just because God knew humanity will fail Him, does not mean He pre-planned it that way. God's prior awareness of what choices we will make does not negate them being our choices. The explanation of the mess we're in lies in God's incredible tolerance in permitting His plans in the world to be executed by beings who may have their own purposes that are not aligned with His. Yet God made allowance for that. He knew this was a possibility. He was fully aware of the potential risks, but His love for humanity was so strong that He couldn't give it up.[2]

Ultimately, only God is perfect. Freedom in the hands of free-will beings—even supernatural ones—can have disastrous outcomes.[3] In this, both satan and a section of the angelic race, along with the entire human race, exercised their free will and chose to rebel against God. But God is a good God. Though He does not need evil as a means to accomplish His purpose, He does have the power to take the evil and the disastrous outcomes of our bad choices and turn them around to produce good,[4] restore the world and reclaim it for His kingdom (Romans 8:28; Revelation 7:17; 21:4).

That's precisely what happened in the Garden of Eden. Adam and Eve missed the goal. They failed to be human in the ideal sense of the word, and God evicted them from His domain in Eden. In effect, deprived of God's presence and stripped of their power and authority as His representatives, they lost paradise. Every human born thereafter was born outside of Eden, alienated from God. But in the words of Michael Heiser, "that was a better outcome than what the serpent had hoped for—human destruction."[5] God wasn't giving up on His plan to have a human family, but rebellion has its consequences.

Satan had incurred the wrath of God, especially considering the central role he played in introducing evil and death into the world. Being naturally endowed with higher intelligence and power, satan then seized power as the prince of this world—the world of failed beings, beings that are disconnected from God. Satan (the fallen cherub, now turned adversary) together with other fallen angels and their offspring, the *Nephilim* (a species of giant humanoids), become a band of supernatural evil beings or gods that oppress and enslave humans.

That's the Bible's depiction of the human condition. The first casualty is the human relationship with God. The intimacy between God and the humans is lost: now they hide from God. The second casualty is human relationship with one another. The man and the woman suddenly realize how vulnerable they are now to each other; they can't even trust each other. So they use makeshift clothes to cover their naked bodies from one another. The third casualty is human relationship with nature. Their "Sabbath rest" in the garden is over. The blessings of God which humanity enjoyed in the garden have been replaced by a world that demands much effort. From now on, it was going to be hard labor:

> "All your life you will struggle to scratch a living from it. It will grow thorns and thistles for you, though you will eat of its grains. By the sweat of your brow will you have food to eat until you return to the ground from which you were made" (Genesis 3:17-19).

So the broken bond between humans and God has had a far-reaching impact on human relationships with one another and with nature, a condition that has persisted throughout history. Now every aspect of life in the real world is going to be fraught with misery, grief, pain and, ultimately, death because of the rebellion and subsequent exile from God's Paradise. And from that very moment things began to rapidly spiral out of control.

Not only was the land cursed, so was womanhood:

> "I will sharpen the pain of your pregnancy, and in pain you will give birth" (Genesis 3:16).

There are three irrefutable facts about life today.[6] The first is that birth and everything associated with childbirth and womanhood is painful. Menstruation is painful, losing one's virginity is painful, pregnancy is painful, miscarriage is painful, vaginal delivery is painful, cesarean delivery is painful, and even weaning a baby is painful. While advancements in medicine such as painkillers, tranquilizers, anesthetics, painless surgeries, and others have improved pain management, the potential risks and side effects can sometimes be greater than the benefits.

My mom once confided to me the intense labor pain she had to endure when she was giving birth to me due to my excessive birth weight and the size of my head which was relatively big. After that throbbing experience, she vowed that that would be her last. As a father, I can still remember the pain my wife had to endure in a 15-hour labor during the birth of our first child. We eventually resorted to a cesarean section to save her life and the baby's. As if that was not enough, two months into breast-feeding, she had an inflammation of her breast tissue which the doctors called mastitis. This caused her excruciating breast pain and swelling for several days. When she got pregnant with our second child, we opted for elective cesarean delivery. In both cases, she had to deal with the pain that comes with C-section, which usually begins after the anesthetics wears out. Birth is indeed painful.

The second fact is that life is hard. There is misery, injustice and poverty in the land. We go through so much just to put food on the table. Depending on the country you live in, some people have to take up two jobs to be able to make ends meet; some can't find a good job even after many tough years of secondary and tertiary education. Even those that manage to get a job or start a business wish it wasn't so stressful and demanding. Our time and energy are often consumed by the need to earn a paycheck, care for our children or aging parents (or both), provide for our security, and fulfill others' needs and expectations of us. Over-worked, we find it increasingly difficult to experience true rest, and the joy and fulfillment that come after a day's work. All over the world, even in rich nations, life is hard for most people.

The third certainty is death. The irony is that, having worked hard and acquired our hard earned wealth, we do not live long enough to enjoy it. We age and die. Having been bereaved myself, I have experienced firsthand the pain of losing a loved one. Three years after I lost my elder sister, my immediate elder brother died. The following year, I lost my mom and my dad consecutively. Well, mine was a little bearable because my parents died at a ripe age, but my siblings died in their prime. But there are many out there who are dealing with the more serious pain and void caused by the untimely death of their loved ones. It can be traumatizing to live with the knowledge that death can come at any time.

This is our reality as human beings on the earth. We were exiled from the place the Lord God had originally appointed us to live. The consequence of being exiled from God's Paradise is the necessity of labor, the experience of sorrow, and the inevitability of death. This means that individuals must work tirelessly to provide for themselves, often accompanied by hardship and distress, until they ultimately confront the inescapable reality of death. In our bid to survive, we sometimes end up cheating, hoarding, trying to undo and control others, or constantly seeking pleasure to numb the pain. Truth be told, many civilizations grew as a result of humans seeking ways to survive and thrive outside of God.

HOMELESS WANDERERS

The nature of the punishment God meted out to the first human family is directly related to those three irrefutable facts. Eve was punished in relation to the family (birth pains), Adam in relation to his work (hardship), and finally death was their ultimate destiny because they were disconnected from the very source of life. The first murder took place within the family as envy and anger in their son Cain gave rise to defiance of the God who warned him not to be offended because He favored Abel's sacrifice. So Cain murdered his brother Abel.

Abel had probably learned from his parents that the only sacrifice acceptable to God was blood sacrifice—the result of a life being taken. God had previously covered the shame of his parents by killing an animal and providing a covering for them from the animal skin. A principle was indirectly being established: blood was shed so that their shame could be covered. So, when Abel appeared before God, he brought an animal sacrifice—the finest of the firstborn lambs from his flock. Cain simply brought fruit and vegetables from his crop, but that was not acceptable to God. Cain was angered by this, and in spite of God's warning, he went ahead and killed his brother.

This incident is a clear manifestation of the effect of the fractured relationship between humans and God, and between fellow humans following the rebellion and exile. The ripple effect of these broken relationships runs through human history. So God's world, which He once declared as good, is now a place where goodness is abhorred and evil is excused by blaming others. The pattern is already set when Adam blames Eve and Eve blames the serpent (Genesis 3:12-13). God responds to Cain's heinous act with a punishment: "Now you are cursed and banished from the ground, which has swallowed your brother's blood. No longer will the ground yield good crops for you, no matter how hard you work! From now on you will be a homeless wanderer on the earth" (Genesis 4:12).

So, following this severe sentence, what became of Cain?

> Cain went out from the presence of the Lord, and dwelt in the land of Nod, on the east of Eden. And Cain knew his wife; and she conceived, and bare Enoch: and he built a city, and called the name of the city, after the name of his son, Enoch. And unto

Enoch was born Irad: and Irad begat Mehujael: and Mehujael begat Methusael: and Methusael begat Lamech. And Lamech took unto him two wives: the name of the one was Adah, and the name of the other Zillah. And Adah bare Jabal: he was the father of such as dwell in tents, and of such as have cattle. And his brother's name was Jubal: he was the father of all such as handling the harp and organ. And Zillah, she also bare Tubalcain, an instructer of every artificer in brass and iron: and the sister of Tubalcain was Naamah. And Lamech said unto his wives, Adah and Zillah, Hear my voice; ye wives of Lamech, hearken unto my speech: for I have slain a man to my wounding, and a young man to my hurt. If Cain shall be avenged sevenfold, truly Lamech seventy and sevenfold (Genesis 4:16-24 KJV).

The above story traces the lineage of Cain and shows some of the consequences of living a life without God. Cain walked away from God's presence, and from his family and settled in the land of Nod (the Hebrew word means "wandering"), east of Eden. He then founded a city, which he named E'noch, after his son. This, of course, was not a city like the modern cities of today; it was most likely a built-up area enclosed within some kind of wall. But it was a city that was secular, ungodly, and restless. We are given in a few words, a picture of the overall development of humanity in the generations that followed Cain after he founded that city.

The direction that the entire line of Cain took was one of striving at self-redemption. Indeed, they were fully aware that there was a curse upon the earth, and that humanity was no longer in the "Garden of God"—under God's government. And in Cain's case especially, the earth no longer yielded her goodness. If the earth was cursed, they would at any rate, through hard work and knowledge, struggle to lessen or overcome the effect of the curse. And by the development of the city, and through advances in agriculture and technological innovations, the seed of Cain could create their own self-government and "paradise garden" with all of its comforts and security, but without any reverence for God.

Cain's descendants like Jabal, Jubal, and Tubal-Cain acquired knowledge and skills in key areas. Jabal's knowledge and skills in civil engineering, architecture and animal husbandry could be deployed to provide housing for the city dwellers and a steady supply of milk, meat, wool and leather. Jubal's musical instruments and musical skills could now soothe its citizenry, the new art serving to entertain fun seekers and distract troubled minds. And Tubal-Cain's knowledge and skills in material science and metallurgy could give the city the weapons needed to defend itself and to make the tools to further subdue the cursed earth.

Ask Cain if he and his descendants were condemned by God to perpetually roam the earth, and you may get a response like: "Well, there's no need for that. I've got it all sorted out in my city, in spite of God's judgment. I will not end up a wanderer. I need no 'mark' of God' to protect me from assassins. I now have fortified walls around me." His quest for survival led to the very first human civilization. Thus Cain's city of E'noch set itself directly against the word of God, and sought to even mitigate or possibly reverse the effects of the curse through science, technology and the arts, without any reverence for God.

But here's the catch. Despite his boasting about his new found city and its developmental strides, Cain and his descendants remained wanderers within their inner selves. Having cut himself off from God, he had severed his roots and taken a new path in self-governance, eastwards from the paradise of Eden. Thus he was condemned to a state of unrest.

This pattern of independence runs throughout history and civilization all the way down to our modern society. A person or society that turns away from God and God's government indirectly turns in itself to unrest and disorder. No person or society will know true peace until it embraces God, because they are cut off from the very source of life. A person or society who lives only a secular life—living only for this world—has only what this world can offer: pleasure, money, position, fame and power. But none of this is permanent. The things of this world can never satisfy the deeper yearning of men and women for inner peace and harmony with their Creator.

We were not made for self-governance and self-dependence. We were made to live under God's rule—in the Kingdom of God. Our pursuit for survival and self-preservation outside of God's care has led us to invent ways of overcoming our hardship and challenges. Injustice, cheating, stealing, corruption, war, oppression, killing, personal enrichment, and many more, are some of the ways we have invented to overcome our hardship. We have succeeded in redefining what's good and what's not good to our self-advantage. From the sparse snapshot of family life among the citizens of the city of E'noch, we observe that Lamech, for example, redefined marriage. The primal law of marriage to one woman had been thrown away as irrelevant, for Lamech was a polygamist. He also continued in the way of Cain and committed murder.

In the line of Cain there is an emphasis on the development of culture and civilization. It's not that there's anything wrong with the development of culture and civilization and technology, but here it is developed for its own sake by Cain's descendants.

Adam and Eve had another son in place of Abel named Seth. When Seth grew up, he had a son and named him Enosh, and this marks a turning point: "At that time people first began to worship the Lord by name" (Genesis 4:26). So in contrast to Cain, in the line of Seth, we see a reawakening towards reverence for God. Some argue that the line of Seth consisted of a laid-back, ignorant and technologically less advanced bunch. On the contrary, we know that the descendants of Seth had a tremendous amount of technology and culture on their side.

For example, when Noah (a descendant of Seth eight generations down the line) and his sons set out to build the ark as commanded by God, a great amount of technical skill would be required to successfully execute such a complex project. It demanded a certain amount of knowledge and skill in physics, marine engineering, boat making, animal husbandry, hygiene, food preservation, among others. They had to develop the technology required to feed thousands of animals and manage the enormous tonnage of animal waste produced on a daily basis on the ark.

So they were technologically advanced, but they did not develop technology for its own sake or for self-advantage. The technology they developed was in alignment with God's will and purpose to survive and to replenish the earth again. They put it under the priority of their relationship with God, and that made a world of difference. Notice how, when the flood waters subsided and Noah and his family could step on dry ground, the first thing he did was to build an altar to God and offer animal sacrifice (Genesis 8:20). We can draw certain conclusions from this observation. Technological developments are not inherently wrong. However, it is when technology becomes disconnected from God's purpose that it becomes evil.

By contrast, what we see in Cain and his descendants is separation from God, and an attempt to mitigate the effects of the curse through technological development. Instead of returning to a relationship with God, they try to construct a parallel worldview without Him. So those early technological achievements emanating from the city of E'noch were mankind's attempts to independently solve one of his biggest headaches—hardship, while ignoring God. But every attempt to solve the problem of hardship in one area somehow multiplies it in other areas. Daily we read in newspapers and watch on our digital screens frightening news about pandemics and disease outbreaks, cyber-attacks, armed conflicts, murders, and the constant threat of terrorist attacks and nuclear holocaust.

The rise of many civilizations throughout human history bears a striking resemblance to the biblical story of Cain and Abel. Throughout the course of human history, numerous individuals, akin to Abel, were ruthlessly murdered to pave the way for the emergence and sustenance of great civilizations.

We have perfected the template of Cain's rebellion: rebel against God (separate ourselves from God), develop advanced civil and military technology, redefine good and evil in our own terms, then sit back and bask in endless fun and pleasure. But are we really happier? A meaningless life—a life that has lost its sense of purpose—a life that has missed its primary goal is a terrible ordeal despite the supposed luxury and the arsenal of technological inventions at our disposal. So, in the words of Tim Mackie, "Sometimes we pull off amazingly good stuff; but just as often, despite our best intentions, we act selfishly and we create evil in the world."[7] Every new invention we pull off just widens the gap between us and the Garden of Eden—the Paradise of God. So we remain stuck as homeless wanderers, drifting farther and farther away in search of answers to our self-inflicted problems of pain, hardship and death. This pattern runs through civilization, from the ancient city of E'noch to the modern city of New York.

In the next chapter, we will explore how the rest of humanity (homeless wanderers), and the generations that followed, set out to manage the consequences that come with their rebellion against God, including hardship and death. We will also continue our discussion on free will in chapter 6.

CHAPTER FOUR

CIVILIZATION AND THE
ILLUSION OF PROGRESS

Human civilization is largely defined by the pursuit of urbanization, technological and economic progress, the establishment of their own standards of good and evil, and the consolidation of power. Rather than seeking partnership with God, nations and cultures often form alliances with rebellious supernatural entities (known as "gods") who exert control behind the scenes. With a determination to improve the human condition and overcome the consequences of their rebellion against God, humanity hope to create a utopian society on Earth, which they envision as their own version of paradise.

There was particular mention in the Book of Genesis of a man named Nimrod (whose name means "Rebel"), who was the grandson of Noah's second son Ham. He began to be a mighty one on the earth, the progenitor of the civilizations of Babel (Babylon), Erech (Uruk), Akkad (Akkadia), and Calneh, in the region of Mesopotamia (Genesis 10:8-10). He was notorious for being rebellious against God and zealously leading people in that direction. The famous Jewish historian, Flavius Josephus, held that it was under Nimrod's direction that the building of Babel and its tower began.

According to Josephus:

> "It was Nimrod who excited them to such an affront and contempt of God. He was the grandson of Ham, the son of Noah, a bold man, and of great strength of hand. He persuaded them not to ascribe it to God, as if it were through his means they were happy, but to believe that it was their own courage which procured that happiness. He also gradually changed the government into tyranny, seeing no other way of turning men from the fear of God, but to bring them into a constant dependence on his power. He also said he would be revenged on God, if he should have a mind to drown the world again; for that he would build a tower too high for the waters to reach. And that he would avenge himself on God for destroying their forefathers. Now the multitude were very ready to follow the determination of Nimrod, and to esteem it a piece of cowardice to submit to God; and they built a tower...The place wherein they built the tower is now called Babylon, because of the confusion of that language which they readily understood before; for the Hebrews mean by the word Babel, confusion."[1]

Nimrod cherished his "independence" of God and saw no need to submit to Him. He believed that through his efforts and bravery, he would overcome the curse of hardship, pain and death placed upon humanity because of their rebellion. Thus, he would procure happiness for himself. He was out to challenge God, to bring the rest of humanity under subjugation to him, and to make a name for himself.

He set out to build a city of a towering architectural masterpiece—a ziggurat. A ziggurat is regarded by scholars as one of Mesopotamia's famous man-made temple complexes. These temple complexes were considered the literal home of the gods, a place where the "heavenlies" (thought to be the demonic realm) and earth intersect, and people experience the presence, not of the creator God but of evil supernatural beings—a complete deviation from God's purpose for the cosmos. Astrological signs usually studded the top of such towers. The architecture of the structure attests to its purpose of existence—to bring the gods down to earth.

So in Babel, Nimrod wanted to unite humanity in the worship and authority of the gods. This was an open rejection of God their creator, a direct affront to God. God had earlier reiterated his original Edenic call after the flood incident for humanity to "Be fruitful and multiply, and fill the earth" (Genesis 9:1 NKJV). But instead of obeying and letting God be their ruler, humanity decided to gather together in a single city and construct the tower with the intention of bringing humanity under the rule of the rebellious supernatural beings (gods) in Babel. Once again, humanity showed a disdain for God and his rule; they had rebuffed God's attempt to partner with them and get humanity back on track with Him.

However, God confounded their language and they were unable to communicate among themselves because of linguistic differences. Therefore, they had no choice but to separate based on their linguistic groupings and migrate to various parts of the world such as Africa, India, China, the Americas, Europe, and other locations in accordance with the boundaries set by God. This led to the formation of distinct nations (a nation in the Bible refers to an ethnic group) as God let all nations go their own way (Acts 14:16). According to Deuteronomy 32:8:

> When the Most High assigned lands to the nations, when he divided up the human race, he established the boundaries of the peoples according to the number in his heavenly court.

The term "heavenly court" in this context refers to the "sons of God," although some versions render it as "according to the number of the sons of Israel." As Michael Heiser rightly points out, the rendition "sons of Israel" cannot be accurate since Israel did not exist as a nation at that time and was not included in the Table of Nations. Heiser further clarifies that these "sons of God" turn out to be rebellious members of God's heavenly court (gods) that humanity sought to ally with at Babel. As a result, God allowed each of these rebellious nations to be controlled by the corrupt sons of God as a judgment from God because of their rebellion against Him.[2]

However, God does something surprising. He decided to raise a new nation for Himself, by Himself. He singled out a man, Abraham, from amongst them in Mesopotamia, and called him to a new partnership with Him that would eventually produce a new nation for Himself, and ultimately a new breed of humanity. From then onwards, the storyline of the Old Testament revolved around the conflict between the new nation and the rebellious nations, as well as the conflict between God and the rebellious sons of God (gods) of those nations.[3] God in His mercies promised that through Abraham, these rebellious nations would be blessed. The new nation would act as a pathway for the nations in rebellion to reconnect with the true God. In Chapter Five, we follow this family of Abraham and see where it leads us. But for now, let's follow the trail of the rebellious nations and see where it takes them.

THE MARCH OF CIVILIZATION
The Mesopotamians (Sumerians, Akkadians, Assyrians and Babylonians) and their close neighbor the Persians continued in the rebellious footsteps of Cain, Nimrod and many others like them. Of course, they were not ready to make peace with God but to use their freedom to define their own standards of good and evil. A Mesopotamian ruler—and indeed most ancient rulers—was looked upon as a steward of the nation for and on behalf of their gods. These people were bent on working with and for their gods toward a mutually beneficial end, and using technology where possible to mitigate the effect of the curse of

hardship upon humanity. They made advances in engineering, medicine, mathematics, astronomy, metallurgy, agriculture, architecture, literature and law.

Mesopotamia is even commonly regarded as the "cradle of civilization." The people lived in cities and developed sophisticated architecture in stone and mud-brick. They invented simple machines including the wheel and axle, the lever, and the pulley system. They applied their knowledge of math in construction projects, in predicting the eclipse and the movement of planets, and in the development of the lunar calendar system. They used copper, bronze, and iron to make weapons such as swords, daggers and spears.[4] In medicine, they used a combination of creams, pills and magic to diagnose and treat illnesses and delay the curse of death. Perhaps two of the most important advances made by the Mesopotamians were the invention of the base-60 numeral system which is still in use today for measuring time, angles, geographic coordinates, and electronic navigation; and the invention of writing using the cuneiform script.[5] With this came the first writings in law (Code of Hammurabi) and literature (Epic of Gilgamesh).

In ancient Egypt, a powerful and technologically advanced civilization, continued the cycle of rebellion against God. Ancient Egyptian society had no reverence or regard for creator God but instead embraced a combination of magic, mythology, spiritualism, astrology, herbology, psychiatry, science, and technology.[6] They created a formal writing system known as hieroglyphs, which has become the precursor for most modern scripts, such as the Latin script (from which the English alphabet and several other language alphabets originated), the Slavic script, and the Arabic script.[7] They made advances in many areas of science and technology such as civil engineering, mathematics, agriculture, anatomy and medicine. They were known for building pyramids and obelisks in worship of their sun god Ra—the Egyptians' greatest deity. In keeping with this tradition, ancient

Egyptian obelisks and modern ones have been erected in most cities around the world.

The Pharaohs ran the empire for and on behalf of their gods. In fact, they were even considered gods by their culture. The Egyptians practiced the earliest known form of neuroscience and alchemy. According to the Egyptologist Wallis Budge, the word "alchemy" (from the Arabic word *al-kīmiya)* means "the Egyptian science."[8] Alchemists attempted to purify and perfect certain ingredients for the purpose of creating the elixir of immortality as well as solutions to cure any disease, and a universal solvent, among others.

The story is the same outside Near-East civilization. In the Indian subcontinent, a civilization emerged in the Indus Valley. Just like other civilizations, they engaged in the usual polytheistic form of worship of gods and goddesses, and in the practice of yoga, meditation and cremation. There was evidence of knowledge of astrology, metallurgy, metrology, mathematics, hydrography, medicine, civil engineering, and sewage management.[9] They were at the forefront of ship building and seafaring technologies among other inventions and discoveries. Jainism, Hinduism and Buddhism all had their roots in the Indus Valley civilization. The Buddha is regarded by some Hindus as the material incarnation (avatar) of Vishnu (one of the principal deities of Hinduism).

Buddhism became so popular that it traveled from India to the Far-East kingdom of China where it enjoyed equal success. In fact, the Chinese civilization has historically been a cradle and host to a variety of the most enduring religio-philosophical traditions that have shaped Chinese culture: Confucianism, Taoism, and Buddhism. But long before the advent of these polytheistic religious traditions, the ancient Chinese were well aware of the one true God, the creator of the universe.

70

Evidence from ancient Chinese pictographic characters (which depict mostly natural objects) provides clues of how the earliest Chinese settlers must have had a fresh revelation of humankind's origins—from creation to the confusion of languages at Babel.[10] The details of these symbols are independent confirmation from extra-biblical sources that these things actually happened. For example, the word for "to create" in Chinese is made up of pictographic characters for "ground" (dust), "mouth" (breath), and "alive" —affirming the Genesis account that God made man from the dust of the ground and breathed life into him, and he came alive. Interestingly, the word for "boat" is made up of pictographic characters for "vessel," "eight," and "people." So a boat is depicted in the Chinese language as a vessel for eight people, as in Noah's ark. The word for "blessed" or "blessing" is made up of pictographic characters to represent "one" or "first" (the first family which represents humanity), "mouth" (breathing person), a "garden," and "God." So in Chinese, just as in Genesis, a blessed person is one who lives under God's rule in the garden, something that humanity lost after they were banished from Eden—the Paradise Garden of God.

Moreover, the emperors of ancient China claimed the mandate of the gods and were deified as "Sons of Heaven" that ruled the empire for and on behalf of their gods.[11] Science and technology made remarkable advancements in ancient China, giving rise to numerous innovations such as the magnetic compass, paper, printing technology, cast iron, matches, the suspension bridge, raised-relief map, propeller, crossbow, south-pointing chariot, and gunpowder.[12]

In the Americas, the ancient civilizations of Mesoamerica (Inca, Maya, and Aztec) were no different from their counterparts in Asia and Africa in terms of religio-philosophical posture and worship of their gods. The Inca Emperors held a status that closely resembled the Pharaohs of Egypt. They constructed structures that resembled pyramids, complete with temples on the summit, for the purpose of worshiping their gods, akin to the ziggurats of Mesopotamia and the pyramids of Egypt. The Mesoamerican pantheon was comprised of a plethora of gods, goddesses, and deities, and they embraced a blend of spiritual practices such as astrology, divination, mythology, as well as more scientific disciplines such as arithmetic, science, and technology.[13] They created impressive feats of engineering, including both above ground and underground aqueducts, artificial lakes, flood prevention barriers, and even pressurized water systems.[14] Their masonry was quake-proof and their agricultural and construction techniques were relatively advanced, as were their writing and astronomical systems.

In Europe, the ancient Greek civilization emerged as a fusion of Greek and Near-Eastern cultures in the Eastern Mediterranean region. The Greeks believed in a pantheon of gods and goddesses and had dedicated places in their homes and temples to offer prayers and offerings to them. They had a deity for nearly every aspect of life. The ancient Greek civilization has had a significant impact on Western culture, including language, politics, education, the arts, philosophy, and science. The Greeks were known for their exceptional education, and no other ancient civilization was as highly educated as they were. Despite their vast knowledge, they knew not the true God, and superstitions and specious beliefs were prevalent in their society. Nevertheless, the Greeks made significant progress in various fields of science, mathematics, philosophy, and knowledge in general. Their civilization produced many prominent sages and philosophers, including Socrates, Plato, Aristotle, Pythagoras, Euclid, Archimedes, and Hippocrates.

Also in Europe, the impact of the Roman civilization on the modern world has been significant, and they were one of the most advanced civilizations of their time, technologically speaking. Their level of urbanization was impressive when compared to other pre-modern societies. Among ancient cities, Rome was unparalleled in its greatness. Before the rise of Christianity, the ancient Romans, like the Greeks, were known for their veneration of numerous deities, some of which were adopted from the Greek pantheon and others from conquered lands. Romulus, the legendary founder and first king of Rome was viewed as a god—the divine persona of the Roman people. They attributed their success as a world power to their collective commitment in maintaining good relations with their gods such as Jupiter, Juno, Minerva and Mars.

But, in spite of their civilized virtues, they displayed repugnant attitudes. Rome, which was then the capital of the world, was immersed in lavishness and public spectacles involving the shedding of blood for entertainment, with the crowd applauding and reveling in the sight. Unrestrained sensual gratification was rampant everywhere, taken to the extreme. What a grotesque display of filth!

For almost a millennium, Roman civilization was sustained by its technological advancements which enabled the expansion of Roman commerce and military prowess. The Romans were particularly skilled in civil engineering, and their civilization was characterized by remarkable progress in technology, architecture, culture, and law that remained unsurpassed for centuries. Among the notable Roman innovations and technological achievements were sophisticated civil engineering techniques (including stonemasonry, arches, and road construction), novel building materials (like concrete), aqueducts, transport, military technology, and certain inventions, such as the mechanical reaper, which remained unrivaled until the 19th century.[15] Above all, the Romans were masters of an advanced legal system and the art of governing a vast empire traversing Africa, Asia, and Europe, consisting of many different races, ethnicities, religions and customs.

When you look back in history, you'll discover that most ancient kingdoms and civilizations were founded and ruled by revered warrior kings who claimed to be part human, part god, and endowed with divine rights and extraordinary knowledge.

Nimrod and Gilgamesh in ancient Mesopotamia, the Pharaohs of ancient Egypt, Romulus and the Caesars of ancient Rome, the emperors of ancient China and Japan, the Obas and Oduduwa of the ancient Bini and Yoruba kingdoms in Nigeria, and a host of others, are all classic examples. Those revered kings and their cohorts were notoriously and fervently rebellious towards God. In term of moral values, they were capricious (i.e. changeable in their values) and given over to delusion and vice. They sought happiness and succor in mundane activities and esoteric beliefs. The Mesopotamians found succor in astronomy and astrology, the Egyptians in magic and alchemy, the Indians in yoga and mindfulness, the Chinese in *kung fu* (martial arts) and *Samatha-vipassana* meditation, the Greeks in mythology, sports and philosophy, and the Romans in paganism and gladiator games.

However, the "happiness" they experienced was merely temporary and sensual, completely unworthy of beings created in God's image. They were quite oblivious of their real misery, deficiency and depravity. As aptly noted by A. W. Pink, "There is scarcely a page in the annals of the world which does not furnish tragic illustrations of the greed and grind, the injustice and chicanery, the avarice and consciencelessness, the intemperance and immorality to which fallen human nature is so horribly prone. What a sad spectacle history presents of our race!".[16]

All of those powerful ancient civilizations from Babylon to Rome, with all their acclaimed power, technology, splendor and glamor came to an end at some point in history. Usually moral decay and corruption weakened them and led to conquest by a stronger nation. Today, they are no more; only their ruins testify of a once-thriving civilization. Since the collapse of the Roman Empire, all through to the end of the medieval period down to the end of the 20th century, many other civilizations and empires in between have come and gone. From the time the nations were dispersed in Babel and throughout most of history, the nations and their kings have been rebellious towards God. They rejected and rebuffed every attempt to partner with God and surrender to

His rule. Instead, they continued to form alliances and associate with the rebellious sons of God (evil supernatural beings), who continued to exercise unseen control behind the scenes.

Fast forward to the digital age of the 21st century, and we are now marching towards one big global civilization. The whole of humankind now is aiming at a single global civilization, determined to overcome its shared challenges and the inherent effects of breaking away from God. Is this another Tower of Babel in the making?

THE ILLUSION OF PROGRESS

We have just seen how, since the fall of man, humankind right from the ancient civilizations of Mesopotamia, Egypt, China, Greece, Rome down to the present global civilization, have invested countless resources (time, capital, energy, labor, etc.) in an attempt to improve the human condition through science and technology. Judging by our achievements over the years, it would seem like we are making progress. The perpetrators of this system would like to think that the trajectory of history is an unstoppable upward march from Edenic confinement to a free society, from barbarism to civilization, from impotence to power, and from ignorance to enlightenment with humans "progressing" from one stage to the next through leaps in our technology and science.

Modern scholars like Ian Morris, Hans Rosling, and Steven Pinker argue fervently for this method of thinking. For example, Steven Pinker in his book *Enlightenment Now: The Case for Reason, Science, Humanism, and Progress*, argues that the enlightenment values of reason, science, and humanism have brought progress, resulting in ever-increasing prosperity, happiness, and peace. In an attempt to indirectly persuade humanity to continue on the path of rebellion against God, Pinker uses well marshaled statistical data to show off in peacock fashion how much "progress" humanity has achieved towards improving the human condition, without the need of God.

"The idea of progress" is a worldview that rests on the notion that the human condition has improved over the course of history and will continue to improve towards a state of perfection if we devote resources to the advancement of knowledge in science and technology, economic development and social organization.[17] It hopes to create one big global civilization, a united humanity, and world peace; and to that end humanity must rid itself of any barriers to this desired state—including belief in God. Continue to look to human reason, they tell us, and keep on advancing and democratizing technology, globalizing the economy, and unifying the political system, and we will have paradise on earth.

Well, Nimrod had a similar vision. He attempted to turn humanity away from God, and unite them in a global government under his own control. The builders of the Tower of Babel boasted about their achievements and progress and the ensuing luxury and pleasure. They were out to make a name for themselves. Any attempt to ascribe it to God or to submit to God was frowned upon and viewed as cowardice. Their actions provoked God's swift intervention. It is said that those who fail to recognize the lessons of history, will fall by the same mistakes. In the same way, the utopian society that globalists look to, once we all renounce God and embrace the "idea of progress," is yet another illusion.

Although we think we are making progress, alas, all our so-called progress is nothing but a downward spiral. We have gone completely off-track, for we are busy chasing the wrong set of goals. Every inch of "progress" we make just adds another mile between us and God (the very source of life).

I once heard the story of a man who was asked to climb a particular tree in 60 seconds in a competition. To everyone's amazement, he did it in half the time, only to realize in the end that he had climbed the wrong tree. He was efficient but not effective. He had missed the goal. We (humanity) have missed the goal completely, for we are sinners headed in the wrong direction (Romans 3:23). The word "sin" may sound odd or religious to modern humans, but it is what it is. The original meaning of the word "sin" isn't religious at all. Ancient archers used it to describe missing the mark when their arrow went off target.[18] In Hebrew, the term "sin" is translated from the word *hatah*, which conveys the concept of "missing the mark" or "straying from the intended path." So in a nutshell, sin is a failure to achieve a goal. But what is the goal?

This brings me to another story of a man who was commissioned by his home government to represent them as ambassador in a faraway country. His mission was clear: to reflect the nation's image of a free market economy. On arrival, the ambassador, rather than work towards fulfilling this goal, chose to redefine his mission and set a completely different agenda. Through hard work and dedication, he made significant progress towards achieving his own goal, that of presenting a centrally controlled economic system. That story to an extent is a metaphor of the human condition.

In the first and second chapter of this book, I did make it clear that God appointed humans as His sole representatives on the earth. Their mandate was to rule over creation in partnership with Him, to extend His rule to the physical world, to reflect His will, His goodness and nature. This is what it means to be human. This is the central goal of humanity. Once we miss this goal, we fail to be truly human. In this way of seeing the world, sin is but a failure to be truly human. The fascinating thing about it is that, for most of the time when people are failing, they either don't know it, or even worse, they think they are making progress.

There's no denying that science and technology have had a profound impact on society throughout history, elevating human power, but also amplifying our imperfections and faults as a species. While it enabled us to have higher standards of living, it also caused us to exploit each other and the environment on an unprecedented scale. It is both a giver of good and an ongoing source of tragedy when it is used by depraved human beings, beings that have completely missed their goal on the planet. It solves a problem at one end, and introduces new problems at another. Every attempt to solve the problem of hardship and misery in one area somehow causes it to mutate in another.

And so, we are caught in this terrible condition that experts call a "progress trap." This is a condition, whereby in the course of pursuing "progress" we inadvertently introduce problems that we do not have the capacity or will to solve, for fear of interim losses in status or quality of life. This is a tragedy that has befallen the human race. Technology itself is not fundamentally immoral, but technology in the hands of immoral men and women is dangerous. The fault is not in our inventions, but in our ethics.

Again, A.W. Pink couldn't have put it better: "Man's separation from God deprived him of no mental or moral faculty, but it took from him the power to use them right so that man was no longer capable of doing anything pleasing to God. The natural man does as he pleases, but he pleases himself only in one direction—selfward and downward, never Godward and upward."[19] Despite all the advancements in science and technology, the one issue that remains unresolved is the deeply flawed and morally bankrupt nature of humanity.

We have ventured into outer space, harnessed our environment, built empires, innovated potent drugs, enhanced food cultivation, fostered broad markets and economic alliances, and amassed vast riches. But have we been able to find answers to the problem of misery, despair, injustice, and most of all, the problem of death in the world? Did the huge increase in human power bring about a corresponding improvement in the general well-being of individual humans? Unfortunately, our reign on earth has so far produced little or no hope for humanity. Today, we can afford to go to space, but we cannot boast of a peaceful home to go to; we produce more food but have less healthy strains for our consumption; we have more but enjoy less; we are wealthier but not healthier; we are smarter but not wiser.

Our achievements are characterized by materialism without morality, beauty without purity, wealth without wisdom, and lust without love. Yuval Harari was honest enough to admit that, "despite the astonishing things that humans are capable of doing, we remain unsure of our goals and we seem to be as discontented as ever. We have advanced from canoes to galleys to steamships to space shuttles—but nobody knows where we're going. We are more powerful than ever before, but have very little idea what to do with all that power. Worse still, humans seem to be more irresponsible than ever. Self-made gods with only the laws of physics to keep us company, we are accountable to no one. Is there anything more dangerous than dissatisfied and irresponsible gods who don't know what they want?"[20]

Rather than humble ourselves and return to God and our original purpose, we have continued in the dangerous path of Cain, Nimrod, and similar notables by trying to construct a worldview that completely disregards God. We continue to think that, through the pursuit of reason and advancements in science, technology, and social organization, we can uplift the human condition. Just like all great civilizations in the past that have risen and fallen, the utopian, secular society we strive to create will inevitably crumble like a statue made of clay. A sad state of affairs indeed! Ultimately, what we need is simply peace with God and a rediscovery of our original purpose.

Where do we go from here? Are we at the stage of no return? Who can rescue us from this mess?

CHAPTER FIVE

GOD'S RESCUE OPERATION

There is a movement among certain scientists to christen our current geological era after humanity by labeling it the Anthropocene. The term "Anthropocene" is derived from two Greek words: anthropo (meaning human) and cene (meaning recent), and is motivated by the belief that our species has caused a permanent and harmful impact on the earth. This impact can be seen in the widespread extinction of plant and animal species, pollution of the environment, significant changes in biodiversity and the atmosphere, and other detrimental effects. The concept has gained traction in recent times, and has been invoked by scholars, archaeologists, historians, and the media alike.

WHEN HUMANKIND RULES

Naming this era after ourselves is no show-off, and really a tongue-in-cheek reminder of our mess. The entire creation bears the brunt of our appalling stewardship. "For we know that all creation has been groaning as in the pains of childbirth right up to the present time" (Romans 8:22). The London based illustrator Steve Cutts summed it up perfectly in his short video called "MAN," a thought provoking animation about the impact of our reckless behavior on this beautiful planet we call home.[1]

In the beginning God made the heavens (the skies or outer space) and the earth (Genesis 1:1). And God described His creation as very good. Food was in abundance and freely available, needs were readily met; in fact, there was no need for money because everything was provided for. Suffering, pain, death and anything evil did not exist. They are simply the consequence of our decision to seize autonomy from God. Someone once said that "When humanity shrugged off allegiance to God, the entire creation by divine permission shook off allegiance to humanity." Every animal that snaps at us, every violent windstorm, every tsunami, earthquake and natural evil that devastates us proves that we are at odds with creation. Injustice, hate, mischief, selfishness, and the demeaning of our human dignity are a reality that we unleash on God's good world and on ourselves.

In effect, the world He once described as very good is now a place where goodness is despised. As pointed out in the Genesis account, humans were set apart from all other creatures as "the image of God" to rule the world by God's definition of good and evil. But, unfortunately, they chose to redefine good and evil in our own terms. We have created for ourselves a world where we have to labor and sweat, cheat and steal, compete and fight in order to survive—in a fanciful competition called "the survival of the fittest."

As a consequence of this fight to be the fittest, the world has been bathed with the blood of the never-ending cycle of wars and massacres. The world is no longer a fair place for everyone. Greed so dominates that people up there don't care about those down below, and when those down below eventually get to the top, they behave exactly like their peers. Everyone wants to outdo the other and exploit them at the slightest opportunity—self-seeking is the name of the game, which has resulted in widespread inequality, unequal distribution of wealth, poverty, and social class. We see this happening not only on a personal and family level, but also in communities, extending to nations and whole civilizations; and the cycle is repeated over and over from generation to generation.

Any intelligent being visiting earth from a "sane world" would be shocked to see the depth of evil, wickedness and chaos that pervades the earth. Despite the huge investment in public policing, the justice system and surveillance technology, evil and human wickedness has proved difficult to contain. Not even religion, technology, education and legislation are sufficient. You may not realize how bad it is because that's the world you have grown up to know—so it would seem absolutely normal to you. But anyone who has lived long enough knows it's a living hell here on the earth, and God hates it.

We might ask why God doesn't just eliminate evil right now. The reason is simple: for God to eliminate evil, He'd have to completely eliminate all of humanity together with the rebellious supernatural beings. That would certainly solve the problem of evil. But it would mean that God's original idea of creating human beings to live and rule with Him was a huge blunder. And an omniscient God doesn't make blunders; His eternal purpose will never be thwarted. He had His plans cut out well ahead of time.

GOD'S REDEMPTIVE PLAN

We might also wish that God had never given humans freedom. But where would we be then? In choosing to give us freedom, God also chose not to make us mindless entities—zombies or automatons. That's the alternative to having free will. But God loved the idea of humanity too much to take away that basic right. And so, after evil entered the world, He devised a means to redeem humanity, restore Eden, and wipe away every tear (Revelation 7:17; 21:4). The story of the Bible is a story about God wanting to heal His world and expunge Evil from within us and out of the earth.

Our story can be likened to a great king who desired to have a large family, but he had just one son. He wanted his only son to have offspring and fill his kingdom and become co-rulers with him. But one day, tragedy struck. His only son and his son's wife acquired the incurable HIV/AIDS infection, and death began to slowly but surely descend on them. They eventually had children before they died but their children were not spared the deadly virus. They had acquired it from their parents from birth, and the cycle would likely continue from generation to generation. In fact, the entire bloodline was polluted with the deadly virus, which looked like death would perpetually reign in the family. The king's hope of having a large family that would be co-rulers with him was completely dashed. He was under pressure to either wipe out his entire progeny and forget about his dream, or step in quickly to save his family and rekindle it.

Well, the king devised a winning strategy. He began afresh with birthing another son of His own, whose blood was uninfected with the incurable HIV/AIDS. Through this offspring of His, the rest of the infected family members would have the opportunity to be cleaned up and saved.

> Although Adam and Eve failed God, and came short of His expectations, God was not giving up on them. He was determined to redeem humanity and restore the lost blessings of the kingdom life in Eden. God first tells the serpent that deceived humanity that, despite its apparent victory, it is destined for defeat. Right in the very act of the rebellion, God made a promise that one day, someone, a son of the woman, was going to come and deal a fatal blow to the serpent's head. However, this triumph will come at a cost as the serpent will also wound His heel (Genesis 3:14-15).

We see glimpses of this redemptive plan in biblical history as God interacts with each successive generation.

FROM PROMISED LAND TO EXILE

In chapter Four, we read about the Tower of Babel rebellion against God led by Nimrod that happened after the flood. As a result, God divided the people by confusing their common language with a diversity of languages, which caused them to be scattered to the ends of the earth. Since they rejected God's attempt to partner with them and restore the lost blessings of the kingdom life in Eden, God had no choice but to move on without them.

God decided to raise a new nation for Himself, by Himself. He singled out a man, Abram ("Exalted father"), who He later renamed Abraham ("Father of all nations") and called into a new partnership with Him. God in His mercies promised that through Abraham, the rebellious nations would be blessed, hence the change in name to Abraham to reflect his new status as the "father of all nations." Abraham's roots could be traced back to Shem, the eldest son of Noah, and he was a native of Ur of the Chaldeans, which was situated in southern Babylonia in modern day Iraq (Genesis 15:7). God's plan through Abraham and his family was to restore the lost blessings of kingdom life in Eden, beginning with the family of Abraham and then to every nation on the earth (Genesis 12:1-3). The blessings of kingdom life in Eden is when God's people live in God's appointed place under God's rule.[2]

The LORD commissioned Abram as follows,

> "Leave your native country, your relatives, and your father's family, and go to the land that I will show you. I will make you into a great nation. I will bless you and make you famous, and you will be a blessing to others. I will bless those who bless you and curse those who treat you with contempt. All the families on earth will be blessed through you." Then the Lord appeared to Abram and said, "I will give this land to your descendants." And Abram

built an altar there and dedicated it to the Lord, who had appeared to him (Genesis 12:1-3, 7).

At this, Abram fell face down on the ground. Then God said to him, "This is my covenant with you: I will make you the father of a multitude of nations! What's more, I am changing your name. It will no longer be Abram. Instead, you will be called Abraham, for you will be the father of many nations…This is the everlasting covenant: I will always be your God and the God of your descendants after you" (Genesis 17:3-5, 7b).

As the nations had declined God's offer to form a partnership, God made the decision to establish a partnership with Abraham instead. It is called the Abrahamic covenant. Upon careful observation, one can discern that the covenant consists of two dimensions: a national aspect, and an international aspect. The national aspect entails God's pledge to bestow upon Abraham a great nation and land for his descendants, while the international aspect involves God's assurance to bless all nations of the world through Abraham. It is one of blessing, both in the narrow sense for the nation that would arise from Abraham's bloodline to inhabit the Promised Land (God's appointed place), and in the broader sense, for all those who would respond to the call of reconnecting with the true God. It is marked by a walk of faith, trusting in God to fulfill His promises.

Miracles happened as Abraham obeyed this promise. Moving into the promised land with his wife, Sarah, his retinue and all his flocks and herds, Abraham became a very prosperous man. One of the miracles was that, although he and his wife had been childless due to old age and his wife being barren, God gave them a son Isaac. From Isaac came Jacob and from Jacob (whom God later renamed Israel) came twelve sons who would be the twelve tribes of Israel. This was to be the backbone of the nation of Israel. To one son Judah, Jacob, the father, prophesied that the scepter of authority would be passed down through his lineage and eventually lead to the ultimate One that God promised would deal a fatal blow to the serpent's head. The one whom all nations will honor.

> "The scepter will not depart from Judah, nor the ruler's staff from his descendants, until the coming of the one to whom it belongs, the one whom all nations will honor" (Genesis 49:10).

From the house of Judah arose David, son of Jesse, whom God appointed King over the nation. A man after God's own heart, David was the person that God chose to establish a partnership with. It is called the Davidic covenant. God's covenant with David encompasses both a national (temporal) dimension, as well as an international (eternal) dimension.

The national (temporal) aspect of the covenant was this. God reaffirmed the promise of the land that He made in His covenant with Abraham and Moses. God then promised to establish a line of kings from David's household to reign over the nation of Israel.

> "And I will provide a homeland for my people Israel, planting them in a secure place where they will never be disturbed. Evil nations won't oppress them as they've done in the past." … Furthermore, the Lord declares that he will make a house for you—a dynasty of kings! (2 Samuel 7:10, 11b).

So far we've seen the national (temporal) aspect of the covenant. But then the promise in verse 16 continues and expands:

> "'… Your house and your kingdom will continue before me for all time, and your throne will be secure forever'" (2 Samuel 7:16).

So the national (temporal) aspect of God's covenant with David opens out into the international (eternal) dimension—the promise of an everlasting kingdom. God made a promise that the Davidic dynasty and kingdom would last forever. This is an obvious reference to the Messiah who will rule the nations forever; the promised seed of the woman who would crush the serpent's head and act as a doorway for the nations in rebellion to reconnect with the true God and regain access to the lost kingdom life in Eden.

We know that King David during his forty-year reign extended the kingdom to its furthest limits to reach the zenith of its power and glory. He was celebrated as a hero and the ideal leader. So could David have been the promised seed of the woman who would crush the serpent's head as mentioned in Genesis 3:15?

No, the evil serpent was not crushed in his time. Yes, David was a man with tremendous zeal for God's kingdom but he was also a man with many imperfections. Neither did the prophecy see fulfillment in the reign of his son, Solomon. Solomon started off brilliantly by being a worshiper of the God of Abraham, Isaac and Jacob. He was blessed by God with such great wisdom and prosperity, that heads of state, even the Queen of Sheba, would visit Jerusalem to admire the magnificent temple, its impressive architecture and all its opulence. But Solomon had one weakness and that was women. He could not resist them and ended up possessing a harem of 700 wives and 300 concubines, which added to his trophies. But, sadly, it turned his eyes away from the things of God and caused him to sin by worshiping the foreign gods of his foreign wives. This was expressly forbidden by the law and in God's personal covenant with him:

> "And as for you, *if* you will walk before me, as David your father walked, with integrity of heart and uprightness, doing according to all that I have commanded you, and keeping my statutes and my rules, *then* I will establish your royal throne over Israel forever, as I promised David your father, saying, 'You shall not lack a man on the throne of Israel.' *But if* you turn aside from following me, you

or your children, and do not keep my commandments and my statutes that I have set before you,
but go and serve other gods and worship them, *then*
I will cut off Israel from the land that I have given
them, and the house that I have consecrated for my
name I will cast out of my sight …" (1 Kings 9:4-7
ESV, emphasis added)

Solomon was assured of a continuing kingdom **if** he followed
the Lord's commands. **But if** he turned aside and worshiped
other gods, like the rebellious nations did, **then** the nation
would be lost. But Solomon had clearly violated the covenant
and dragged the people into idol worship with all its detestable
practices.

On the Mount of Olives, east of Jerusalem, he even
built a pagan shrine for Chemosh, the detestable
god of Moab, and another for Molech, the detestable
god of the Ammonites. (1 Kings 11:7).

Molech, the god of the Ammonites, and Chemosh, the god of
the Moabites, were associated with child sacrifice. In addition,
altars were built for Ashtoreth, the goddess of war and sexual
love in the region.

God was merciful to Solomon for the sake of his father, and
the throne was not removed from him in his lifetime. But upon
his death, there was a revolt against his son, Rehoboam, and the
kingdom was split into two. Ten of the twelve tribes formed the
Northern Kingdom or Kingdom of Israel, and the remaining two
tribes, Judah and Benjamin, formed the Southern Kingdom or
Kingdom of Judah. Israel, led by its new ruler, Jeroboam, went
into apostasy by devising its own places of worship (no longer
at the temple of Jerusalem), its own feasts and its own forms
of worship.

The succession of kings in both kingdoms fluctuated
between the worship of the true God, Yahweh, and the gods of

the surrounding region. In Judah, there were kings who were deemed godly, namely Asa, Jehoshaphat, Jotham, Hezekiah, and Josiah. In contrast, in Israel, only one king, named Jehu, was considered godly. However, despite his virtuous acts, Jehu remained attached to some false gods. These godly kings made attempts to destroy the high places and reinstitute the worship of the true God. But, by and large, both kingdoms declined spiritually, morally and hence materially. God warned them of the consequences of their disobedience and breaking the terms of partnership. Portraying Himself as a Husband to them, He simultaneously berated them for their "spiritual adultery" and tried to woo them back to Him as their faithful husband. But the warnings were taken lightly.

Then the inevitable judgment fell. The Northern Kingdom, Israel, was overrun by the Assyrians, a fierce warring nation. The ten tribes were taken into exile from their God-appointed place and scattered throughout the Assyrian Empire, which history records as "the ten lost tribes of Israel." The Assyrians succeeded in ending the sovereign status of the Northern Kingdom (Israel) forever.

The Southern Kingdom struggled on for a period of time, but then it too was conquered and the armies of Babylonian King Nebuchadnezzar destroyed the temple in Jerusalem. A significant portion of the population, along with their ruler King Zedekiah, were taken into exile in Babylon. Zedekiah made history as the last King of Judah from the Davidic line that ruled the Southern Kingdom (Judah).

Can you see a clear parallel between exile from God's Paradise (the Garden of Eden) and exile from the Promised Land? The Promised Land was bestowed upon them as a gift, with the condition that they remain faithful to their covenant relationship with God. However, they willingly violated their alliance with God, and served other gods, resulting in exile from their God-appointed homeland. The Southern Kingdom of Judah was exiled to Babylon, the very city where humanity unanimously rejected God. In a way, the condition of exile embodies the human condition. We find ourselves trapped in a cycle where our rejection of God and moral failures result in a "Babylonian captivity" that we cannot break free from. We can only hope that someday we will return to our God-appointed place where we enjoy God's blessings free from the shackles of enslavement.

So now, it seems like all hope is lost as there are no more kings from David's line to possibly fulfill God's promise. But God remains committed to fulfilling His promise and hasn't given up. During those trying times, God sent certain individuals called "prophets" who continually reminded everyone that cared to listen to the promise that the serpent crushing King would come; and that He will defeat evil and restore the lost kingdom life. God's word through the prophets rekindled the hope that someday, a king will come and rescue them from the Babylonian exile they had brought upon themselves.

In fact, one of those prophets whose name was Daniel was so specific about the timing of the arrival of the coming King. Daniel, who was also taken captive to Babylon and served as an advisor to the king, records that the exile would last 70 years as prophesied by Jeremiah. He predicted that from the time of the decree to rebuild Jerusalem until the arrival of the expected Messiah it would be 483 years (Daniel 9:25).

> "Know therefore and understand,
> *That* from the going forth of the command
> To restore and build Jerusalem
> Until Messiah the Prince,
> *There shall be* seven weeks and sixty-two weeks;
> The street shall be built again, and the wall,
> Even in troublesome times" (Daniel 9:25 NKJV).

Now a biblical "week" is often interpreted as a year, so 69 weeks (seven weeks + sixty-two weeks) amounts to 69 x 7, or 483 years.

But sadly, none of those prophets (including Daniel himself) witnessed its fulfillment in their lifetime, and after the demise of Malachi (last of the old block of prophets), there was a long period of prophetic silence that lasted about 400 years. This period saw the emergence of notable world figures and influencers. A few decades after Malachi's final message from God, a renowned Greek philosopher named Socrates rose to prominence and began impacting the world with his philosophical ideas and teachings.[3] Socrates was succeeded by his student Plato, and later by Aristotle. Other notable figures that emerged during those 400 years of prophetic silence include Buddha, Confucius, Alexander the Great (who was tutored by Aristotle), Julius Caesar, and Pompey—during whose time the nation fell again into the hands of another imperial power—the Roman Empire. And the ordeal of being in exile endured, but this time it took place within the confines of their own homeland.

HERE COMES THE SERPENT CRUSHING KING

After the long years of silence, a new prophet—an austere character called John the Baptist suddenly emerged as a forerunner of the serpent crushing King. On one fateful day around AD 27–29 according to scholarly estimates, while baptizing followers in the Jordan River, he announced the long-awaited good news: "'Look! The Lamb of God who takes away the sin of the world! ... I did not recognize him as the Messiah, but I have been baptizing with water so that he might be revealed to Israel'... I didn't know he was the one, but when God sent me to baptize with water, he told me, 'The one on whom you see the Spirit descend and rest is the one who will baptize with the Holy Spirit.' I saw this happen to Jesus, so I testify that he is the Chosen One of God" (John 1: 29, 31, 34-35). Wow! It had been a very long wait—thousands of years in the making since the fall of humanity for the promised seed of the woman.

His Hebrew name is *Yeshua HaMashiach* (Jesus the Messiah), the chosen King. Okay, but ... wait a minute! Was this truly the one who would restore the lost blessings of kingdom life in Eden to the nations in an everlasting covenant? Was this the seed of the woman, the serpent crushing King? Besides John's testimony, what other evidence do we have to establish that He was the One? We know because He fulfilled everything that was written about the Messiah in scripture.

Here are the key prophecies that were fulfilled:

He fulfilled Daniel's prophecy.
Daniel foretold that it would take 483 years from the decree to rebuild Jerusalem until the expected Messiah would arrive. Although there were four decrees, it is uncertain which decree Daniel was referring to, and what calendar system he was using (Babylonian or Jewish). The first decree was issued by Cyrus and allowed Zerubbabel and others to begin rebuilding Jerusalem (Ezra 2:1). This was followed by another decree by Darius, which allowed more exiles to return. Artaxerxes I issued two decrees: The first, which was issued around 457 BC, allowed Ezra and others to return and rebuild (Ezra 7:1-10), while the second issued around 444 BC, enabled Nehemiah and many others to return (Nehemiah 2:4-11).[4]

The general consensus among Bible scholars is that by taking the decree issued to Ezra by Artaxerxes I in 457 BC as the starting point, the 483 years referred to in Daniel's prophecy ends around AD 27–29 (the widely accepted date for the baptism of Jesus, when John announced Him as the Messiah). Isn't it remarkable that the Messiah arrives precisely on schedule, just as Daniel had predicted?

The Chosen One would need to come from the lineage of David.

God promised King David that his throne would be estab-lished forever:

> "Your house and kingdom will endure before me forever, and your throne will be established forever" (2 Samuel 7:16 CSB).

In the very first chapter of Matthew the direct descent from Abraham through David to the Messiah is mentioned in one short succinct line:

> This is a record of the ancestors of Jesus the Messiah, a descendant of David and of Abraham (Matthew 1:1-16).

He would have to be born in Bethlehem.

The prophet Micah predicted that He would come from the little town of Bethlehem. Now how does anyone pre-arrange their own birth?

> But you, O Bethlehem Ephrathah, are only a small village among all the people of Judah. Yet a ruler of Israel, whose origins are in the distant past, will come from you on my behalf (Micah 5:2).

This prophecy was confirmed by the wise men before King Herod:

> King Herod was deeply disturbed when he heard this, as was everyone in Jerusalem. He called a meeting of the leading priests and teachers of religious law and asked, "Where is the Messiah supposed to be born?"

"In Bethlehem in Judea," they said, "for this is what the prophet wrote: ..." (Matthew 2:3-5, emphasis added).

There would be divine confirmation.

God confirmed Jesus as His Son, when He was baptized by John the Baptist in the Jordan:

> When Jesus was baptized, he went up immediately from the water. The heavens suddenly opened for him, and he saw the Spirit of God descending like a dove and coming down on him. And a voice from heaven said, "This is my beloved Son, with whom I am well-pleased." (Matthew 3:16-17 CSB).

Jesus was to be the sacrificial lamb.

The Prophet Isaiah spoke of the coming Messiah as the sacrificial lamb without blemish or defect, the one that would be the ultimate sacrifice for our sins:

> He was oppressed and treated harshly,
> yet he never said a word.
> He was led like a lamb to the slaughter.
> And as a sheep is silent before the shearers,
> he did not open his mouth.
> Unjustly condemned,
> he was led away.
> No one cared that he died without descendants,
> that his life was cut short in midstream.
> But he was struck down
> for the rebellion of my people. (Isaiah 53:7-8).

Jesus' ministry would be confirmed by scripture.

Right after being tested in the wilderness, Jesus went to the synagogue and, reading from the Book of Isaiah, He announced the fulfillment of this prophecy and the start of His ministry:

"The Spirit of the Lord is upon me,
for he has anointed me to bring Good News
to the poor.
He has sent me to proclaim that captives will
be released,
that the blind will see,
that the oppressed will be set free,
and that the time of the Lord's favor has come."

He rolled up the scroll, handed it back to the attendant, and sat down. All eyes in the synagogue looked at him intently. Then he began to speak to them. *"The Scripture you've just heard has been fulfilled this very day!"*
(Luke 4:16-21, emphasis added).

His ministry would be confirmed by eye witness reports.

All four Gospels and eye witness accounts in the Book of Acts report that He went around preaching the good news that God's reign had arrived. He demonstrated it by confronting the effects of evil on people by healing them and forgiving them of their sins, restoring sanity and order into their lives. Further, He exercised sovereignty over nature and the forces of evil by commanding the storms to be still and the dead to rise. He was the ultimate image of God—a true representation of what it means to be truly human.

Jesus' message to the world was that their basic need was a change of heart and a change of government, from self-government to God's government, from self-rule to God's rule.

The government will rest on his shoulders. And he will be called: Wonderful Counselor, Mighty God, Everlasting Father, Prince of Peace. His government and its peace will never end. He will rule with fairness and justice from the throne of his ancestor David for all eternity (Isaiah 9:6-7, emphasis added).

Jesus' message resonated with the common people, who had for a long time been yearning for freedom from oppression. He went about telling them to make a U-turn and reverse the course of their lives because God's government had arrived. But Jesus did not exactly use the word "government." He used the word "kingdom," and the way He presented God's kingdom shocked everybody. The people were expecting a militant king to defeat the current imperialist regime of Rome and, like a benevolent dictator, bring about a political kingdom. Instead, He described His kingdom as one that would invade this present evil age and transform the lives of men and women, delivering them from the power of sin, sickness and death, and bringing them into the right relationship with God.

He said many radical things that ran counter to our normal propensities. For instance, you live under God's reign when you give your total allegiance to Him. When you give your total allegiance to Him, you reflect God's will and His true nature. You respond to evil with good by loving, not just your friends and the lovable, but also your enemies, forgiving them and seeking peace. He spoke of God in the most intimate of terms, calling Him "*Abba*," an Aramaic word which translates to "Daddy"! (Mark 14:35). "*Abba*" signifies the close, intimate relationship of a father and his child, as well as the childlike trust that a young child puts in his daddy.

But this noble mission did not go unchallenged. Jesus' authority and influence threatened the religious leaders of the day to the point that they finally decided to have Him executed. Jesus did not put up any resistance when the time came for God's will to be fulfilled. He saw the sin and the utter depravity of the people of His day as just one small part of the entire human condition. He assured His followers that He was going to crush the serpent's head and defeat evil by taking the full weight of humanity's sin on to Himself and giving His life in an act of sacrificial love.

But why did it have to be Jesus and not any virtuous man to be our Savior?

Because, for the sacrifice to be acceptable to God, it had to be a totally sinless one without the slightest blemish of sin. Only Jesus among all men could qualify for that. How so?

Jesus was sinless because He was not conceived in sin like the rest of humankind. His was a virgin birth overshadowed by the power of the Holy Spirit:

> And the angel answered and said to her (Mary), "The Holy Spirit will come upon you, and the power of the Highest will overshadow you; therefore, also, that Holy One who is to be born will be called the Son of God" (Luke 1:35, emphasis added).

His sinlessness was confirmed by the following scriptures:

> For God made Christ, who never sinned, to be the offering for our sin, so that we could be made right with God through Christ (2 Corinthians 5:21).

> This High Priest of ours understands our weaknesses, for he faced all of the same testings we do, yet he did not sin. (Hebrews 4:15).

So Christ as the sacrificial Lamb had to become that sin for us on the cross.

> All of us, like sheep, have strayed away. We have left God's paths to follow our own. Yet the LORD *laid on him the sins of us all* (Isaiah 53:6, emphasis added).

He received the full brunt of the Father's wrath through the terrible pain and humiliation He endured. David, in one of his psalms speaks prophetically of the Messiah's punishment:

> But You have cast off and abhorred,
> You have been furious with Your anointed.

You have renounced the covenant of Your servant;
You have profaned his crown by casting it to
the ground.
You have broken down all his hedges;
You have brought his strongholds to ruin.
All who pass by the way plunder him;
He is a reproach to his neighbors.
You have exalted the right hand of his adversaries;
You have made all his enemies rejoice.
You have also turned back the edge of his sword,
And have not sustained him in the battle.
You have made his glory cease,
And cast his throne down to the ground

The days of his youth You have shortened;
You have covered him with shame (Psalm
89:38-45 NKJV).

But paying the penalty for us with His life was not enough. Jesus had to break the power of sin and death. That meant He had to overcome death. Jesus took on the evil serpent and all the forces of darkness by challenging them to do their worst. He was going to let evil exhaust all of its power on Him, using its only real weapon: death. When Jesus died on the cross, the serpent was gleeful, thinking it had finally crushed Him. But if he had heard the Genesis prophecy right, it said that he the serpent would only **wound His heel**. And so when it seemed like the serpent had won, he was in for the shock of his life: Jesus rises from the dead! And now Jesus has the ultimate power over evil and death. He opened up a way for anyone to escape from the serpent's grip over sin and death. Jesus' death and resurrection was the final crushing of the serpent's head that robbed him of his power (Hebrews 2:14).

Jesus' victory over the evil serpent is analogous with Neo's victory over the evil Agent Smith and his cohorts in the final battles of the Matrix Trilogy movie. The Agents were guardians and masters of the Matrix, who had all the keys to the virtual world of the Matrix. After Agent Smith succeeded in killing Neo, it seemed like it was all over and the Agent had won. But, surprisingly, Neo miraculously bounced back to life in the Matrix, and could immediately decode the Matrix codes all around him.

Neo paid the ultimate price of death by allowing Agent Smith to exhaust all of his power on him in order to destroy him and rescue humanity. He allowed the Agent to infect him with his malicious code before he eventually crushed him. Neo's death and "resurrection" helped him gain total mastery of the Matrix, and render the authorities (Agent Smith and co) powerless. Now he had the keys to the Matrix program that enslaved humanity to a humdrum existence. Neo defeated Agent Smith, just as Jesus defeated the evil serpent (satan).

The risen Christ now holds the keys of death and Hades (Revelation 1:18). Now, as rightly noted by N.T. Wright, "The Jesus in question has, as His credentials, the fact that He 'was dead', and is 'alive forever.' Like someone whispering to us that they know the secret way out of the dungeon where we have been imprisoned, He says, 'I've got the keys! The keys of death and Hades—I have them right here! There's nothing more you need to worry about.'" The price of sin has been paid in full, and divine justice is satisfied.

At the time of writing, my son, who was six years old, posed a thought-provoking question to me: "Dad, if Jesus came to save the world, why did He limit Himself to spreading His message only in Israel? He should have traveled the world." This caught me off guard, and I asked him what he thought. He suggested that perhaps Jesus wanted his followers to carry His message to the far corners of the world, given that He had limited time on earth. I concurred, acknowledging that he had grasped the idea perfectly.

Indeed, Jesus' charge to His followers was to go out and keep announcing this good news of the arrival of God's kingdom (which represents the life in Eden that was lost) to the world, and to invite everyone to give their allegiance to Him, so they can experience in practical terms the reality of the defeat of evil in their daily lives. Today, Jesus' power over evil and death is still available to us to begin confronting the effects of evil in our own lives. This is indeed the greatest cheering news of all, and certainly worth sharing.

OUR PROPER RESPONSE

So Jesus' death and resurrection has opened up a way for us to be set free from the grip of the evil serpent, and to reconnect with God and experience kingdom life again. Now the big question is: how does one enter into that experience? What demands does God's kingdom make on us to qualify? Does one enter the kingdom by merely making a verbal confession, repeating a creed or doing a lot of penance? The kingdom makes only one fundamental demand: a decision from the heart.

Our decision is to repent and openly acknowledge Jesus as the Lord of our lives. Jesus' message to the world is to repent for the Kingdom of God has arrived (Matthew 3:2). The plain meaning of "repentance" is a change in one's way of thinking. It means to change direction in one's life and make a decisive commitment to the Kingdom of God and the Lordship of Jesus. Repentance is not some shallow apology but entails a total change of heart, a complete turning away from our sins. We may still struggle with sin, but this is the start of the turnaround.

The Kingdom of God does not require us to produce the life or power it needs; it provides them for us. It also doesn't expect us to attain the righteousness it demands, rather it bestows us with its own righteousness. The Kingdom of God does not set up moral standards and only grants admission to those who meet them. The Kingdom of God requires only one thing: a decision to repent and receive the kingdom as presented by Jesus.[5] By doing so, you receive its life, power, righteousness, blessings, and the destiny that awaits those who embrace it.

When Peter first announced the good news of the arrival of God's kingdom to the people of his day, the Bible tells us that "they were cut to the heart and said to Peter and the other apostles, 'Brothers, what shall we do?' Peter replied, 'Repent and be baptized, every one of you, in the name of Jesus Christ for the forgiveness of your sins. And you will receive the gift of the Holy Spirit…'" (Acts 2:37-38). According to Romans 10:9-10:

> If you openly declare that Jesus is Lord and believe in your heart that God raised him from the dead, you will be saved. For it is by believing in your heart that you are made right with God, and it is by openly declaring your faith that you are saved.

So you are declaring your belief that Jesus is the Son of God and that He died for your sins and rose again. When you make Him Lord, you are saying that He rules over every area of your life. When you say that with a sincere heart, you are saved. Once saved, and have received the gift of the Holy Spirit, which is the confirmation of God's personal presence filling your life, the next step is to undergo a process of mentorship (discipleship), so that you can grow in the Word of God and be fruitful in the kingdom.

A man once approached Jesus and said, "Lord, I will follow You, but first let me say goodbye to my family" (Luke 9:61). Of course, there's nothing wrong with saying goodbye to your loved ones if you choose to fully dedicate your life to following Jesus. But Jesus replied to him, "Anyone who puts a hand to the plow and then looks back is not fit for the Kingdom of God" (Luke 9:62). In other words, Jesus is highlighting the need for a decisive commitment. The man who approached Him was willing but hesitant. There is no room for foot-dragging. If you wish to respond to the Kingdom of God and its demands upon your life, there must be no hesitation, no looking back. You must let go of what you left behind and not cling to the past. Remember Lot's wife (Luke 17:32).

Sometimes the decision which God's kingdom demands can come at great cost. Despite this, God's kingdom is a priceless treasure worth giving up all you have for, if need be, just to possess it. A wealthy young man once approached Jesus and asked, "Good Teacher, what should I do to inherit eternal life?" (Luke 18:18). This young man was expressing the common human desire for immortality. After determining the man's sincerity, Jesus told him that a decision was necessary. Seeing that the man's attachment to his wealth was hindering him from making the decision, He said, "Sell all that you have and follow Me."

Now, giving up wealth is not a requirement for entry into God's kingdom. However, in this particular instance, it was necessary to remove a hindrance. Wealth is not inherently evil, but it becomes so when it prevents a decision for the kingdom. Anything, be it wealth, career, or family, that obstructs one's decision for God's kingdom must be set aside. If a person's loyalty to wealth, position, career, ambition, or even another person surpasses their loyalty to God, their priorities must shift. All other interests must become secondary to the rule of God.

The Kingdom of God may even cost a man his very life. Jesus said, "If you refuse to take up your cross and follow me, you are not worthy of being mine" (Matthew 10:38), and, "If any of you wants to be my follower, you must give up your own way, take up your cross daily, and follow me" (Luke 9:23). In the Roman era, the cross was a tool of execution, similar to the electric chair, scaffold, gas chamber, lethal injection, or bullet. Your cross is the means of your dying to your flesh life, and the rulership of self. The act of taking up your cross and denying oneself could therefore mean facing physical death or making some sacrifice. This does not mean that every follower of Jesus must face an untimely physical death, but it does mean that—and I express this with caution—if faced with a choice between death and loyalty to Christ and His kingdom, one should be prepared to choose death. That is the ultimate consequence of one's allegiance. Many have made this ultimate sacrifice out of love and loyalty to Jesus and His kingdom.

The future has arrived in the present. The life of the age to come is available to us now. So, what then shall we do? Simply put: repent, accept and declare Jesus as the Lord of your life. Admit your rebellion against God, regret your misdeeds, let God's grace guide you to turn your life around, and demonstrate your commitment to change through your actions. The Kingdom of God is here and requires total surrender to God's rule. Embracing and living this truth requires complete trust in God.

CHAPTER SIX

FREEDOM OF THE WILL

———————

A vital aspect of human significance is recognizing ourselves as free and accountable beings with moral responsibility. Based on this understanding, we freely make choices and bear moral responsibility for them and the actions that stem from them, while being aware of the alternatives open to us. However, today, this understanding is increasingly under attack in the popular scientific narrative, and in popular culture that includes the mainstream media.

The reason may not be far-fetched. Nobody wants to take responsibility for his or her actions anymore. They would rather blame it on the environment, biochemistry, genes, or external forces—anything but themselves. People are clutching at straws, latching on to anything that attempts to prove that free will does not exist. People are looking to find reasons why God is not just in penalizing them for their "bad choices" and rewarding others for their "good choices." "If our choices aren't made freely, why should God penalize or reward us for them?" they ask. To be clear, there is no dispute over the existence of will: humans certainly have a will. The issue at hand is whether this "will" is free or not.

DOES NEUROSCIENCE DISPROVE FREE WILL?

The debate on free will has been going on for millennia. However, in recent times, some cognitive neuroscientists and scholars have become increasingly bullish in their claim that all human actions can be explained by an "unbreakable chain of cause and effect." They came into the free will discourse, claiming to have decisively resolved the matter with a single sweeping statement that portrays human behavior as a result of a continuous chain of neuron firings, leading to involuntary thoughts and actions that stretches back to our birth and beyond.[1] Their actions are gradually undermining our understanding of ourselves as free and accountable beings with moral responsibility.

One experiment that is frequently cited as evidence that science has proved that free will is an illusion, and humans are not the authors of their actions is Libet's experiment. Scientists claim that the experiment proves that our conscious choice is, in reality, an ex post facto awareness of what has been decided unconsciously. In other words, the "brain decides" to act before the person is conscious of it.

It all started in 1964 when two German scientists in an experiment monitored the electrical activity in the brains of volunteers for several months. The participants had wires fixed to their scalp and had only one task to perform: to randomly tap their fingers as it pleased them up to 500 times a visit. The purpose of the experiment was to search for signals in the participants' brains that preceded each finger tap. In order to successfully collect data on what happened in the brain just before the finger tab, they invented a technique called "reverse-averaging." This technique allowed them to see for the first time the brain preparing itself to create a voluntary movement. The outcome was a burst of neuron activity called "readiness potential" (German: *Bereitschaftspotential*).[2] The two scientists who discovered it both believed in free will, and simply wanted empirical data of how the brain works to freely generate an action versus the idea of the brain just being a passive organic machine that merely produces thoughts and actions.

However, in 1984 the American physiologist, Benjamin Libet, used the readiness potential to make the case that the brain shows signs of a decision *before* a person consciously acts.[3] His findings triggered a new wave of debate in scientific and philosophical circles. Suddenly, the world went crazy with the idea that our choices are determined by something outside of our own perceived preference. Despite his findings, Libet himself did not interpret his experiment as evidence for the non-existence of free will. Rather, he pointed out that the conscious will retains the right to veto any conscious action of the subject. But there was an unresolved hidden puzzle in one aspect of Libet's findings that slipped by for years: what if Libet's conclusions were based on a flawed premise, despite the fact his observations were correct?

In 2012, Aaron Schurger, a researcher at the National Institute of Health and Medical Research in Paris, set out to solve the puzzle.[4] He realized that the readiness potential's rising pattern wasn't a sign of the brain preparing to move at all, but something much more incidental. He and his team repeated a version of Libet's experiment and found that what Libet's study seemed to suggest was just an illusion. According to Schurger, "What looks like a pre-conscious decision process may not in fact reflect a decision at all. It only looks that way because of the nature of spontaneous brain activity."[5] It turns out the readiness potential isn't what we thought it was after all. Schurger received an award for upending a long-standing idea. Now, researchers are looking beyond the readiness potential in their search of evidence to question the concept of free will.

Given that the issue of free will is so fundamentally important to our view of who we are, a claim that our free will is an illusion should be based on concrete evidence. As at the time of writing, such evidence does not exist.[6] Notwithstanding the gaps in science, free will skepticism is spreading like wildfire around the world. This has far reaching practical implications for civilization. What would a society without free will and moral responsibility look like?

REVERSE-ENGINEERING FREE WILL

No doubt, cognitive science and neuroscience are attempting to teach us some things about our fallen nature and the limits of our freedom of choice, and will certainly try to come up with more studies in the future. Indeed, the narratives pushed out there about the illusion of free will and moral responsibility from the evolving field of cognitive neuroscience is grossly exaggerated. But the implications are deep.

Research has shown that when people stop believing in free will, they stop seeing themselves as blameworthy for their actions, and begin to act less responsibly.[7] They become less willing to learn from their mistakes, and more willing to embrace whatever fate an exploitative social or political system may have decreed for them.

According to a study, there has been a more than twofold increase in the number of court cases that use evidence from neuroscience in recent times—mostly in the context of defendants arguing that their brain made them do it.[8] In other words, people can now get away with crimes because neuroscience tells them they are not responsible for them. If this mind-set is carried to its logical conclusion, it may result in the abolition of the structures of the justice system such as laws, courts, police and prisons, while crime or vice reigns supreme. This is a recipe for moral anarchy. In an article published on *The Atlantic* magazine, Cambridge University philosopher, Stephen Cave noted that "In every regard, it seems, when we embrace determinism, we indulge our dark side."[9]

The mind is certainly under siege by modern science. There is a proliferation of new technologies that make it easier to hack our brains, read our thoughts, exploit our inherent vulnerabilities, and manipulate our desires. But the development and invention of these new mindware technologies are not proof that free will does not exist. If anything, they point to something more sinister: an attempt to hijack our minds, undermine or mess with our individual and collective free will, strip humans of their power to freely make choices, and stealthily steer our behavior in a defined direction. Technology ethicist, Tristan Harris, coined the phrase "human downgrading" to describe the damaging effect of these technologies on human capacity and freedom. According to Harris, "All of our minds can be hijacked. Our choices are not as free as we think they are." [10]

"Surveillance capitalism" is the term used to describe the monetization of personal data captured through the monitoring of a user's interaction with digital technology. This includes digital technologies that are both internal and external to our bodies. According to Harvard scholar, Shoshana Zuboff, "surveillance capitalism begins by unilaterally staking a claim to private human experience as free raw material for translation into behavioral data, which can be manipulated to alter your behavior".[11] A professor of the public understanding of technology, John Naughton, noted that "These behavioral modification processes are meticulously designed to produce ignorance by circumventing individual awareness and thus eliminate any possibility of self-determination ... It usurps decision rights and erodes the processes of individual autonomy..."[12] What will become of human societies if these ominous clouds of technology gathering overhead are fully realized? Are we all going to be turned into automatons and servants to AIs?

Already experts are predicting that free will is destined to crumble as machines know people better than people know themselves. Unequal knowledge about you (from other sources versus yourself) produces unequal power over you. The real challenge lies in the power imbalance in what is known about you. Sun Tzu once said that "If you know neither the enemy nor yourself, you will succumb in every battle."[13] One way to get around this erosion of your basic right is to insist on the protection of your privacy when using digital technology. If you are not in control of your privacy, you will always be at risk. Privacy reduces the ability of others to know you and then use this knowledge to manipulate you for their own profit. It puts knowledge about you in your own hands. Knowledge about you in your own hands is power for you. But in today's technology driven world, keeping your privacy is easier said than done. This is why some experts are of the opinion that "anyone who processes our data to create knowledge about us should be legally obliged to give us back that knowledge."[14] What machines tell us about ourselves is for us to benefit from using, not for others to profit from abusing.

TRUE FREEDOM

One thing is certain about our fallen human nature: we have a tendency to engage in wrongdoing due to our flawed nature. This idea is acknowledged by the apostle Paul, who stated that "I have discovered this principle of life—that when I want to do what is right, I inevitably do what is wrong" (Romans 7:21). Nevertheless, this does not eliminate our moral accountability for the actions we take, whether they are right or wrong. To be morally accountable for our actions is to accept that we have done wrong, make efforts to put right anything that went wrong, and resolve not to do it again. As humans, we clearly do have the capacity to do this, and that's what really matters.

The concept of free will is central to biblical understanding of the human person. God endowed us with freedom to enable us to function as His representatives here on earth. Without genuine freedom to make real decisions, we cannot genuinely love God; otherwise, it cannot be considered authentic. For decisions like love or obedience to be authentic, they must be made against a truly possible alternative. Genuine love can never be fully expressed without intrinsically weaving into it the freedom of the will. In the movie *Bruce Almighty*, God tells Bruce, who thinks being God is easy, to take the reins for a while and do whatever he wants with it. God gives only two rules: The first is, "You can't tell anybody you're God." And the second is, "You can't mess with free will." Frustrated after his girlfriend broke up with him, Bruce says to God in a loud tone, "How do you make someone love you without affecting free will?" And God responds in a soft tone, "Hey, welcome to My world, son. If you come up with an answer to that one, let Me know."

The alternative to free will is a set of creatures that simply comply but never choose to express the genuine sentiment and reality of love. God could have created human beings that always did the right thing, never hurt anyone, and never disobeyed. But instead He chose to give us freedom. If God's ultimate command is for us to love Him with all of our passion, and to love our neighbors as ourselves, then free will is a necessary component to make that happen. But this portends great danger because of the risk of abuse.

This is exactly why evil—both moral and natural—reigns in our world today. All of humanity, and a part of the angelic realm abused this freedom, with the rebound in all of creation. But then again, it's far better to have free will with the genuine risk that some will end up being evil, than to live in a world without choice. So are we now going to coexist with evil forever? Not at all. There is hope for an evil free society. God had His plans cut out well ahead of time. God had devised a means to stamp out the resident evil. The entire story of the Bible is about God's determination to restore creation back to what it used to be—the "very good" state of man and nature.

He began by taking care of the penalty of sin in the death and resurrection of Jesus. He has also taken care of the power of sin when He gave us the Holy Spirit. And He will take care of the presence of sin and death in Jesus' second coming and His millennial reign and beyond, when the darkness of sin and death will be no more. In the end, a new world will emerge, free of evil. God is going to make sure that no one pollutes it. He is going to make sure that no evil being gets into it (Revelation 21:27).

But how can God prevent it from being polluted? Who would be fit enough to inhabit that new world?

First off, let me begin with the bad news. No human being is qualified to inhabit it except one—the only life lived in whom God was well pleased—Jesus. None of us is good enough for God because of our natural propensity to do wrong (Romans 3:23). Is this propensity to do wrong in our nature? The answer is yes; sin is encoded deep in our nature. We have a sinful nature that puts us out of step with God even before we are born. This sin nature is obvious in all our new-borns or children. You never had to teach them to be selfish; they instinctively exhibit it. You never had to teach them to lie; it is an inherent ability which they freely manifest.

Our spontaneous tendency to do wrong stems from this nature which we inherited from Adam. This is not a God given tendency. It was acquired after Adam and Eve ate the forbidden fruit and acquired the knowledge of good and evil (Romans 5:12). This willful transgression instantly changed human nature—as evidenced by the sudden realization of their nakedness before a holy God. Adam and Eve instinctively gained experiential knowledge of evil without learning about it. This knowledge of evil is passed from one generation to another as inherited knowledge or instinct. On the other hand, the knowledge we acquire through learning is not genetically passed from one generation to another. But, surprisingly, it is the knowledge we acquire through learning—and by that I mean the experiential knowledge we gain from God's word—that can combat the inherited sin nature in us (Romans 12:2).

We will never experience true freedom until we have been set free from the bondage and power of sin over our lives. Anyone willfully living under the bondage of sin is condemned to eternal damnation. This is the destiny that awaits the entire human race. The only permanent solution for dealing with sin nature is to get rid of it. The good news is that Jesus paid the ultimate price for sin. Through the blood of Jesus, the power of the Holy Spirit, and the knowledge and application of the Word of God in our lives, we can experience the freedom to live above the inherited sinful nature in us (2 Timothy 3:16; James 1:21).

This means that no one should face eternal damnation anymore. No one should be punished for their immoral behavior, or the tendency to do so, whether it was freely made or not. The only reason anyone would be punished is because they exercised their free will and rejected Jesus. In Jesus, we now have the opportunity to experience a new kind of nature and become new creations. God's great plan is to replace the sin nature in us by God's nature. God will eventually replace this corrupt earthly body with a new kind of body, free from the corrupt nature, so that we can be fit to go into that new world without polluting it.

God has decided that only those who are willing to be changed, those who have responded to the message and demand of God's kingdom and pledged allegiance to it, can go and live in that new world. He will put the earth right again and give it to those who have been willing to be put right themselves. And having been in this world and having experienced the devastating effect of evil, they will never want to experience that again. God has promised to make those willing vessels perfect just like Him and restore His image in them to make them fit to inhabit the new world. A world where goodness and true love exists in its purest form, and where the redeemed will love and worship God out of their own free will. Those who reject this offer have automatically enlisted themselves in the class of "endangered species," and one day, they will have to face the obvious consequence of their decision—eternal separation from God.

The first part of this book explored how God created the cosmos and humans as His chosen partners to carry forward His will for the whole creation. The second part took us on a brief tour of how humanity failed in this task and how God provided a means of redeeming us from our fallen state. The third and final part will look at how God's redemptive effort pays off with new humanity's renewal of partnership with God, and the eventual fulfillment of God's will for the whole creation.

PART III

HUMANITY RENEWS PARTNERSHIP WITH GOD

Where is history headed?
What does the future hold for our species
amidst the rising threat of AI?
Which species could replace the current
human species in the future?

CHAPTER SEVEN

HOMO SAPIENS: AN ENDANGERED SPECIES

———————

The United Nations' Intergovernmental Science-Policy Platform on Biodiversity and Ecosystem Services (IPBES) released a report in 2019 on the global state of biodiversity. The report, among other things, warns that the planet's life-support systems are approaching a danger zone for humanity.[1] This is because the rate of species extinction due to the human impact on the environment is accelerating, and around 1 million animal and plant species are now threatened with extinction.

Be that as it may, it is also critical to emphasize how plants and animals are not the only groups threatened with extinction. In fact, the most endangered species of all has been the species to which all of us humans claim to belong—Homo sapiens. Yes, that's right—you and I are now an endangered species! This may come as a surprise to many.

Some time ago, I watched one of the episodes of Jimmy Kimmel Live, a popular American late-night talk show that airs on the ABC television network. Jimmy and his team, wanting to raise awareness of the UN biodiversity report, asked random people in the street if they were worried about one endangered species in particular— "Homo sapiens." The responses were quite hilarious. One of the respondents suggested that we find a way to live separately with the Homo sapiens, in a way that doesn't affect either species. Another responded thus: "It's not the fact that I don't like Homo sapiens; it's just that we've always lived without them, so we don't know anything at all." Another respondent was asked if she had seen a Homo sapiens before, and her response was "Yeah, I saw one once at the zoo," and she described it as fury, big and gorilla-looking.

Well, it was obvious the respondents had no idea who was being referred to as Homo sapiens. They assumed it was some kind of higher animal species out there. Little did they know they were being asked about the potential extinction of the extant human species, to which they themselves belong.

But, on a more serious note, we appear to have reached a tipping point in our existence as a species. We are now at a precipice, and our reign and domination on the earth is about to take a steep downward turn. As we inch closer to the edge of history, Homo sapiens will be relegated to the background, until they eventually vanish from the face of the earth. A new kind of human species will suddenly emerge to take center stage. This is both good news and bad news, depending on which side of the divide you belong.

Now, I guess you are probably wondering how I came to this conclusion. Well, such an outcome has long been predicted in the Bible. And, surprisingly, it has also been predicted by scientists and philosophers. Stephen Hawking in 2017 warned the world that if humanity doesn't leave earth and colonize suitable planets in the next five centuries or so, we may well go extinct.[2] Yuval Harari once said that "We are probably one of the last generations of Homo sapiens. I think that *Homo sapiens* as we know them will probably disappear within a century or so."[3] Oxford University philosopher Nick Bostrom also noted that "Unless the human species lasts literally forever, it will some time cease to exist. In that case, the long-term future of humanity is easy to describe: extinction."[4]

But how is this possible you may ask? It's hard to imagine that a species that has consistently dominated the planet for thousands of years and multiplied in number, approaching a population of 8 billion (at the time of writing) can be threatened with extinction. Well, let me make myself clear. I am not insinuating that our species will become extinct because of the inevitable effects of climate change or the destruction of the Earth's biodiversity according to the UN report. I am not insinuating that our species will become extinct because of a nuclear cataclysm or artificial intelligence (AI) overthrow. Although those are real existential threats, they are not the kind of extinction I am referring to.

Our species will become extinct because it is going to be replaced by one that has been transformed or upgraded to an entirely different kind of being. According to Nick Bostrom, "There are two different ways in which the human species could become extinct: one, by evolving or developing or transforming into one or more new species or life forms, sufficiently different from what came before so as no longer to count as Homo sapiens; the other, by simply dying out, without any meaningful replacement or continuation."[5] I agree with Yuval Harari that "The next big revolution in history will be the transformation of our bodies and our minds, and it will replace Homo sapiens with a very unique kind of being." At the core of this pursuit is the desire to conquer mankind's greatest enemy—death, and to acquire immortal bodies.

This new kind of human species has been called various names by different groups: Transhuman, Posthuman, Humanity+, Human 2.0, Homo Deus, Glorious Man, New Creature are some current nomenclatures. I choose to call it Homo Novus and I will elaborate on this in the next chapter. For now, let's deal with the big question, "How exactly will Homo sapiens be transformed or upgraded into a unique kind of being? Is it going to be by the process of evolution or by creation? Is it going to be by man's own effort or by God's power? Is it going to be by technological breakthrough or by divine intervention?" Deep questions. Whatever name you choose to call this new kind of human species is heavily dependent on what you think or believe to be the answer to those questions.

UPGRADING THE HUMAN SPECIES
From my research on the topic, I can summarize four main explanations about how our species will be upgraded and transformed into a different kind of being or species.

Bioengineering
The first explanation is based on bioengineering—the application of the life sciences and engineering principles in the transformation of the human species. Bioengineers have lost patience with the good old natural selection process, which they consider "slow, uncontrolled, and unpredictable." Natural selection is now being supplemented by a fast and controlled technology-driven unnatural selection directed by human engineering. Bioengineers are determined to shortcut the natural selection process by deliberately rewriting the genetic code of Homo sapiens, rewiring its brain circuits, and even growing entirely new human body parts in order to create a new kind of human species. The result will be the creation of an intrinsically new kind of being who might be quite different from the rest of the Homo sapiens species. These views have also been expressed by many scientists and philosophers, including Yuval Harari in his book *Homo Deus: A Brief History of Tomorrow*.

Gene editing is the technique that lets scientists rewrite the human genetic code. With this technique, scientists are able to insert, modify, delete or even replace the DNA in the genome of a living organism. It has been the invention of a powerful easy to deploy gene-editing tool known as CRISPR (clustered regularly interspaced short palindromic repeats) that makes this possible. CRISPR can be described as the "Photoshop" of gene editing. With this tool, scientists can potentially rewrite the natural human genetic code by altering the DNA in sperms, eggs, or embryos—known as germline editing—thereby producing unique human creatures called 'designer babies' (genetically modified babies). The idea of producing designer babies may sound futuristic, but the reality is, designer babies are already here with us. In 2018, Chinese scientists led by He Jiankui stunned the world when he revealed that he and his team had edited genes in human embryos to produce the first designer twin babies known by their pseudonyms, Lulu and Nana. At the time of writing, Lulu and Nana are in their toddler stage and are living a normal undisturbed life.[6]

Bioengineers are currently engaged in the manipulation and alteration of human cells with the aim of eradicating or reversing the effects of aging and treating age-related illnesses. The ultimate objective is to reengineer the human body to enable it to have an unlimited lifespan, achieved through complete rejuvenation to a state of healthy youthfulness, using cutting-edge technologies such as tissue rejuvenation, stem cells, regenerative medicine, molecular repair, gene therapy, pharmaceuticals, and organ transplantation. Advocates of this view are of the opinion that bioengineering will revolutionize not just one aspect of the human body, but the whole of it.

The concern is, when we alter the fundamental building blocks of life, we are inadvertently changing the very nature of our humanity. This obviously raises a lot of ethical concerns. Even now, the editing of genes in human embryos is a hugely controversial endeavor. Some scientists are worried that the changes made in the gene could be passed on to generations unborn, and could ultimately affect the entire gene pool. Nonetheless, in years to come—who knows? People may have the liberty to transform themselves and their children in ways that might be quite different from the extant human species. Although the transformation or upgrade that comes from bioengineering may likely augment our bodies and cognitive abilities, they are still made up of materials that are subject to deterioration and death. In other words, a human body that has been engineered or re-engineered through biotechnology is not imperishable.

Cybernetic upgrade

The second explanation involves merging human and machine, resulting in the creation of a "cybernetic organism," commonly referred to as a "cyborg". This technology can be used to help one regain lost function such as vision, hearing, or mobility. It can also be used to enhance human abilities beyond the ordinary natural limitations through the integration of specific technological components into the body. It is the enhancement aspect that is the primary focus of the Cyborgism movement. It is believed that incorporating cybernetic enhancements into our bodies will enhance our physical and mental capabilities, enabling us to acquire additional organs, senses, and capacities. It is hoped that through cybernetic enhancements, we can transform ourselves into superhumans who possess abilities that far surpass those of existing humans to the extent that we no longer strictly qualify as human under the current standards.

According to proponents of this view, becoming cyborgs is essential to maintain human relevance in an era dominated by artificial intelligence. They argue that the fusion of humans and technology could produce a synergy that surpasses the capabilities of artificial intelligence. Their vision is for a future where our brains are implanted with a brain-computer interface (BCI) and memory chips, eliminating the need for external computing devices. This would blur the distinction between humans and machines even further.

Using a brain-computer interface (BCI) enables one to gain direct access to the digital realm. This would allow us to surpass our physical and mental limitations and essentially become cyborgs. This implies that individuals would have computer chip implants in their brains. By connecting the BCI to the internet, the human brain can be further improved, allowing for expanded collaboration between individuals across different locations. Currently, researchers are working on linking our neocortex (that region of the brain responsible for higher mental functions) to a synthetic neocortex in the cloud. Once this is accomplished, our thinking may be dominated by the synthetic neocortex, and we may even be able to back up our brains to the cloud. The goal is to enhance human intelligence, memory, and potentially extend the capabilities of the human brain.

The notion that cyborgs and BCI exist only in fiction is now a thing of the past. There are several individuals who have already become real life cyborgs and are leading their daily lives. These individuals have utilized advanced technologies such as bionic eyes and ears, prosthetic limbs, insulin pumps, and other bodily implants to augment their abilities. Neuralink, a brain-computer interface (BCI) startup co-founded by Elon Musk, is set to begin human trials of their BCI chip.[7] Upon successful completion of the trials, the product will be released to the general public. Brain networks, though still in their early stages, have also been shown to be technically feasible in labs. However, all these technologies are faced with various unresolved safety, security and ethical challenges, including freedom of choice, personal identity, privacy, and accountability issues.

The risk lies in the possibility that the BCI technology, which offers individuals direct access to the digital realm, can also give unauthorized parties, such as corporations or hackers, access to their brain data and innermost thoughts. This poses a significant danger to our shared humanity if our brains can be monitored, compromised, or aggregated in the same manner as our daily online activities. Imagine a world where individuals are arrested or discriminated against solely on the basis of their random thoughts and desires. Merging the human brain with a computer would completely redefine what it means to be human forever. And again, just like bioengineered bodies, cyborgs are made up of perishable earthly materials that are still subject to deterioration and death.

Mind upload

The third explanation is based on a concept called "mind upload," whereby the essential contents of a person's mind are transferred to a non-biological hardware carrier. It involves scanning a person's physical brain structure to create an emulation of the mental state (including memories, emotions and personality) and copying it in a digital form to a computer-based platform, a robot body, a simulated environment, or perhaps a cloned body. The goal is to cheat death via digital immortality. The idea of separating a person's consciousness and transferring it to another medium (even if they are physically dead) is being actively explored in science and philosophy. It also features prominently in numerous science fiction novels, films, TV shows, and games.

This idea in part stems from the classic philosophical concept of mind–body dualism which sees the mind and body as distinct and separable. Unlike classic philosophical dualists, modern-day dualists don't claim that the mind (some call it soul, consciousness, or mental self) is non-material and impervious to manipulation. Instead, they take cues from the software-hardware dualism found in the domain of computers, where information-based software can be easily transferred from one disposable hardware environment to another.

These modern thinkers consider the human body analogous to disposable computer hardware, and the mind analogous to software installed in the hardware environment. They regard the mind as "the information state of the brain," and is immaterial in the same sense as the information content of a data file or the state of a computer software currently residing in the work-space memory of the computer. Data specifying the information state of the neural network can be captured and copied as a "computer file" from the brain and re-implemented into a different physical form."[8] Scientists are currently exploring ways to capture and transfer this "brain software" or mind to alternative or perhaps more advantageous hardware environments.

The concept of mind upload is not merely a hypothetical proposition. Given how much interest and effort is already directed towards this goal, proponents of this view maintain that mind uploading is inevitable. There are ongoing attempts by organizations in the United States and European Union to, among other things, map the human brain, and develop mind upload technologies. In the U.S., for example, the BRAIN Initiative (Brain Research through Advancing Innovative Neurotechnologies) was set up with the goal of "supporting the development and application of innovative technologies that can create a dynamic understanding of brain function."[9] The scientists participating in this project hope to eventually create a map of the tens of billions of neurons present in the human brain.

In the EU, the Blue Brain Project and the Human Brain Project (HBP) attempt to use electronic methods to, besides other things, build what they call "high-fidelity reconstruction of the human brain."[10] Scientists involved in this project hope to create a machine that exhibits human-like behavior or intelligence. Similar brain mapping projects exist in Japan (Brain/MINDS project) and China (China Brain Project), all in an attempt to develop technologies for human brain mapping, and ultimately develop brain-inspired AI technology.

Furthermore, the 2045 Initiative founded by Russian entrepreneur Dmitry Itskov aims to create technologies that enable the transfer of even an individual's personality to a more advanced non-biological carrier. It also hopes to extend life to the point of immortality. The initiative provides a roadmap (that spans from 2015-2045 with milestones at periodic intervals) for transforming Homo sapiens into a different kind of species.[11] The final stage is the creation of an immortal radiant humanity with a light body similar to a hologram. The concept of an "immortal radiant humanity with a light body similar to a hologram" is often associated with beings that are considered to be highly advanced or evolved. These beings are often depicted as having transcended physical limitations and possessing incredible powers, such as the ability to manipulate energy or reality.

As lofty and promising as the idea of mind uploading and digital immortality may sound, it is not an easy task. It raises many ethical and moral questions. For example, who would have access to a person's digital self? How would it be used? Would it be able to make decisions, and if so, who would be responsible for those decisions? These are all important questions that would need to be answered. The implication of digital immortality is that power systems must not fail, servers must not crash, and digital security must be guaranteed. In contrast to the physical brain, most scientists agree that the human mind and the concept of consciousness is something that we still don't fully understand. In theory, the process is understood, but in practice, it is still far from being feasible. It relies on a technology that has not yet been developed, indicating that a significant amount of progress needs to be made before it can be realized. It may take decades of hard work before scientists have a detailed map of the human brain.

But if it is eventually achieved, would this mean that we can upload consciousness into a computer or more advantageous hardware? Would it truly be you? The consequence is that we will cease to be humans as we know it. There are genuine concerns that if we succeed in uploading our brains to the computer, we may lose our mental faculties or consciousness in the process. But, even if everything goes well, the so-called "advantageous bodies" are not immune to death. They can still be crushed to death by vehicles running over them, or via the destructive power of bombs, plus a host of other threats. This, according to Harari, "will probably make them the most anxious people in history."

Both the first, second and third explanations discussed are based on technological breakthroughs anchored on human intervention. Behind the human intervention approach to a new humanity is a group of people that call themselves "transhumanists." Transhumanism is a "techno progressive" movement that advocates for the use of technology in order to transform the human organism radically, with the ultimate goal of becoming "transhumans." The term "transhumanism" suggests that it has roots in the concepts and values of humanism, yet the addition of the prefix "trans" connotes a meaning that extends beyond humanism. In humanism, humanists strive to eliminate the role of God. But in transhumanism, transhumanists want to gain godlike abilities and become God themselves.

Transhumanists are devoted to the concept of an evolved human future where technology is employed to overcome our biological limitations and physical restrictions, potentially blurring the line between humanity and computers. Transhumanists support the so-called NBIC convergence—the unification of nanotechnology, biotechnology, information technologies and cognitive science (NBIC), as well as evolving technologies such as artificial general intelligence (AGI), 3D bioprinting, simulated reality, and mind uploading. They hope to leverage these technologies to become more than human. Organizations that directly or indirectly seek to promote the ideas and ideals of transhumanism with the goal of helping to prevent human extinction include Humanity Plus (H+), Foresight Institute, The Future of Humanity Institute, The Institute for Ethics and Emerging Technology (IEET), The Machine Intelligence Research Institute, the Mormon Transhumanist Association, and others.

Transhumanists look forward to the day when artificial intelligence (AI) surpasses human intelligence. That will be a pivotal moment when machines become smarter than humans, and humans (realizing their limitations) eventually merge with machines (robots and computers). This is what scientists refer to as technological singularity. According to Encyclopaedia

Britannica, "The idea of the singularity is a powerful inspiration for people who want technology to deliver a new spiritual and material reality within our lifetimes." [12]

The term "Singularity" was borrowed from Mathematics by John Von Neumann in 1950 to describe his vision of a forthcoming technological explosion that would surpass the limits of human affairs. Vernor Vinge later popularized this concept in his 1993 essay *The Coming Technological Singularity*, wherein he predicted that machines equipped with artificial intelligence would surpass human intelligence at an incomprehensible rate.[13] Ray Kurzweil, a prominent figure in the transhumanist movement, also explores these ideas in his 2005 book *The Singularity Is Near: When Humans Transcend Biology*. Here, he predicted that humans will leave their biological bodies behind and their intelligence will be transferred to machines. Kurzweil is so confident of his singularity predictions that he set the date 2045 for it to happen. Kurzweil has a reputation for accuracy in technological predictions, with his past forecasts having an 86% success rate. Will he be right about the singularity too?

A supporter of Kurzweil has admitted that the concept of singularity, with its promises of eternal happiness, youth, and god-like abilities gives him hope, and it's the only reason left for him to continue to live in this world. Many transhumanists are holding out for that moment with a carefully designed regime of exercise, dietary changes, longevity supplements, and even regenerative blood transfusion from young people (reminiscent of the days when ancient Romans rushed to consume the blood of young men and slain gladiators to rejuvenate themselves).[14] They hope these measures will sustain them until the singularity finally comes. In fact, some have even gone as far as paying for cryonics services. These services involve placing their bodies in sub-zero temperatures to pause the dying process, with the hope of being revived and brought back to life once these technologies become fully available in the future.[15]

There has been intense debate surrounding the potential advantages or disadvantages that the singularity could bring to humanity. Stephen Hawking, Elon Musk, Nick Bostrom, and other tech leaders and experts have expressed concern that full artificial intelligence (AI) could result in human extinction. The implication here is that humanity's desperate attempt to use technology to prevent human extinction or transform the human organism may in itself end up being our greatest undoing. We are unknowingly and indirectly creating our way to our own demise. "There is a way that seems right to a man. But its end is the way of death" (Proverbs 14:12 NKJV).

Divine intervention

The fourth explanation is that the human being will be completely upgraded and transformed into a unique kind of being by divine intervention. This divine intervention will take place at the return of Jesus the Messiah to planet Earth. It will be the most revolutionary event in history. The first human to ever experience this kind of bodily transformation or upgrade was Jesus Himself. When Jesus rose from the dead, He became the pioneering first member of a glorious new humanity—the Homo novus species. His victory over death opened a way for us (Homo sapiens) to become that new kind of human.

Resurrection from the dead is the defining event in God's ultimate plan for the inauguration of a new humanity. God will not allow evil and death to have the final say in His creation. He has promised to put the world right again and restore all things, including humanity. It begins with the transformation of the human spirit, and culminates in the total transformation of the human body. The new upgraded (resurrected) body will be vastly superior to the old. The old one was frail, corruptible, and mortal, while the new one will be glorious, incorruptible, and immortal. Imagine having a body with multi-dimensional properties that are not subject to the laws of physics, that defy gravity and distance, that are able to seamlessly pass through walls and travel at the speed of thought, and capable of inhabiting both planet Earth, outer space and God's space.

There has never been anything like it in history. The best bioengineered body, the most advanced cyborg or a completely non-biological human body will look extremely lowly and inferior alongside it. In fact, it would be utterly unfair to even attempt to subject the two to a head-to-head comparison. It's like trying to compare charcoal with a diamond—they are simply incomparable. Jesus in His incarnation showed us how to be truly human. He restored humanity's original calling to preside over creation in partnership with God, and to live forever. Now His resurrection opens the door for everyone to partake in this new reality. As part of God's final intervention to recreate the world, God will grant the faithful followers of Jesus—those who have been willing to be made right with God—a new kind of body—a glorious immortal kind. "He will take our weak mortal bodies and change them into glorious bodies like His own, using the same power with which He will bring everything under His control" (Philippians 3:21). This is not something anyone should dare to miss. The future is indeed very bright. Blessed is he who partakes in this new reality!

As you can see, all four explanations agree that the future of humanity is not to be Homo sapiens anymore. But opinions differ as to how this future humanity would be realized—whether it will be by human/technological or divine intervention. If this future human transformation—whether by divine or human effort—is anything to go by, it is a clear sign to any discerning mind that the days of Homo sapiens are numbered. His history is winding down to its final obsolescence.

Similarly, our present universe is also under the bondage of decay. It has become too polluted, both physically and morally, to recover. Its days are also numbered—it has a sentence of death on it (Isaiah 65:17). Scientists call it the second law of thermodynamics—in which the fixed amount of energy is becoming less and less usable. According to this law, disorder, characterized as a quantity known as entropy, always increases. Once entropy reaches its peak, there would be no more room for usable energy or heat to exist, and the universe would die from "Heat Death," or what is now known as the "Big Freeze." As N.T Wright rightly noted, "The world that began with the Big Bang is heading either for the Big Cool-Down, as energy gradually runs out and the universe expands into the cold dark beyond, or for the Big Crunch, as gravity reasserts itself and everything slows down, stops, and then rushes back together again."[16]

CHAPTER EIGHT

HOMO NOVUS: THE EMERGING SPECIES

––––––––––

Death by far is humanity's greatest enemy. As soon as we are born, we are old enough to die. Death is no respecter of age. Ever since God sentenced humanity to death as a result of our rebellion against Him, our struggle against death has been our most enduring fight. Humanity's quest for the elusive elixir of immortality continues unabated. Throughout history we have continued to battle this arch enemy, albeit in our own strength, hoping that someday we would gain victory over it.

THE QUEST FOR IMMORTALITY

According to the historian, Flavius Josephus, Nimrod the infamous lead architect of the tower of Babel once vowed that he would avenge himself on God for bringing death on their fore-fathers. Through his efforts and bravery, he would overcome the curse of death placed upon rebellious humanity, and achieve happiness. He failed on all fronts.

In the *Epic of Gilgamesh*, one of humanity's oldest tales, the title character embarks on an epic quest to attain immortality. After many trials, he eventually hears of a flower on the ocean floor that will restore his youth. And, despite a warning from the only people ever granted immortality by the gods—that his quest will ruin the joys of life—Gilgamesh plucks the flower from the watery depths. Unfortunately, his success doesn't last. Gilgamesh inevitably loses the flower, and eventually, like all mortals before and after him, dies.

Alchemy, with its roots in ancient Egypt, was driven in part by this same quest for immortality. One of the main goals of alchemy, aside from the transmutation of metals, was the creation of a panacea to cure any disease, and to attain physical immortality. Interestingly, the word "panacea" which has become a regular English word for "remedy," was actually the name of the goddess of universal remedy in Greek mythology. Panacea was the daughter of Asclepius (the ancient Greek god of medicine). Alchemists in various ages and cultures have sought the means of formulating the elixir.

In ancient China, Chinese alchemists developed their own unique alchemical techniques with the goal of creating an elixir. It is said that many emperors, nobles, and officials consumed what they thought were elixirs of immortality to extend their lives, not knowing that they were poisonous and ended up dying. Qin Shi Huang, the first emperor of unified China, had long harbored the obsession of ruling forever. He sent Taoist alchemists with hundreds of young men and women to find him this "elixir of life." As he aged with no hope in sight, he became desperate and started ingesting potions containing the highly toxic mercury sulfide made by his alchemists to prolong his life. His quest for immortality led to an early grave. What he feared most came upon him without mercy.

Similar stories exist in other ancient cultures and civilizations such as India, Greece and Rome and, by extension, the whole of Europe. In medieval Europe, for example, alchemists swindled aristocrats by promising to defeat death and deliver immortality, all to no avail. This eventually gave birth to what is now the science of chemistry. Scientific alchemists dropped the Arabic prefix "al," and the word "chemy" or "chemistry" replaced alchemy as a term for the scientific study of physical and chemical processes. However, alchemy retained its ancient mystical and philosophical flavor, which eventually gave rise to the modern day concept of alchemy.

For thousands of years, our forebears rummaged the spiritual and natural world for guidance and remedies to ease pain, cure diseases, and revive the sick. Modern Western medicine, which has its roots in the ancient Greek temples of Asclepius (god of medicine), has become one of humanity's most powerful weapons to push back death and extend our lifespan. Through a mix of superstition, trial and error, and a gradual accumulation of empirical knowledge, a form of science evolved that we know today as medicine. The discovery of the invisible death armies we call germs (bacteria, viruses, and fungi) that cause disease, and the invention of antibiotics and vaccination was a pivotal moment in humanity's fight against death. The ancient medical approach known as humorism, which was thought to explain the cause of disease, gradually gave way to the modern day germ theory of disease.

So we thought we had finally acquired the tools to defeat death. But, sadly, in spite of our wonderful achievements in the field of medicine, we still haven't conquered death. According to Yuval Harari, "So far modern medicine hasn't extended our natural life span by a single year. Its great achievement has been to save us from premature death, and allow us to enjoy the full measure of our years."[1]

However, up to this point, all efforts by humanity to overcome the curse of death have been unsuccessful. Everyone in history who invested money, energy and time in the hope of acquiring immortality all met the Grim Reaper. And yet the dream of physical immortality and everlasting life hasn't ebbed. In the 21st century, Silicon Valley capitalists and the rich around the world are on the match again for immortality and even divinity. Follow the money as they throw millions of dollars at immortality research and anti-ageing startups. Many are pitching their hope on the promise of technology and profit-driven capitalists to defeat death and deliver immortality to the benefit of humanity. They look forward to the day when they can upgrade their bodies and upload the content of their brains to computer systems.

Again, to quote Yuval Harari, "We don't need to wait for the Second Coming in order to overcome death. A couple of geeks in a lab can do it, given enough time and money." Really! His statement reminds me of the famous saying by Winston Churchill: "Those who fail to learn from history are doomed to repeat it." If there's anything we can learn from history, it is that all those who embarked on this journey share something in common: they failed. What most people fail to realize is that no amount of human knowledge and technology can help us escape God's decree that we are dust and to dust we will return in our appointed time (Genesis 3:19). Yes, the technology developed along the way may help us solve some difficult health challenges, and possibly slow the aging process and improve life expectancy; nonetheless the quest to conquer death as a technical problem will ultimately prove to be futile.

But the good news is that God has already made a way for humanity. Jesus in His resurrection has won us the age-long coveted victory over death, and He invites everyone to come drink from His "elixir of life" (John 4:14). While the tech companies and their geeks seek to achieve immortality, God is offering us something more than immortality. He is offering us eternal life—God's own life. Immortality is merely about quantity, and that's about it. An immortal life that is completely disconnected from God leaves you utterly desolate. But eternal life is not just about quantity; it is also about quality. The good things we experience and the source of supply play a vital role in its quality. The emphasis is placed on "the excellence of the meal" presented (eternal life), as well as "the caliber of the person" who provides and enjoys it with you at the dining table (The Lord Himself). Eternal life is a life that is directly connected to God—the very source of life—and lavished with endless goodness. This is the greatest gift of all. It's a big deal.

Why would any rational being want to put their faith and hope in human interventions and the promise of technology to produce a new life in the here and now? One indisputable fact about humans and the technology we create is that we are fallible. Throughout history, there have been numerous instances where humans and technology have failed to meet expectations. In contrast, God has a proven track record of fulfilling His promises without fail. When God makes a promise, it can be trusted completely, as He always follows through on His word. So who would you rather trust: God or Yuval Harari and "a couple of geeks in a lab"?

THE UPGRADE HAS ALREADY BEGUN

Unbeknown to many, the upgrade of the Homo sapiens species has already begun—but not in the way you would expect. A brand new humanity is on the rise, and those who are willing to be made right with God are pressing into it. God is making new men and women and transforming them into a new kind of human species—the Homo novus species. Homo novus is a Latin word for "New man" or "New human."

Ancient usage suggests that Homo novus was a political term used in the Roman Empire to describe a man from outside the senatorial elite in Rome, who was successfully elected as consul—the highest political office of the Republic. Modern usage of the term is aptly captured by the Lexico online dictionary, which defines it as "a man who has recently risen from insignificance to a position of importance or higher social standing." Renowned Bible teacher David Pawson, often used this term to describe a new kind of human species that would replace the extant Homo sapiens species.

This Homo novus is the sign the new creation has begun, and we are living in it right now. God is calling and transforming ordinary men and women from a state of insignificance and unworthiness into a new higher class of human species. God is transforming the old death-riddled Homo sapiens race into a new life-filled Homo novus race. It is an inside-out process that begins with the transformation of the inner man, and culminates in the transformation of the outer man—the human body (John 3:3-6). There are two human races on earth today: you are either of the old humanity in Adam (Homo sapiens) or you are of the new humanity (Homo novus) in Christ (1 Corinthians 15:22).

We were all born Homo sapiens. Our old bodies came to us from the earth through Adam. Through our Creator God, Adam was the first man of the Homo sapiens species and through our Creator God again, we can become Homo novus. Our new body will come to us from heaven through Jesus, the first man of the Homo novus species (1 Corinthians 15:47). Blessed indeed is he who partakes in this transformation!

As noted in previous sections of this book, in the opening pages of the Bible, God appointed humans to rule the world on His behalf. But when they rebelled, God promised that one day a human would come to defeat evil and death at the root, and open up a way for the emergence of a new humanity that will be God's faithful partners, forever. The biblical story led us on a search for that new humanity. This promise reached its fulfillment in Jesus when God raised Him from the dead. Now resurrection is not the same as resuscitation or re-incarnation. It does not mean that your soul continued surviving in some non-bodily sense, and gained immortality in heaven. Resurrection means a new bodily life on earth after a period of being bodily dead.

The risen Jesus is human but a new kind of human. While His resurrected body was physical, it was physical in a way that was clearly different from ours. He had a transformed physical body with immortal properties: one that could live in God's space

136

(heaven) and our space (earth), one that could live and rule with God forever. Jesus is the new humanity that we are called to become. He didn't only come back to life, but also continued to live on.

In the first creation, God began with heaven (the skies or outer space) and earth, and ended with humankind. The new creation is in the reverse order. He is recreating humanity first, and then He will end with making a new outer space and earth for them to live in. The order is reversed in order to give as many of us as possible the opportunity to be part of the new creation, even though we have rebelled against Him.[2]

THE RESURRECTION

There are some people who are still skeptical about the historical validity of the resurrection narrative. Did Jesus actually rise from the dead? What scientific evidence do we have to prove that this event took place? Well, to be fair, we haven't got any scientific evidence to show Him rising from the dead. But don't be too quick to jump on that. As you are likely aware, the realm of scientific proof is restricted to observable phenomena or laboratory replicable experiments.

In the case of Jesus' resurrection, scientists were not there to observe it, and it cannot be replicated in a laboratory, making it impossible to prove or disprove. While Jesus' followers cannot provide His living body as evidence, skeptics cannot produce His dead body or bones. If Jesus' followers could present His living body and let people see Him, it would provide compelling evidence. Similarly, if skeptics could locate Jesus' dead body or remains in Israel or Palestine, it would support their argument.[3] However, to date, neither side has been successful in finding any evidence.

So what kind of evidence can we then produce? The answer is simple: legal evidence.[4] We have both an historical account of eyewitness testimony and circumstantial evidence for the resurrection of Jesus.

John, one of Jesus' disciples couldn't have put it any better when he said, "What we have heard, what we have seen with our eyes, what we have observed and have touched with our hands is what we're declaring unto you" (1 John 1:1-2). In other words, John was basically saying "We were eyewitnesses. We were there." When John went into the tomb and noticed that the long linen wrappings (burial napkins) used to wrap His body (as was the custom in those days) was still wound round but lying flat by itself—and the burial face-cloth (turban) used to wrap His head was not lying with the other linen cloths, but was still wrapped round and round in a place by itself. If it is true that Jesus' body was stolen, the perpetrator would have had to take the body along with the wrappings or spend time unwrapping it, leaving behind a trail of evidence as the pattern of the wrappings would have been disrupted. However, there is no indication that either of these scenarios occurred. When John observed these things, he knew at that point that he wasn't witnessing a natural event at all. Something supernatural had happened. And he believed without any doubt that Jesus had risen from the dead (John 20:3-9).

There are troves of eyewitness accounts in the Gospels (Book of Matthew, Mark, Luke, and John), and in the letters of Paul, of Peter, and of James, the brother of Jesus, that testify to the resurrection. Paul writing to the Corinthians introduced the list of witnesses:

> I passed on to you what was most important and what had also been passed on to me. Christ died for our sins, just as the Scriptures said. He was buried, and he was raised from the dead on the third day, just as the Scriptures said. He was seen by Peter and then by the Twelve. After that, he was seen by more than 500 of his followers at one time, most of whom are still alive, though some have died. Then he was

seen by James and later by all the apostles. Last of all, as though I had been born at the wrong time, I also saw him (1 Corinthians 15:3-8).

It is hard to simply dismiss the testimony of over 500 eyewitnesses. Paul indirectly challenges his audience to investigate this claim and seek out evidence for themselves that Jesus rose from the dead. That's why he mentions the eyewitnesses. In fact, Paul boldly puts his credibility on the line when he mentions that most of them were still alive at the time of his writing, which means they were accessible and could be interviewed directly. The curious thing is that when you read the witnesses of Matthew, Mark, Luke and John, you will observe slight differences in their accounts. Does that inconsistency show error? No, legal experts would agree that those slight differences are, in fact, a key pointer to the authenticity of the eyewitness testimony. This should convince any discerning mind that they were all telling the truth—independently. If they all told exactly the same story without the slightest variation, then it's likely they had made up the story and were colluding. It's just common sense, isn't it? So, yes, we have real documented eyewitness testimony—each in their own words highlighting their own perceptions.

But, even if we didn't have any eyewitness testimony, circumstantial evidence abounds for any fair inquirer to consider. David Pawson once said that "The eye-witness testimony plus the circumstantial evidence is far stronger that the evidence that Julius Caesar invaded England in 55 BC."[5] For example, the historical record indicating that women were the first to discover Jesus' empty tomb serves as evidence supporting the authenticity of the Scriptural account rather than it being a fabrication. Since the testimony of women was usually not respected in that culture, it would have been more likely for men to report discovering the empty tomb if the account was fictitious and an attempt was being made to concoct a credible lie about Jesus' resurrection.

Aside from this argument, Jerusalem was the hardest place in the world to convince anyone that the resurrection took place if it wasn't true. Anyone could easily confirm the "empty tomb" for themselves by merely strolling to the graveside. The entirety of early church preaching was centered on the historical fact of Jesus' resurrection. If they weren't convinced about the empty tomb, the disciples would have reasoned with the skeptics of the day, and not continued to defend something they weren't absolutely sure of. However, on virtually every occasion that preaching and teaching occurred, the resurrection of Jesus from the dead was the central truth being communicated because it had changed human history and could not be ignored.

Moreover, the preaching of the good news of the resurrected Jesus did not bring the disciples prestige, wealth or social status; instead, they were beaten, stoned, thrown to the lions, tortured, and even crucified. Yet, they remained unstoppable. The only plausible explanation is that the disciples were convinced beyond any shadow of doubt they had seen the resurrected Jesus.

But, by and large, the most remarkable circumstantial evidence was the transformational effect the resurrection story had on the characters of the disciples and everyone else that heard it. Prior to the resurrection, Jesus' disciples were timid, afraid, defeated, and cowering behind locked doors fearing the Jewish leaders might have them executed as well. After the resurrection, however, they started acting like conquerors, no longer crouching down in fear. They were all radically trans-formed into bold witnesses to what they had heard and seen, even to the point of laying down their lives for their convictions. You can imagine the revolution. This is quite remarkable. If the disciples were making up Jesus' resurrection, would they have lived and died for such a lie they themselves cooked up? To be fair, neither a transformed life nor even a person's willingness to die for their beliefs proves the person's beliefs are true. However, it is difficult (if not impossible) to account for the enduring con-viction of the disciples if they had not seen the resurrected Jesus.

140

James, the brother of Jesus, who didn't follow Jesus during His ministry years was radically transformed after his encounter with the risen Christ. How did it come about that this man, who openly displayed skepticism and even antagonism towards Jesus, would become one of the pillars of the Christian community in Jerusalem, even at the cost of his own life? One would have expected to find James anywhere but in the so-called "deluded circle" of Jesus followers. This is profoundly astonishing, to say the least. Even Paul, a sworn enemy of the followers of Jesus, who had vowed to suppress the movement, was himself suppressed and assimilated by it after a remarkable encounter with the risen Jesus Himself. Again, this can only be described as a miracle.

Furthermore, Jesus' disciples, including James and Paul, were not alone in this life-changing experience. If indeed the resurrection is true, then it means Jesus is still alive and it's possible to meet Him. By putting your trust in Him and declaring loyalty to Him, He guarantees forgiveness of your sins and a fresh start. I encourage you to take this step and witness the incredible transformation in your life. This would serve as the most compelling proof of the reality of the resurrection in your own personal experience.

Countless lives have been transformed by the risen Jesus in Jerusalem, Judea, and the entire territory of the Roman Empire since the movement began, and continues to this day all around the world wherever this good news is proclaimed. Where there is discord, He brings harmony; where there is hate, He brings love; where there is error, He brings truth; where there is despair, He brings hope; where there is brokenness, He brings healing. Sinners have found forgiveness in the sight of God. Even devoutly religious folks have seen their religious burdens lifted. Families and relationships have been restored. Lives have been transformed. The list is endless.

Ask me how I know? He did it for me too. I am a living example of a life that has been heavily influenced by the risen Jesus.

Ever since I encountered Him and received His personal presence (the Holy Spirit) in my life in my early teenage years, I have never walked alone. He has over the years helped me to navigate through the challenges that life throws at me—with all its temptations and lures of the flesh—to live for Him. There were times I felt like following the lead of my flesh and doing things my own way, but He always pulled me in the right direction. If it were not for Him, there is no telling how far and deep I would have wandered into sin and darkness had I pursued my own way. And He is not finished with me yet. The fire of God's personal presence through the person of the Holy Spirit continues to burn ceaselessly in my heart. It started with a spark and now it has engulfed me entirely. And the more I know Him, the more I need Him, the more I yield to Him, and the more He transforms me from the inside out, until one day, when this body is exchanged for the resurrected body, I become perfect, just as He is.

You too can experience this transformation in your life if you give your allegiance to Him. This transformation of the inner man is the first phase of the upgrade to the Homo novus species. The revolution blazes on. Men and women from every nation, tribe and tongue are embracing the risen Jesus as their Lord and King, and experiencing a new life in Christ (2 Corinthians 5:17). "In Christ" simply means that you are united with Jesus, and you have now become what He is. You are now part of the Christ race—the Homo novus.

There's no one that can convince you better than the skeptic. George Lyttelton and his cousin Gilbert West were eminent Englishmen and learned minds from Oxford University, who were convinced that the resurrection was false and needed to be convincingly refuted. They decided to individually study and write down what they discovered to prove that Jesus was dead. Lyttelton investigated the conversion of the apostle Paul on the road to Damascus, and West studied what history said about Jesus' resurrection from the dead.[6] When they came back together to compare notes, one said to the other,

"I'm rather embarrassed to meet you," and the other asked why. He said, "I've discovered He did rise from the dead. The evidence has convinced me"—to which the other replied, "You don't know how relieved I am that you said that, because the evidence has convinced me too!"[7]

They could not refute the fact; rather they were transformed by what they discovered, and together they experienced forgiveness and a new life in Christ. West went on to publish the book *Observations on the History and Evidence of the Resurrection of Jesus Christ* (1747), for which Oxford University awarded him the honorary Doctor of Laws degree.

Albert Henry Ross, better known as Frank Morison, was an English advertising agent who was skeptical regarding the resurrection of Jesus. He set out to analyze the sources and to write a short paper entitled *Jesus—the Last Phase* to demonstrate the apparent myth. However, while carrying out his research, he too came to be convinced of the truth of the resurrection. That truth transformed him, and he experienced forgiveness and the new life in Christ. Thereafter, he wrote the book *Who Moved the Stone?* (1930). It was said that many came to embrace the new life in Christ after reading the book.[8]

Lee Strobel is an American investigative journalist and a graduate of Yale Law School. Strobel had formerly been an atheist and was compelled by his wife's conversion and allegiance to the risen Jesus to debunk claims about the historicity of Jesus' resurrection. He used the tools he had used in his investigative writing to attempt to prove his case. However, Strobel was unable to debunk the claims to his satisfaction; instead, he was transformed by what he discovered, and he too pledged allegiance to the risen Jesus and embraced the new life in Christ. Isn't that amazing? Strobel went on to publish the book *The Case for Christ: A Journalist's Personal Investigation of the Evidence for Jesus* (1998). It became one of the best-selling works of Christian apologetics of all time, and also earned him an honorary doctoral degree.[9] A motion picture adaptation of the book was released in 2017.

So, since we are surrounded by such a great cloud of witnesses, why isn't everyone persuaded? The answer is apparent: they are unwilling to consider the evidence. Why do they refuse to do so? Because they are not willing to confront the possibility of altering their way of life that comes with the discovery of the truth. But they love the darkness more than the light, and refuse to go near it for fear their dark ways will be exposed (John 3:19-20). If only they would consider the evidence with an open mindset, they would come to the realization that everything Jesus said is true. However, such a realization would demand a change in their way of life, and hence, they are reluctant to embrace it. The point here is not about winning a debate, "But these are written so that you may believe Jesus is the Messiah, the Son of God, and by believing you may have life in His name" (John 20:31).

The consequence of Jesus' resurrection is that one day all those who believe in Jesus—those who put their absolute trust, faith and hope in Him—will be resurrected to life and given brand new immortal bodies just like the risen Jesus. This is the second and final phase of the upgrade to the Homo novus species.

The existence of every human being can be divided into three distinct phases. The first phase, known as life before death, encompasses one's time here on earth in a physical body. If you are in the physical body and reading this, it means you are still in the first phase. However, after death, one transitions into the second phase, which is life after death or the disembodied phase. During this stage, the individual exists as a conscious spirit without a physical body. The third and final phase is referred to as "life *after* life after death" by N.T. Wright, and is the re-embodied phase where the individual is once again embodied in a physical form. Nobody but Jesus has entered the third phase.

We pass from the embodied to the disembodied phase as individuals on different dates. However, many individuals will transition from the disembodied phase to the re-embodied phase simultaneously on a particular date, which can either be during the first or second resurrection. The first resurrection is reserved for the faithful followers of Jesus and leads to physical immortality and everlasting life. This event is expected to take place at the Second Coming of Jesus. The second resurrection, on the other hand, is intended for the rest of humanity who reject Jesus and leads to judgment and the second death.

We trust that even if we die, God's power will transform our dead bodies and raise us up into the new creation where evil and death no longer have power over us. The faithful followers of Jesus who have already died will be the first to receive their new bodies. Those still alive will not die at all, but will receive their new bodies instantaneously, in the blink of an eye (1 Corinthians 15:52). On the potential impact of the resurrection on the cosmos, N.T. Wright noted that:

> Every force, every authority in the whole cosmos, will be subjected to the Messiah, and finally death itself will give up its power. In other words, that which we are tempted to regard as the permanent state of the cosmos—entropy, threatening chaos, and dissolution—will be transformed by the Messiah acting as the agent of the creator God. If evolutionary optimism is squelched by, among other things, the sober estimates of the scientists that the universe as we know it today is running out of steam and cannot last forever, the gospel of Jesus Christ announces that what God did for Jesus at Easter he will do not only for all those who are 'in Christ' but also for the entire cosmos. It will be an act of new creation, parallel to and derived from the act of new creation when God raised Jesus from the dead.[10]

The impact of Jesus' resurrection extends far beyond our immediate reality. It offers us forgiveness for our past mistakes and gives us hope for the future. This pivotal event confirms that God has approved the sacrifice made by Jesus on the cross, and the divine punishment for humanity's sins has been satisfied. One man did it wrong and got mankind in trouble with death; another man did it right and got mankind out of it. But more than just getting us out of it, He got us into eternal life! (Romans 5:18-19). One small step out of the tomb for a man, one giant leap ahead for mankind. The future and hope of the human race and the universe, stepped out of the tomb on that fateful resurrection morning. The ending is a new beginning with Jesus and the new humanity reigning and ruling together in a united heaven and earth. What a wonderful future!

But again, it does require a radical change in you. Entering the new universe in your current form would result in pollution and disorder, much like what we have done to our existing universe. Before you get a new body, you need a new spirit (God's spirit) within you (Psalms 51:10). Before you get a new spirit, you need to show repentance towards God and receive forgiveness for your sins through Jesus. The good news is that God is able and willing to do just that for you, using the same power He used to raise Jesus from the dead. He is already doing that for many. The inner trans-formation and upgrade to the Homo novus species happens when you hear the message about the life, death and resurrection of Je-sus, and you respond to it. The real action comes next: He will then ignite the kingdom life within you by the power of the Holy Spirit within you, changing you from the inside out. The Holy Spirit is the river of life flowing out from God that fills you up with God's own life. This transforms you into a new kind of human species, al-lowing you to bear fruits of love, goodness, faithfulness, kindness, self-control, joy, peace, patience, and creating beautiful things in the world that bring life to others. Humans (Homo sapiens) can repro-duce only human (Homo sapiens) life, but the Holy Spirit gives birth to a new kind of being—Homo novus—a truly living breath-ing human species.

God is doing all of these amazing things to prepare you for the "age to come" while still in this one. But remember that the "age to come" has already broken into the "present age." The new creation is here, taking form even when we can't see it. The Kingdom of God is the "age to come" and it's already here; but instead of transforming our bodies and the external political order, it is first of all enlisting its citizens and transforming their lives. The Kingdom of God is here: it can be entered into now, though not in full yet. One day it will be pushed forth into life, like a new baby emerging from the womb. George Eldon Ladd puts it this way:

> The Kingdom of God belongs to The Age to Come. Yet The Age to Come has overlapped with This Age. We may taste its powers and thereby be delivered from This Age and no longer live in conformity to it. This new transforming power is the power of The Age to Come; it is indeed the power of the Kingdom of God. The Kingdom of God is future, but it is not only future. Like the powers of The Age to Come, the Kingdom of God has invaded this evil Age that men may know something of its blessings even while the evil Age goes on.[11]

The Age to Come, depicted by the dotted horizontal lines at the top of Figure 2.0, commenced following the resurrection of Jesus, coexisting with the present era of evil, and will persist until its complete establishment upon the Second Coming of Jesus as depicted by the solid horizontal lines.

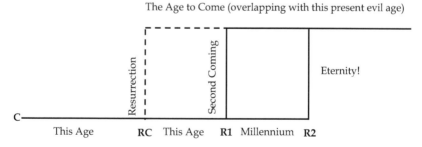

C = Creation | RC = Resurrection of Christ
R1 = First Resurrection | R2 = Second Resurrection

Figure 2.0 | This evil Age Vs. the Age to Come

THE REAL "USELESS CLASS"

Jesus once told a story about the Wheat and the Weeds to His listeners. This is what He said:

> "The kingdom of heaven may be compared to a man who sowed good seed in his field. But while people were sleeping, his enemy came, sowed weeds among the wheat, and left. When the plants sprouted and produced grain, then the weeds also appeared. The landowner's servants came to him and said, 'Master, didn't you sow good seed in your field? Then where did the weeds come from?'" 'An enemy did this,' he told them. "'So, do you want us to go and pull them up?' the servants asked him. "'No,' he said. 'When you pull up the weeds, you might also uproot the wheat with them. Let both grow together until the harvest. At harvest time I'll tell the reapers: Gather the weeds first and tie them in bundles to burn them, but collect the wheat in my barn'" (Matthew 13:24–30 CSB).

In explaining the meaning of this story, Jesus said:

> "The one who sows the good seed is the Son of Man; the field is the world; and the good seed—these are the children of the kingdom. The weeds are the children of the evil one, and the enemy who sowed them is the devil. The harvest is the end of the age, and the harvesters are angels. Therefore, just as the weeds are gathered and burned in the fire, so it will be at the end of the age. The Son of Man will send out his angels, and they will gather from his kingdom all who cause sin and those guilty of lawlessness. They will throw them into the blazing furnace where there will be weeping and gnashing of teeth. Then the righteous will shine like the sun in their Father's kingdom. Let anyone who has ears listen" (Matthew 13:37–43 CSB).

It is clear from the above story that anyone who is not part of God's kingdom is considered a weed or chaff, something of no value. But you have the opportunity now to transition from "weed" to "wheat." You have the opportunity now to turn in your old life for a kingdom life. You have the opportunity now to upgrade from Homo sapiens to Homo novus and become part of the new human race. When harvest time comes, everyone who fails to seize this opportunity will face the consequence of their choice. They will become nothing but waste or chaff—worthless. At harvest time, Jesus will separate the chaff from the wheat with His winnowing fork. Then He will clean up the threshing area, gathering the wheat into His barn but burning the chaff with never-ending fire (Matthew 3:12). This is the "useless class."

With Harari we have a different take. He predicts that technological developments might split humankind into a small elite of upgraded superhumans and a massive underclass of useless Homo sapiens, which he calls the "useless class." Yes, many people risk losing their jobs and means of livelihood due to increasing levels of automation and all. But there is even a greater risk, and not even the so-called "small elite of upgraded superhumans" will be spared. And that is the risk of becoming eternally useless. Those who fail to upgrade to the Homo novus species will be the real "useless class." God's train will dash away to eternal glory with the new humanity, leaving behind in eternal condemnation the chaff or "useless class." Jesus once said, "And what do you benefit if you gain the whole world but lose your own soul? Is anything worth more than your soul?" (Matthew 16:26).

Moreover, Jesus warns those who now enjoy the greatest economic and social advantage—the superclass—to humble themselves and upgrade to the new life He offers, or face an irreversible downgrade. Get ready for the great reversal. "Some who seem least important now will be the greatest then, and some who are the greatest now will be least important then" (Luke 13:30). Those at the bottom of the ladder—the so-called underclass or useless class, as Harari calls them—will suddenly find themselves at the top.

You are faced with two upgrade choices: You can either choose to upgrade through technological transformation and become "Homo Deus" or through divine transformation and become "Homo Novus." The former option promises to offer digital immortality, which is based on human design, while the latter option promises physical immortality (eternal life), based on God's design.

I leave you with a popular Nigerian proverb that says "The fly that fails to take heed of wise counsel is doomed to follow the corpse into the grave." And just like Morpheus said to Neo in The Matrix movie, "I can only show you the door. You're the one that has to walk through it." The Bible says it more bluntly: "The way of a fool is right in his own eyes, but he who heeds counsel is wise" (Proverbs 12:15). The decision is entirely yours, but it's important to keep in mind that this choice will have ever-lasting consequences, and you must be prepared to embrace the outcome of your decision.

But here's an insight on how things may unfold: A powerful technologically advanced global superpower will arise in the future and completely dominate the whole world. The people of this global superpower may try to upgrade or strengthen themselves by merging with machines. But just as iron does not mix with clay, the merging of humans and machines will not hold together (Daniel 2:43). A rock cut from the mountain, though not by human hands, will crush them into pieces. Then like chaff on a threshing floor, the wind will blow them all away without a trace. But the rock will become a great mountain that covers the whole earth (Daniel 2:34-35). That rock is the Kingdom of God. The God of Heaven will set up a kingdom that will never be destroyed or conquered.

When Jesus traveled to Jerusalem shortly before His death, His disciples approached Him privately one day and said, "Tell us, when will these things happen? And what is the sign of your coming and of the end of the age?" (Matthew 24:3). Similarly, while they were having the Passover meal some hours before His arrest, He told His disciples, "I'll not be drinking wine from this cup again until that new day when I'll drink with you in the kingdom of my Father" (Matthew 26:26-29). Just before Jesus' departure from the earth after His resurrection, His disciples again asked Him; "Master, are you going to restore the kingdom to Israel now? Is this the time?" (Acts 1:6). We know it was not the time then.

But there are more surprises ahead! In the next chapter, we will explore these deep questions and examine more thoroughly the concept of the Kingdom of God and its supremacy over all other kingdoms.

CHAPTER NINE

GOD'S SOVEREIGNTY OVER SUPERPOWERS

H umanity is in search of a utopian society. A utopian society is one that is characterized by benevolent governments that ensure the security, safety and general welfare of its citizens. It's a society anchored on equity and trust, which treats its citizens with dignity, a society where citizens live in health and abundance, and in a safe environment without fear, a society where citizens have absolute control over their circumstances and environment. We all desire and long for that kind of society even though it has so far eluded us.

The search for utopia and the ideal society is as old as humankind itself and runs through civilization. It has led to the invention of all kinds of ideologies and socio-economic and political systems such as monarchy, democracy, communism, totalitarianism, progressivism, egalitarianism, humanism, trans-humanism, intentional community, universal basic income, among others. Surprisingly, some of these ideologies have also been the source of untold mass poverty, injustice, terror, oppression and destruction. Those are nothing but signs of dystopia—a dysfunctional society quite the opposite of what society yearns for. More often than not, the future is often presented in our current film and literature menu as a dystopian society.

The pursuit of utopia, in any shape or form, indicates that there is undoubtedly within every person's heart a craving and an empty space that is designed specifically for God. This craving and vacuum cannot be satisfied by anything that is created, but only by the Creator Himself. There is a deep longing within us for a return to Eden (God's paradise or kingdom), but we want God out of it. The renowned French mathematician and physicist, Blaise Pascal, while reflecting on this truth noted thus:

> What else does this craving, and this helplessness, proclaim but that there was once in man a true happiness, of which all that now remains is the empty print and trace? This he tries in vain to fill with everything around him, seeking in things that are not there the help he cannot find in those that are, though none can help, since this infinite abyss can be filled only with an infinite and immutable object; in other words, by God Himself.[1]

Every time we exclude God from the equation, the ultimate outcome tends to be dystopian and results in more misery for humanity.

Our world is perpetually faced with a choice between a society characterized by liberalism and one that is dictatorial. This entails a choice between a world order based on distributed decision making, and one based on centralized decision making. It's a choice between democracy and dictatorship, between a liberty that could lead to anarchy and self-destruction, or controls that make life more difficult. Some countries have embraced dictatorship and totalitarian control, while others have embraced liberal democracy, which in itself is gradually falling apart due to the growing influence of modern technology.[2] Which system of governance, democracy or dictatorship, is better suited for humanity and likely to emerge as the dominant one?

In the hope of a better society, people sometimes demand a change of government, by which they mean a change of political party or politician such as president or prime minister, or even a complete change in the system of government. Interestingly, Jesus' key message to the world echoes the same sentiments. He said that the basic need of the world is a change in government, and that He was sent to bring about that change. He used the term "Kingdom of God" to describe the kind of change in government that He is bringing (Luke 4:43). The Kingdom of God is a theme that runs through the entire Bible, and even throughout this book.

EMERGENCE OF THE KINGDOM

In the opening pages of the Bible, it was expressed as the Sabbath rest or the Garden of Eden (God's paradise garden). God's ultimate will is to see His kingdom fully restored and reestablished on the earth and for humanity to regain access to Eden and enjoy God's Sabbath rest once again. Jesus once said, "don't be afraid, little flock. For it gives your Father great pleasure to give you the Kingdom" (Luke 12:32). "Come to me, all of you who are weary and carry heavy burdens, and I will give you rest" (Matthew 11:28).

Humankind was not made for democracy or to run themselves; neither were they made for dictatorship or to be under someone else's authoritarian control. They were made for the Kingdom of God. They were made to be under a just and benevolent divine King. This is the only way that society will flourish. We were made to be subjects of the life-giving King. This is the only way to find fulfillment and to reach our full potential.

The world is in dire need of good leadership—an individual capable of effectively managing and controlling society while granting its citizens complete freedom within those parameters. We are constantly searching for a political figure or political institution that can strike the ideal balance between control and liberty in our social structures. Regrettably, the perfect person or system remains elusive and unattainable. This reality has led to many citizens harboring deep skepticism towards politicians and some have lost all faith in their government and governing institutions.

I remember watching an interesting BBC documentary some years ago titled *The Power of Nightmares*. The narrator, Adam Curtis, hit the nail on the head in his opening lines: "In the past, politicians promised to create a better world. They had different ways of achieving this, but their power and authority came from the optimistic visions they offered their people. Those dreams failed and today people have lost faith in ideologies. Increasingly, politicians are seen simply as managers of public life, but now they have discovered a new role that restores their power and authority. Instead of delivering dreams, politicians now promise to protect us from 'nightmares.' They say that they will rescue us from dreadful dangers that we cannot see and do not understand."

There's no one who can create a better world for us except the Lord Jesus. When He does, there will for the first time be a harmonious balance between complete control and absolute freedom. In this new world, righteousness, peace, and joy will prevail, creating a perfect society.

So does this imply that the only message we can offer people in our present unstable world is "Don't worry; wait for the kingdom and for Jesus to return and fix everything?" If that's the case, it's discouraging news. It's not practical for us to continue living as we are because there's a possibility we won't be alive by the time Jesus returns. But here's where the message of the Kingdom comes into play: The Kingdom of God has already invaded this present age so that men may know something of its blessings even in this corrupt age. While we await Jesus to return and seize the reins of power and establish the fullness of His Kingdom here on earth, you can still enter the Kingdom now. You can come under His rule and government now, and as you do so, you will experience true freedom through the liberating influence of the Holy Spirit working within you (Romans 8:2).

Freedom is such a popular buzzword but it's certainly not the opportunity to do as it pleases your heart and flesh. It may seem right in your eyes, but it's a slippery slope that leads to nothing but enslavement to sin and self-destruction. Real freedom is having the ability to do what satisfies God, and having the freedom to choose to live in accordance with His will, and to be the kind of person that is morally upright. Until you find the Holy Spirit and the freedom that comes with being filled with the Spirit of God, you cannot be truly free to live a life that pleases God. Therefore, genuine freedom is having the opportunity to be righteous and live according to God's will. God has promised the Holy Spirit as a gift to anyone who repents of their sins, and welcomes Jesus as Lord and King over their life.

Because we do not really know what it is like to live in a perfect kingdom, under a just and benevolent divine King, we sometimes tend not to immediately see the good in the news that the Kingdom of God has arrived. First off, let me shed more light on what a kingdom is. In its basic form, a kingdom is simply a group of people ruled by a king or queen. David Pawson was spot on in his description of a kingdom as "a people ruled by one man, and that one man's will is law. He has no government to debate his will; he simply declares his will. He rules and reigns by inheritance. He is king because he is the son of a father who was also king. He has no cabinet and certainly there is no opposition. He is not put into that position by a vote nor can he be voted out of that position."[3]

Now that is certainly a powerful position for anyone to occupy. We know from history that people who occupied or come close to wielding such a level of power mostly abused it and used the power to exploit citizens for their selfish gain. But guess what? It would be a totally different story if that position is occupied by a good and perfect king. It takes a perfectly good

156

king to create the sort of utopian society that humanity longs for. There is only one man in history that fits that profile with excellence. You guessed right—Jesus. He is the good and perfect king.

Jesus' credentials are unparalleled in history. He existed before birth, He chose to be born, He was born of a virgin (virgin birth), He is perfect in all His ways, He was the only human ever-lived in whom God was well pleased, He resurrected from the dead (with an immortal body), He left the world about 40 days after He died (every other human exit the world the moment they die). Which other human in history possesses this kind of credential? The challenge is, because we never encounter perfection in human existence, it is almost impossible for us to comprehend what a perfect king in Jesus means. Once you gain that understanding, you will immediately appreciate why the message of the literal arrival of God's kingdom on earth ruled by Jesus Himself is such cheering news.

But the full benefit and glory of the Kingdom of God belongs to the age to come and it's set in sharp contrast to this present age. In this age there is suffering and death; in the age to come, there will be goodness and eternal life. In this age there is evil; in the age to come, righteousness will displace all evil. The age to come will completely obliterate the present political order of power and greed. The world will witness the dawn of a new era in human history. Even creation eagerly awaits the arrival of the age to come because at that time the natural world will be liberated from its bondage to decay (Romans 8:21-22). The natural order will be restored to its proper operation and potential.

In order to bring about the new era, this present one would have to be brought to a close. Contrary to what most people think, it is not going to be a sudden takeover where the world comes to an end. It will only transition into a new era through a gradual process that gets more intense as it nears the grand finale. It is akin to the deceleration process of an aircraft that is preparing to land—things will get more and more intense as it approaches and engages the runway. This portends huge consequences for the human race (especially those alive during the active transition period), the environment, and the present world order. It is said that "crisis occurs at the cusp of change." Bringing this present era to a close and ushering in a new one is certainly a big change, and big change attracts big crises. The future is bright and beautiful, but things will get worse before they get better, really dark and ugly before they get bright and beautiful. So fasten your seat belt. It is going to be the most turbulent ride in human history.

There has never been anything like it before, and there will never be anything like it afterwards. It's akin to the birth pains that bring forth a glorious new creation, rather than the final agonies of a dying creation. The intense turbulence leads to a joyous outcome. The Bible refers to that final day as "the day of the Lord." The sad thing is that most people are just living out their lives, oblivious of what is coming. The God of the universe is sovereign over all earthly kingdoms and their kings. He is the God of history—the divine authority over the course of history. As the saying goes, history is His-story (a tale of His actions and interventions), and He has promised to put the world right. He is determined to fulfill His promise to His people. God will overthrow all earthly kingdoms and replace them with His own kingdom.

When Jesus traveled to Jerusalem shortly before His death, His disciples approached Him privately and said, "Tell us, when will these things happen? And what is the sign of your coming and of the end of the age?" (Matthew 24:3 CSB). Anyone with precise answers to these questions would be the possessor of the greatest secret in human history. Concerning that day and hour, Jesus made it clear that no one knows—no one except the Father. But, thankfully, He gave us signs to look out for; these signs provide clues that His coming is near, so that we can be ready to receive Him.

In responding to the questions of His disciples, Jesus makes reference to predictions in a book written many years ago by a prophet named Daniel. When Babylon conquered Jerusalem, Daniel was only a youth when he was exiled to Babylon to serve in the palace of Nebuchadnezzar the King of Babylon.

One night Nebuchadnezzar had a dream of a great and terrifying statue whose parts were mostly made of different metallic materials. The head of the statue was pure gold, its chest and arms were silver, its belly and thighs were bronze, its legs were iron, and its feet were partly iron and partly ceramic clay. We notice at once that the metallic materials are arranged in decreasing order of quality (possibly a depiction of depreciation in moral quality and glory) and increasing order of strength. Then the dream showed a stone that broke off, without a hand touching it, and it struck the statue on its feet of iron and clay, and crushed them. The wind carried them away, and not a trace of them could be found. But the stone that struck the statue became a great mountain and filled the whole earth.

Anxious to understand his dream, the king summoned his advisers to tell him the dream and its interpretation. Unfortunately, no one could do it except Daniel. Daniel told the king that God had revealed the mystery to the king to let him know what would happen from Nebuchadnezzar's day to the future down to the very last days. Daniel went on to provide the interpretation thus:

> "...You, O king, *are* a king of kings. For the God of heaven has given you a kingdom, power, strength, and glory; and wherever the children of men dwell, or the beasts of the field and the birds of the heaven, He has given *them* into your hand, and has made you ruler over them all—you *are* this head of gold. But after you shall arise another kingdom inferior to yours; then another, a third kingdom of bronze, which shall rule over all the earth. And the fourth kingdom shall be as strong as iron, inasmuch as iron

breaks in pieces and shatters everything; and like iron that crushes, *that kingdom* will break in pieces and crush all the others.

Whereas you saw the feet and toes, partly of potter's clay and partly of iron, the kingdom shall be divided; yet the strength of the iron shall be in it, just as you saw the iron mixed with ceramic clay. And *as* the toes of the feet *were* partly of iron and partly of clay, *so* the kingdom shall be partly strong and partly fragile. As you saw iron mixed with ceramic clay, they will mingle with the seed of men; but they will not adhere to one another, just as iron does not mix with clay. And in the days of these kings the God of heaven will set up a kingdom which shall never be destroyed; and the kingdom shall not be left to other people; it shall break in pieces and consume all these kingdoms, and it shall stand forever. Inasmuch as you saw that the stone was cut out of the mountain without hands, and that it broke in pieces the iron, the bronze, the clay, the silver, and the gold—the great God has made known to the king what will come to pass after this. The dream is certain, and its interpretation is sure" (Daniel 2: 36-45 NKJV).

Daniel's interpretation of the dream makes it clear that the statue symbolized successive kingdoms or empires which were to dominate the course of world history. But in the end all these earthly kingdoms would be crushed by God's kingdom, which would endure forever. Before we discuss these kingdoms in detail, let's look at a similar vision this time given to Daniel himself as recorded in Daniel chapter 7:

In my vision that night, I, Daniel, saw a great storm churning the surface of a great sea, with strong winds blowing from every direction. Then four huge beasts came up out of the water, each different from the others.

The first beast was like a lion with eagles' wings. As I watched, its wings were pulled off, and it was left standing with its two hind feet on the ground, like a human being. And it was given a human mind.

Then I saw a second beast, and it looked like a bear. It was rearing up on one side, and it had three ribs in its mouth between its teeth. And I heard a voice saying to it, "Get up! Devour the flesh of many people!"

Then the third of these strange beasts appeared, and it looked like a leopard. It had four bird's wings on its back, and it had four heads. Great authority was given to this beast.

Then in my vision that night, I saw a fourth beast—terrifying, dreadful, and very strong. It devoured and crushed its victims with huge iron teeth and trampled their remains beneath its feet. It was different from any of the other beasts, and it had ten horns.

I watched as thrones were put in place
and the Ancient One sat down to judge.
His clothing was as white as snow,
his hair like purest wool.
He sat on a fiery throne
with wheels of blazing fire,
and a river of fire was pouring out,
flowing from his presence.
Millions of angels ministered to him;
many millions stood to attend him.
Then the court began its session,
and the books were opened.

I continued to watch because I could hear the little horn's boastful speech. I kept watching until the fourth beast was killed and its body was destroyed by fire. The other three beasts had their authority taken from them, but they were allowed to live a while longer.

As my vision continued that night, I saw someone like a son of man coming with the clouds of heaven. He approached the Ancient One and was led into his presence. He was given authority, honor, and sovereignty over all the nations of the world, so that people of every race and nation and language would obey him. His rule is eternal—it will never end. His kingdom will never be destroyed (Daniel 7:2-14).

Most Bible scholars agree that Daniel's vision in chapter 7 parallels Nebuchadnezzar's vision in chapter 2. Both came from God Himself. When you compare these visions, you would see some correlations which provide a clearer and more detailed picture of the identity of the successive kingdoms or empires which must dominate the world stage before the Kingdom of God finally obliterates them and takes center stage forever. Let's now explore the identity of the successive kingdoms that the different parts of the statue symbolize.

THE HEAD OF GOLD: THE BABYLONIAN EMPIRE

Daniel clearly identified the head of gold as Babylonia under the leadership of Nebuchadnezzar. Addressing Nebuchadnezzar, he said, "He [God] has made you the ruler over all the inhabited world and has put even the wild animals and birds under your control. You [Nebuchadnezzar] are the head of gold" (Daniel 2:38, emphasis added). We can compare this to the winged lion in Daniel's vision and also see a reference to Babylonia under the leadership of Nebuchadnezzar. This is what Daniel saw: "The first beast was like a lion with eagles' wings. As I watched, its wings were pulled off, and it was left standing with its two hind feet on the ground, like a human being. And it was given a human mind" (Daniel 7:4).

The lion symbol was characteristic of Babylon under Nebuchadnezzar. It represented the king of Babylon. The depiction may have been inspired by the Mesopotamian lion, which used to roam in the region—remember the story of the lion's den in Daniel 6:16? Recall that in 1876 some archaeologists discovered in the ancient city of Babylon a stone-based statue of a lion called

"The Lion of Babylon" (now a national symbol of Iraq), which is believed to have been built by Nebuchadnezzar.[4]

Ishtar, the ancient Babylonian goddess, was also associated with lions. It's a known fact that the Ishtar Gate entrance to the city of Babylon was adorned with dragons, bulls, and lions on blue-glazed brick, symbolizing the gods, Marduk, Adad, and Ishtar respectively. A reconstruction of the smaller frontal segment of the Ishtar Gate is on display in the Pergamon Museum in Berlin. Ezekiel (who also lived in Babylon during the Jewish exile) described Nebuchadnezzar the king of Babylon as a great eagle with broad wings and long feathers (Ezekiel 17:1-11).

All these associations lend credence to the view that the winged lion represents Babylon under Nebuchadnezzar. The expression "And it was given a human mind," may refer to Nebuchadnezzar regaining his sanity after God took it from him for seven years (Daniel 4:16; 4:28-37). It is noteworthy that Daniel makes no mention of Babylonia in chapter 8, because it was already deposed as an empire at this point (Daniel 8:1).

Nebuchadnezzar's 43-year reign over Babylonia (605–562 BC) saw the empire grow into a world superpower and capital of the world, making him the ruler of much of the then civilized world as predicted by Daniel. In an attempt to conquer Egypt, Nebuchadnezzar crushed pockets of resistance posed by some kingdoms along the way including the Phoenicians, Arameans, Arabs, and the southern kingdom of Judah. Nebuchadnezzar deposed Jehoiakim the then king of Judah, and deported a select part of their population and members of the royal line (which included Daniel) to Babylon. Nebuchadnezzar's military conquests and a flourishing economy, art and sciences gave rise to a golden age in Babylon.

After securing his empire, Nebuchadnezzar devoted most of his time to infrastructural developments, and construction and refurbishment projects within the city. He is credited with building the famous Hanging Gardens of Babylon, ranked as one of the Seven Wonders of the Ancient World.

Nebuchadnezzar's reign ended in 562 BC, many years after Daniel's prophecy was given. Several kings succeeded him, but in 539 BC after about 66 years of world dominance, Babylon was conquered and taken over by the Medo-Persian empire.

CHEST AND ARMS OF SILVER: THE MEDO-PERSIAN EMPIRE

Daniel did not specifically name the kingdom represented by the chest and arms of silver in Daniel chapter 2, but it is not hard to figure out if you follow history. When Cyrus the Great conquered Babylon during the reign of Belshazzar, it should be clear to any discerning mind that Daniel's prediction was being fulfilled—"But after you shall arise another kingdom inferior to yours" (Daniel 2:39b). Think of inferior in terms of degradation in quality (possibly moral quality or glory) from gold to silver, not in terms of strength or military might. And when you compare Daniel chapter 2 with chapters 7 and 8, the identity becomes clearer:

> Then I saw a second beast, and it looked like a bear. It was rearing up on one side, and it had three ribs in its mouth between its teeth. And I heard a voice saying to it, "Get up! Devour the flesh of many people!" (Daniel 7:5).
>
> As I looked up, I saw a ram with two long horns standing beside the river. One of the horns was longer than the other, even though it had grown later than the other one ... The two-horned ram represents the kings of Media and Persia" (Daniel 8:3, 20).

Daniel explicitly identified this kingdom in chapter 8 as Media and Persia. Observe the similarity in the expression, "It was rearing up on one side," and "One of the horns was longer than the other, even though it had grown later than the other one." This most likely refers to the Persians' advantage over the Medes. The Persians came up later, but were stronger, and absorbed the Medes in a completely bloodless victory.

The three ribs in the mouth of the bear most likely refers to the three major kingdoms that Cyrus the Great (founder of the empire) conquered: The Median kingdom (550 BC), the Lydian kingdom (546 BC), and Babylon (539 BC). According to a Wikipedia article, "His empire took root with his conquest of the Median Empire followed by the Lydian Empire and eventually the Neo-Babylonian Empire."[5] The empire greatly expanded under Cyrus' successors, stretching from parts of the Balkans (Eastern Bulgaria–Paeonia and Thrace–Macedonia) and Southeast Europe in the west, to the Indus Valley in the east, making it one of the largest the ancient world had ever seen to that point.[6] Indeed, it devoured the flesh of many people (i.e. conquered many nations) as predicted by Daniel.

Thus, the second empire represented by the chest and arms of silver, the bear, and the ram as predicted by Daniel was the Medo-Persian Empire, also known as the Achaemenid Empire. However, despite its military might and over 200 years of dominion over the entire civilized ancient world, this empire was conquered by another and eventually came to an end.

BELLY AND THIGHS OF BRONZE:
THE GREEK EMPIRE

> While I was watching, suddenly a male goat appeared from the west, crossing the land so *swiftly* that he didn't even touch the ground. This goat, which had one very large horn between its eyes, headed toward the two-horned ram that I had seen standing beside the river, rushing at him in a rage. The goat charged *furiously* at the ram and struck him, breaking off both his horns.

The shaggy male goat represents the king of Greece, and the large horn between his eyes represents the first king of the Greek Empire. The four prominent horns that replaced the one large horn show that the Greek Empire will break into four kingdoms, but none as great as the first (Daniel 8:5-7, 21-22, emphasis added).

History tells us that the Greeks conquered the Medo-Persian Empire. Daniel chapter 8 explicitly identified the shaggy male goat as the Greek Empire. Ancient Greeks were known for keeping long beards like the shaggy male goat (a goat with long, thick, unkempt hair) as a sign of honor and wisdom. Alexander the Great—the first king of the empire, is clearly in view here as the "very large horn." Again when you compare Daniel chapter 8 (shaggy male goat with very large horn) with chapter 7 (four winged leopard) and chapter 2 (belly and thighs of bronze), you will see a striking correlation:

"Then the third of these strange beasts appeared, and it looked like a leopard. It had four bird's wings on its back, and it had four heads. Great authority was given to this beast" (Daniel 7:6). "… a third kingdom, represented by bronze, will rise to rule the world" (Daniel 2:39). A leopard is built for speed and strength. It is **fast** and **ferocious** and kills its prey with one **swift** bite to the neck. According to National Geographic, leopards are "super springy" and "can leap 6m forward through the air."[7] Similarly, the beast of chapter 8 (the shaggy male goat) was described as "crossing the land so **swiftly that he didn't even touch the ground**" and "charged **furiously** at the ram." Can you now see the striking similarities in their characteristics?

This aptly describes Alexander the Great, who conquered the known world at an alarming speed. And as if that was not enough, he also set his eyes on Babylon, and that put him on a warpath with Darius III, king of the Medo-Persian Empire. For Darius III, the stakes were really high—the loss of Babylonia would likely spell the end of the entire Medo-Persian Empire, and so he couldn't afford to lose. According to historical records, in 331 BC Alexander the Great and King Darius III faced each other in a decisive battle, and Alexander the Great conquered the Medo-Persian army in its entirety and overthrew King Darius III.[8]

As documented on Wikipedia, "By the age of thirty, Alexander the Great had created one of the largest empires in history, stretching from Greece to northwestern India. He was undefeated in battle and is widely considered to be one of history's greatest and most successful military commanders."[9] This confirms the word of God to Daniel that "a third kingdom, represented by bronze, will rise to rule the world."

Then look at what happened:

> "The goat became very powerful. But at the height of his power, his large horn was broken off. In the large horn's place grew four prominent horns pointing in the four directions of the earth" (Daniel 8:8).

Alexander died a sudden death in the old palace of Nebuchadnezzar, in Babylon, at the young age of 32—just at the height of his power. Following his death, there was a series of conflicts among Alexander's generals over the control of the empire. This eventually settled into four stable power blocks known as the Hellenistic kingdoms: The Ptolemaic Kingdom (Egypt and parts of North Africa), the Seleucid Empire (Syria and Mesopotamia), the Kingdom of Pergamon (Turkey), and the Greco-Bactrian Kingdom (Afghanistan, Uzbekistan, Tajikistan, Turkmenistan, and the Indian subcontinent). This again confirms the word of God to Daniel "that the Greek Empire will break into four kingdoms" as depicted by the "four prominent horns" (kings), "four bird's wings" (kingdoms), and "four heads" (kings). These four kingdoms lasted for about 200-300 years before the Roman Empire began to conquer them.

LEGS OF IRON: THE ROMAN EMPIRE

"Following that kingdom, there will be a fourth one, as *strong as iron*. That kingdom will smash and crush all previous empires, just as iron smashes and crushes everything it strikes.

"Then in my vision that night, I saw a fourth beast— terrifying, dreadful, and very strong. It devoured and crushed its victims with *huge iron teeth* and trampled their remains *beneath its feet*" (Daniel 2:40, 7:7b, emphasis added).

Although Daniel did not specifically name this fourth kingdom, he described it as having "legs of iron" and "strong as iron" in chapter 2, and "crushed its victims with huge iron teeth" and "trampled their remains beneath its feet" in chapter 7. Daniel's description was a fitting picture of what the Roman Empire became. History tells us that the Romans conquered the Greek Empire. The Roman military leveraged the strength of iron in every way and that in part made them very effective. Virtually all the Roman military personal equipment including helmet, breastplate (muscle cuirass), greaves (legs of iron), spears and javelin was made of iron. The Romans emerged as the dominant world empire or superpower after they conquered and swallowed up the various fragments of the Greek Empire and other smaller kingdoms in a series of battles.

This was predicted by Daniel: "That kingdom will smash and crush all previous empires, just as iron smashes and crushes everything it strike." In fact, the writer of the book of Revelation, John, clearly identified this kingdom as the city on seven hills— an allusion to Rome (Revelation 17:9); and described it thus: "Now the beast which I saw was like a leopard, his feet were like the feet of a bear, and his mouth like the mouth of a lion" (Revelation 13:2b). As you can see from previous sections of this chapter, the leopard, bear, and lion represent the Greek, Persian, and Babylonian kingdoms respectively. Recall that Babylon (lion) was conquered by the Persian Empire (bear), the Persian

168

Empire was, in turn, conquered by the Greek Empire (leopard); then the Greek Empire was conquered by the Romans. John is simply saying that the Roman Empire is the sum total of all of those kingdoms (Greek, Persia, and Babylonian).

Incidentally, it was during the reign of the first Roman emperor Caesar Augustus that Jesus (the promised King whose kingdom lasts forever) was born. Interestingly, despite popular demand and expectation, Jesus did not attempt to crush the Roman Empire; instead He concentrated on inviting men and women to become loyal citizens of His kingdom. Thereafter the Roman authorities crushed Him as demanded by the Jewish leaders of the day. But God reversed their verdict by doing something extraordinary and unprecedented—raising Him from the dead!

The Roman Empire was a vast kingdom. "At its height, it stretched from Italy through Europe to the British Isles, across North Africa, down through Egypt and up into Mesopotamia and across Anatolia" in modern-day Turkey.[10] According to the Guinness World Records, the Roman Empire is considered to have been the longest-lasting empire in all of recorded history, lasting for almost 1500 years.[11] It eventually collapsed following the fall of the surviving eastern wing of the empire to the Ottoman Empire in AD 1453. But it appears not to have totally eclipsed. Daniel foresees a reemergence of this same fourth kingdom towards the end of history.

FEET OF IRON-CLAY: THE REVIVED ROMAN EMPIRE

It's obvious that the ancient Roman Empire isn't the last empire to dominate the world before the Kingdom of God finally takes over. Since the fall of the ancient Roman Empire to date, many more empires and superpowers have come and gone. And as I write, there are still global superpowers that dominate our times. We also know that Jesus did not crush the ancient Roman

Empire in His first coming, nor has He physically taken over world affairs yet.

So, continuing from the Roman Empire, there is yet another powerful future superpower that will dominate this world towards the end of history. It will be the last earthly kingdom that will rule over this world. Its reign will be very brief and brutal; and its downfall will pave the way for the ascendance of the Kingdom of God in its full glory. How do I know this? We know from Nebuchadnezzer's dream that the stone cut from a mountain (the Kingdom of God) did not strike at the "legs of iron." It struck at the "feet of iron mixed with clay." "As you watched, a rock was cut from a mountain, but not by human hands. It struck the feet of iron and clay, smashing them to bits" (Daniel 2:34). This alludes to the Revived Roman Empire in the latter days. The presence of a noticeable differentiation in both the anatomy (feet and toes), and the material composition (iron mixed with clay) provides compelling evidence that this is, in fact, a separate kingdom. Daniel characterizes this kingdom as exceedingly savage. In fact, the Angel who revealed the true interpretation of the vision to Daniel explicitly stated that "It will be different from all the others. It will devour the whole world, trampling and crushing everything in its path" (Daniel 7:23). The presence of iron in its feet shows that this kingdom retains the strength of iron, and is related to the kingdom represented by the legs of iron (ancient Roman Empire).

In fact, this depiction of the last empire as an extension of the ancient Roman Empire (Daniel 7:7-13) is quite a puzzling portrayal. There must be something God is trying to communicate to us here, and this calls for wisdom and understanding. This future empire (iron mixed with clay) is a reemergence of the ancient Roman Empire (legs of iron). We will delve deeper into this idea in the next chapter.

The consensus among historians is that the ancient Roman Empire held the title of the world's first superpower, and according to Daniel, it will reemerge in the future as the world's final superpower. But there is more. Firstly, Daniel tells us that the **feet and toes of iron mixed with clay** is an indication that the kingdom shall be divided; but the strength of the iron shall be in it. Recall that the Babylonian Empire was a single unit throughout its existence. The Medo-Persian Empire was twofold—Media and Persia. The Greek Empire in its final form was fourfold—it was split into four. And the Roman Empire in its final form according to Daniel, will be a "ten-toed" kingdom. This can be likened to the ten horns depicted in Daniel 7:7: "It was different from any of the other beasts, and it had ten horns." What do these ten horns signify? This kingdom is divided into ten parts, or has ten kings. These ten parts and their kings will eventually relinquish their political power to one man (Revelation 17:13)—a single political authority with the strength of iron.

Secondly, Daniel tells us that the **iron mixed with clay toes** indicates that this kingdom shall be partly strong and partly fragile. And thirdly, he tells us that the **iron mixed with clay** analogy indicates that "they" will mingle or merge with the seed of men; but will not hold together, just as iron does not mix with clay. Whatever is implied here as "they" must be a stronger entity that has the strength of iron merging or mingling with a weaker entity—the seed of men (clay).

> "Whereas you saw the feet and toes, partly of potter's clay and partly of iron, the kingdom shall be divided; yet the strength of the iron shall be in it, just as you saw the iron mixed with ceramic clay. And as the toes of the feet were partly of iron and partly of clay, so the kingdom shall be partly strong and partly fragile. As you saw iron mixed with ceramic clay, they will mingle with the seed of men; but they will not adhere to one another, just as iron does not mix with clay" (Daniel 2: 41-43 NKJV).

So what exactly is going on here? Is Daniel foreseeing a society made up of extant (normal) human species (clay) and super intelligent humanoid machines (iron)? As I have elaborated in previous chapters, all that is certainly plausible in our present generation.

We are already cohabiting with intelligent machines (AI) in our society. These machines are growing in intelligence at an exponential rate and will someday, according to experts, get to a point where they become far more intelligent than humans. Some technology experts are of the opinion that the only way humans can survive or remain relevant at that point is to upgrade their bodies and brains, and their physical and intellectual abilities by merging with those super intelligent machines (AI) to become superhuman, or Homo deus, as Yuval Harari calls it. The technology to make this merger possible is already being perfected and will be available to anyone who can afford it in the near future.

But the question is: how many people can afford it? Such upgrades are likely to be expensive and within reach of only the privileged few. This may result in the division of humanity into two parts akin to a caste system. One part will be as strong as iron, the other part will be as fragile as clay. Aldous Huxley's *Brave New World* predicted this kind of caste division in society and the struggle to maintain social stability. Yuval Harari also noted that this kind of scenario may result in "the most unequal societies that ever existed."[12] Could this be the division that Daniel was alluding to when he said that "the kingdom shall be divided ... while some parts of it will be as strong as iron, other parts will be as weak as clay"? (Daniel 2:42). If so, then what this could mean is that the citizens of this future world superpower will try to strengthen themselves by merging with super intelligent machines (AI). But just as iron does not mix with clay, the merger of humans and super intelligent machines (AI) will not hold together (Daniel 2:43).

The Bible tells us that this future world superpower (the revived Roman Empire) will be global and totalitarian, which means that democracy will be obliterated. It will demonstrate great power and authoritarian control that far outweighs the record of previous empires, as well as gross decadence in moral quality unparalleled in history. The consolidation of authority under one entity is feasible because, for the first time in human history, we live in a truly globalized world. Given that nearly all of the necessary institutions and technologies for governing a globalized world are already in place, and given the growing array of global challenges such as pandemics, nuclear proliferation, climate change, and emerging technologies, the idea of a world government is certainly a plausible notion.

There are already insinuations from different quarters of the need for a world government and a world leader to effectively tackle the many global challenges bedeviling the world. Global challenges, they say, require global policies and solutions. And global policies and solutions, they say, require a global leader to enforce it. Who could such a global leader be? Daniel refers to this world leader as the "little horn" (Daniel 7:8)—we will discuss this in more detail later. He will rise from the ashes of a global chaos and seize power on the promise of utopia and Pax Romana (Roman Peace) evolving into world peace. Aldous Huxley in his book *Brave New World* calls this kind of empire the "World State"—depicted as a perfect society equipped with the most advanced technology to maintain order and control.

But don't be fooled. What may seem like world peace and utopia, will turn out to be a dystopia and the greatest distress the world has ever known and will ever know. The actions of this "little horn" will then trigger a decisive response from God, which will usher in a new dawn in human history.

THE ROCK THAT CRUSHES ALL EARTHLY KINGDOMS

"As you watched, a rock was cut from a mountain, but not by human hands. It struck the feet of iron and clay, smashing them to bits. The whole statue was crushed into small pieces of iron, clay, bronze, silver, and gold. Then the wind blew them away without a trace, like chaff on a threshing floor. But the rock that knocked the statue down became a great mountain that covered the whole earth" (Daniel 2:34-35).

> "During the reigns of those kings, the God of heaven will set up a kingdom that will never be destroyed or conquered. It will crush all these kingdoms into nothingness, and it will stand forever. That is the meaning of the rock cut from the mountain, though not by human hands, that crushed to pieces the statue of iron, bronze, clay, silver, and gold" (Daniel 2:44-45b).

> "I continued to watch because I could hear the little horn's boastful speech. I kept watching until the fourth beast was killed and its body was destroyed by fire" (Daniel 7:11).

The final world superpower and its leader (the little horn) will unleash unprecedented hostility and oppression against the people of God, and he will conquer them. But his actions will provoke a response from the almighty God. God will pass a judgment against the little horn and He will authorize Jesus the Messiah to step in and save the day. When Jesus was responding to His disciples concerning their question on when these things would happen, and what would be the sign of His coming, and the end of the age, He clearly told them that immediately after the hostility of those days, the sign of the Son of Man will appear in the sky. There will be deep mourning among all the peoples of the earth, and they will see the Son of Man coming on the clouds of the sky with power and great glory (Matthew 24:29-30).

Jesus is the rock that will crush the final world superpower and its leader into pieces, and bring its civilization to an end as predicted by Daniel. He will immediately seize the government and become the King of the whole world. The great mountain that covered the whole earth is the Kingdom of God taking over the whole world. Jesus will usher in the Kingdom of God which replaces the kingdom of the little horn. His kingdom will last forever.

The Second Coming of Jesus is clearly in view here as recorded in the referenced scriptures above—not the first coming as some may want to think. The quiet and humble entrance of Jesus into the world at His incarnation doesn't fit in with the language of "Son of Man coming on the clouds of the sky" and "crushing" these other kingdoms into pieces, and the "wind blowing them away like chaff without a trace." As noted earlier in this chapter, Jesus never crushed the Roman Empire during His time on earth, even when it was suggested to Him. And there are still many other human kingdoms in existence today that have not been crushed and wiped out. In general, many Jews did not expect that the Messiah would come twice. They expected that God's kingdom would completely take over from the human kingdoms once the Messiah appeared, but they didn't realize that the Messiah's coming would happen twice. From that first coming of the Messiah, God's kingdom would be sown in the hearts and minds of men for generation upon generation for at least 2000 years alongside other earthly kingdoms, until the Second Coming of Christ, when it will be manifested in its complete form and take over the whole world.

Interestingly, just as the Messiah would come twice, the same empire in power during His first coming (the Roman Empire) would re-emerge to continue their dominion over the world for a little while. Recall that, whereas Julius Caesar was the first ruler, the Roman Empire officially began during the reign of Caesar Augustus, coinciding with the birth of Jesus. Note also how Jesus began His ministry by proclaiming the arrival of the Kingdom of God. It is this revived empire and its notorious leader, the beast (the little horn), that Jesus will finally confront and destroy (Daniel 7:11; Revelation 19:15, 20). From then on, the Kingdom of God will completely take over the affairs of the world. This is the mystery of the Kingdom of God that was hidden from man for ages but now revealed. Isn't that amazing?

> Thank you, Father, Lord of heaven and earth. You've concealed your ways from sophisticates and know-it-alls, but spelled them out clearly to ordinary people. Yes, Father, that's the way you like to work (Matthew 11:25-26 MSG).

But why did God make those revelations known to Daniel, knowing that he wouldn't be alive to witness all the events unfold? Well, it's obvious that those revelations were not only meant for Daniel himself but for later generations. Other prophets such as Jeremiah, Ezekiel, Isaiah, Joel and Apostle John in Revelation also spoke of God's kingdom overthrowing all other kingdoms. First-ly, these prophecies were primarily given as an encouragement to God's people to remain faithful even in the face of intense persecu-tion and death threats, knowing that God is in control of the nations and world events, and would fulfill the promise of His Everlasting Kingdom. Secondly, they are also a call to world rulers to acknowl-edge and honor God as the supreme ruler of the universe, who be-stows kingdoms to whomever He pleases. By doing so, they can display humility and behave justly.

For modern readers proffering a worldview that complete-ly ignores God, this is a call to recognize, trust, and respond to God and embrace His kingdom, despite the allure of technology, transhumanism or utopia. History shows that all the powerful empires that existed in the past have all been reduced to ashes. Likewise, the powerful empires and superpowers that lord it over us today, and the ones that will emerge tomorrow, will one day burn down to ashes and disappear. In the end, only one kingdom will remain standing, the Kingdom of God. Do not invest your life in **ashes**. Invest your life in the kingdom that endures forever—the Kingdom of God. There isn't much time left. The countdown to the emergence of the final global super-power—the one world government and the end of civilization has already begun.

CHAPTER TEN

COUNTDOWN TO THE FINAL WORLD SUPERPOWER (THE REVIVED ROMAN EMPIRE)

Since antiquity, the notion of a single political authority for all humanity has been contemplated, proposed and even attempted by some kings and world leaders. One of the well-known early proponents of this notion is the medieval Italian poet and philosopher Dante Alighieri. Dante in his book *De Monarchia* (The Monarchy) proposed a single universal monarchical authority over the earth, to enable mankind to realize a state of universal peace and well-being. Dante believed that a supreme world ruler with absolute power over all the earth would not engage in aggression because he is already in control. Rather, his reign would bring an end to the threat of war (present and future), and help establish a new era of enduring peace throughout the world.

IN PURSUIT OF A GLOBAL EMPIRE

Unfortunately, noble as it sounds, this utopia has proven to be one of mankind's most elusive goals throughout history. The position of a supreme world ruler over the earth comes with great power. And, according to an ancient adage, "with great power comes great responsibility," and great responsibility requires the highest of moral standards and maturity. Such a person is expected to exhibit a vast measure of humility, self-control, love, intelligence and, where possible, certain superhuman abilities. If that kind of power falls into the wrong hands, it can potentially ruin everything. It is difficult to find a man whose resume ticks all the boxes, and more. Who is worthy to receive such great power, and the glory and honor that come with it without succumbing to pride and with it corruption?

After the flood in Noah's day, God's vision and instruction for humanity was to spread across the whole earth. Instead, humanity decided to violate this order by coming together to build themselves a great city and what seemed like the world's first skyscraper (Genesis 11:3-4). That city is what we have all come to know as Babylon. Earlier we saw how a rebellious Nephilim-like figure (a mix of human and angelic race) named Nimrod was the leader of those who attempted to build the city and its imposing tower. We know this because Nimrod's kingdom included the city of Babel or Babylon (Genesis 10:10-12). They had access to the most advanced technology known to man at that time, including the knowledge and ability to make bricks and use tar in construction projects, in order to make their dream a reality. Nimrod's vision was to build a world empire in opposition to God, and to establish himself as the single political authority for all humanity.

But these rebellious actions of theirs triggered a decisive response from God. God intervened and brought the project to an end, scattering the people across the region. Today, Babylon, with its founder Nimrod, stands as an archetype of humanity's collective rebellion against God and His rule. Babylon has now become the symbol of a global worldly system that is completely opposed to God.

Other ancient Mesopotamian, Egyptian, Chinese, and European dynasties, at one time or other, also aspired to preside over a global empire. The ancient Chinese, for example, had a particularly well-developed utopian vision of a unified global government which they called "the Great Unity." But, it never materialized. The Pax Romana—a roughly 200-year period of sustained Roman imperialism, relative peace and security across much of the known world at the time, is seen by advocates of world government as a great accomplishment and model for tackling present global challenges. If the Roman model is fully adopted for the entire world, the consequence will be the birth of a world empire whose power and control is vested in one man. And the Bible tells us that this one man will set himself up as god and demand worship and total submission from his subjects—the citizens of the world.

Although the Roman Empire is long gone, some experts are of the opinion that the empire never truly died but its progeny exist in various forms. A number of empires and political unions have claimed various forms of successorship to the Roman Empire, using the same name, or a variation of it, and in some cases a completely different nomenclature to describe themselves.

In the East, the most notable claimants of the continued Roman Empire have been the Byzantine Empire (395–1453), also referred to as the Eastern Roman Empire. It was followed by the Ottoman Empire (1453–1922), the Russian Czardom (1547–1721) and, by extension, the Russian Empire (1547–1917). In fact, The Russian Czardom declared Moscow to be the Third Rome and successor of the Byzantine Empire after the fall of Constantinople to the Ottoman Turks in 1453. This claim was strengthened by the marriage between Ivan III of Russia and the niece of Constantine XI, the last Byzantine emperor. Ivan III styled himself Czar, a Russian word for Caesar.

In the West, the most notable claimant to Rome has been the Holy Roman Empire (800-1806). This followed the coronation of the Frankish king, Charlemagne, as emperor in December 800 by Pope Leo III; it continued until its demise during the reign of Francis II (1792–1806). The German Empire (1871–1918) in turn claimed lineage (via Otto I) from the Holy Roman Empire. Nazi Germany subsequently called itself the Third Reich (Empire), which alluded to the claim that Nazi Germany was the successor to the earlier Holy Roman Empire (considered as the First Reich) and German Empire (considered as the Second Reich).

The formation of the European Union (EU) is seen by many as a modern-day attempt to revive the Holy Roman Empire and, by extension, the Roman Empire. Nonetheless, the world is changing and evolving rapidly, and the EU is not exempt to the threat of breaking up, following the pull out of Great Britain, the Russian-Ukraine war, and other unfolding factors. Who knows what will become of the EU in the near future? Will it wax and forge ahead because of strong leadership from France and Germany, or will it wane and fall apart because of weaker member states? Time will tell.

As I write, there is growing opinion to support the notion of the United Nations (UN) and the post-World War II world order as the successor to the Roman Empire. The two most ambitious efforts to date to institute some form of world government are the League of Nations and its successor, the United Nations. These two bodies grew directly out of the traumatic experiences of two world wars. The UN was established after World War II to, among other things, maintain international peace and security, prevent wars from happening, arbitrate armed conflicts, and ensure a better future for the world. But it is no secret that, since its creation in 1945 to date, there have been countless wars and ongoing national and international conflicts. Just look around you and you will find injustice, broken promises, human right abuses, genocide, unrest, poverty, pandemic, recession, terrorism, civil wars, climate crisis; the list is endless. These trends continue in spite of the organization's huge annual budgets and lofty manifestos. What does this portend for the future of the world?

In fact, it appears the post–World War II world order built on democracy is gradually falling apart. The conflict between autocracy and democracy has accelerated. We are living at a time in history where democracy is under its greatest threat ever.[1] In many parts of the world, democracy and support for democratic principles have backtracked and there is a growing call for more authoritarian governments, using the environment and pandemics, as arguments.[2] What will emerge when the post-World War II world order ends remain to be seen. Whatever happens, we know from the word of God that at the climax of history, a sweeping global autocratic empire led by a powerful dictator will rise to take control of the world. The Bible refers to this dictator as "the beast" or "the little horn."

There are two similar but distinct figures in the Book of Daniel that were described as the "little horn." Incidentally, these two little horns play a role in the first and second coming of the promised Messiah respectively. The first little horn preceded the first coming of the Messiah, and the second little horn will precede the second coming of the Messiah. These figures are nothing but the apotheosis of the spiritual conflict between the forces of good and evil. In fact, one of the incredible insights we gain from studying the Book of Daniel is the understanding that earthly conflicts are a reflection of heavenly conflicts between the forces of good and evil.

THE FIRST LITTLE HORN: ANTIOCHUS EPIPHANES

The first little horn emerged from the Seleucid Kingdom—one of the four kingdoms that sprang out of the Greek Empire following the death of Alexander the Great. "Then from one of the prominent horns came a small horn whose power grew very great. It extended toward the south and the east and toward the glorious land of Israel" (Daniel 8:9).

From history, we can identify this first "little horn" as Antiochus IV Epiphanes—a member of the Greek Seleucid dynasty. His accession to the throne was controversial, and his reign brutal. He seized power after he murdered the legitimate heir to the throne, and immediately assumed the name Antiochus IV Epiphanes (which means "God Manifest") when he ascended the throne. He even claimed to be the incarnate of the Greek god, Zeus. It was apparent that satan was the invisible force behind him. His influence and power extended towards Egypt (South), Persia (East), and the land of Israel.

Antiochus had a mercurial temperament, and demonstrated an unusual level of arrogance and cruelty which earned him the nickname Epimanes (which means "The Mad One"). While he did things that captivated the hearts of the common people, he proved to be a despot of a high order. He took Jerusalem in 167 BC and enforced the hellenization on the Jews in an attempt to exterminate the Jewish faith. Although some Jews succumbed, others vehemently objected to his hellenization policies, and he started to use force, including capital punishment, to drive it.

Antiochus issued decrees forbidding many traditional Jewish practices such as temple sacrifice, circumcision, observance of Sabbaths, and other Jewish festivals. He also attempted to deny them access to their holy books and prevent them from keeping God's laws. The greatest affront to the Jews was when he plundered the temple and desecrated it by erecting an altar to the Greek god, Zeus Olympios (an act often described as the "abomination of desolation"), and forced the Jews to sacrifice pigs right there in the altar. Thousands who refused to abandon their faith and follow his dictates were tortured and massacred.

Daniel predicted that "His army will take over the Temple fortress, pollute the sanctuary, put a stop to the daily sacrifices, and set up the sacrilegious object that causes desecration. He will flatter and win over those who have violated the covenant. But the people who know their God will be strong and will resist him" (Daniel 11:31-32).

Never before had there been such a flagrant attempt to totally wipe out the Jewish faith and culture! It was so horrible that it gave rise to the Maccabean revolt led by Judah Maccabee (a Levite from the line of Aaron). Antiochus had crossed the red line. His cup was full, and he must face God's judgment. And that he got in full measure. Antiochus was struck with a mysterious incurable bowel disease that came with sharp internal tortures. In the midst of these tortures, worms also ate up his body while he was still living, and he gradually rotted away. No man could endure to carry him due to the intolerable stench that emanated from him; and he ended up dying a miserable death (2 Maccabees 9:5-28). A death similar to that of Herod Agrippa, persecutor of the early Christians (Acts 12). This is what Daniel wrote about him:

> It even challenged the Commander of heaven's army by canceling the daily sacrifices offered to him and by destroying his Temple. The army of heaven was restrained from responding to this rebellion. So the daily sacrifice was halted, and truth was overthrown. The horn succeeded in everything it did (Daniel 8:11-12).

> He will be a master of deception and will become arrogant; he will destroy many without warning. He will even take on the Prince of princes in battle, but he will be broken, though not by human power (Daniel 8:25).

In the end, Jerusalem was reclaimed and the temple was rededicated to God. This historic victory is celebrated annually to this day by the Jews in a festival called Ḥanukkah. Had he succeeded in his attempt to wipe out the Jewish faith and, by implication, the Hebrew language, the holy books, the cultural heritage, he would have tactically made it impossible for the promised Messiah to come and fulfill His mission. But God's will and purpose always prevail, and he did not succeed. The Seleucid Empire eventually fell to the firepower of the Romans.

The Maccabean family ruled Judea autonomously under the name Hasmonean dynasty for about a century until they were deposed and replaced with the Herodian dynasty (whose founder from the line of Esau converted to Judaism) by the Romans. It was during this period that the Messiah was born. Through diplomatic means, the Hasmonean and Herodian dynasties secured significant favors and concessions for the Jews from the Romans, including exclusion from Roman military service, and permission to follow their Jewish laws, customs and religion both in Judea and in the diaspora (other parts of the Roman world)—something that Antiochus Epiphanes had vehemently denied them. These concessions remained in effect throughout the Messiah's lifetime, and provided the right setting for Him to effectively carry out His ministry. Antiochus foreshadows the second little horn that is to emerge at the end of history.

THE SECOND LITTLE HORN: THE BEAST OF REVELATION

The second and final little horn emerges from the fourth beast described in Daniel chapter 7. This little horn sprouts from the stump (remains) of the ancient Roman Empire and stands in sharp contrast to the green sprout that grows from the stump of the Davidic kingdom (Isaiah 11:1). This little horn and the empire he represents also correspond to the feet of iron mixed with clay described in Daniel chapter 2—the **revived** Roman Empire, which is the final world superpower.

> Then in my vision that night, I saw a fourth beast—terrifying, dreadful, and very strong. It devoured and crushed its victims with huge iron teeth and trampled their remains beneath its feet. It was

different from any of the other beasts, and it had ten horns. As I was looking at the horns, suddenly another small horn appeared among them. Three of the first horns were torn out by the roots to make room for it. This little horn had eyes like human eyes and a mouth that was boasting arrogantly (Daniel 7:7-8).

There is also a reference to this particular little horn in the New Testament, albeit with another name. Paul described him as the "man of lawlessness" or "man of sin" (2 Thessalonians 2:3–10), while John, the author of the Book of Revelation saw him as "the beast from the sea" (Revelation 13:1-10). The sea in Jewish tradition represents the dark forces of chaos that stand in the way of God's plans.

But the title by which most people identify him is "the antichrist," which is a term found only in the Epistles of John. Nowhere in the Book of Revelation is the word "antichrist" mentioned. The prefix "anti" (can mean one of two things. The most common meaning is "against" or the "opposite of." But, the second meaning, surprisingly, can be "another," "an alternative," or "in place of"—more like an alternative Christ or another Christ rather than a completely hostile world ruler. It's obvious it is this second meaning that John had in mind when he used the word antichrist (Greek: *antíkhristos*). This is because, according to John, there are many antichrists that are already in the world. John may have been inspired by Jesus' prediction that false christs (Greek: *pseudokhristos*) and false prophets are going to pop up everywhere to deceive people (Matthew 24:24).

> For *many* deceivers have *gone out into the world* who do not confess Jesus Christ as coming in the flesh. This is a deceiver and *an antichrist* (2 John 1:7, emphasis added).

So in his Epistle, John was not specifically referring to the "man of lawlessness" or "the beast" who is to come. The Epistle was written in response to dissenters that John called antichrists, false prophets, or false teachers, who, rejecting the idea that God would come in human form in the person of Jesus, were promoting an alternative christ rooted on Greek philosophy. All these antichrist and false prophet figures will culminate in the final figure that John in Revelation calls "the false prophet." So the real hostile figure is the one that John calls "the beast from the sea," who, ironically, proclaims himself to be God.

In Revelation, John describes this beast as "like a leopard, his feet were like the feet of a bear, and his mouth like the mouth of a lion" (Revelation 13:2b). As we noted in the previous chapter, the leopard, bear, and lion represent the Greek, Persia, and Babylonian Empires respectively. Recall that Babylon (lion) was conquered by the Persian Empire (bear), the Persian Empire was in turn conquered by the Greek Empire (leopard), and the Greek Empire was conquered by the Romans. In short, John is saying that the beast and the empire he represents is the sum total of all of the past empires (Greek, Persia, and Babylonian).

So who exactly is this end-time little horn? How can we unravel his identity? Let me begin by saying that the identity of the beast is not really something anyone should focus their attention on at this stage because it is still an unfolding story. When the time is right, his identity will be disclosed, and everything will become clear. What matters more is what system you give your allegiance to here and now in the run-up to the end. Is it to be the world system based on the one world new order or God's eternal kingdom? The warning is loud and clear: do not be deceived! My concern is that when that time comes, and the beast is finally revealed, many will already have been swept away by the great wind of deception that will blow across the world. And for that reason, I am going to give some attention to the identity of the beast.

Attempts to unmask the identity of this mysterious individual have been the subject of numerous sermons, debates, presentations, articles, and books, and have led to all kinds of conjecture. Interestingly, John gave us valuable clues as to the identity of this figure. It was a riddle that I suppose was well understood by his original audience at the time.

> Wisdom is needed here. Let the one with understanding solve the meaning of the number of the beast, for it is the number of a man. His number is 666 (Revelation 13:18).

In ancient days, alphabets served both as letters and numerals, whereby each letter of the alphabet was assigned a numerical value. The most familiar example of this dual function can be found in the Roman numeral system. The Greek and Hebrew languages operated similarly. Because of this dual use of alphabets, cryptogram-based riddles or puzzles were common in ancient cultures. In ancient Hebrew such cryptograms were known as *gematria*. Summing up the numerical equivalents of these letters gives a numerical value to a word or name.

According to historical accounts, during the first century, the followers of Jesus who lived in the Roman Empire, specifically during John's time, used to the number 666 as a code name for the notorious Roman emperor, Nero Caesar.[3] This implies that the original recipients of the Book of Revelation were acquainted with the person to whom John was hinting when he wrote, "for it is the number of a man. His number is 666." Many Bible scholars have also come to conclude with a satisfying degree of confidence that the number 666 was a reference to the nefarious Nero Caesar. In his book *Revelation For Everyone*, N. T. Wright noted that "it is more or less certain that the number 666 represents, by one of many formulae well known at the time, the name NERO CAESAR when written in Hebrew characters."[4]

Using the Hebrew gematria, the name Nero Caesar, if spelled according to Hebrew characters, adds up precisely to the number 666. The Book of Revelation was originally written in Greek. The Greek version of the name Nero Caesar (Kaisar Neron) translit-erated into Hebrew as Qsr Nron (רסק ןורנ), and yields a numerical value of 666, as shown on the table below:[5]

Resh (ר)	Samekh (ס)	Qoph (ק)	Nun (נ)	Vav (ו)	Resh (ר)	Nun (נ)	Sum
Q	S	R	N	R	O	N	
200	60	100	50	6	200	50	666

Table 3.0 | The number of the beast (Qsr Nron)

Of course the Arabic numerals (our modern number system) were only invented in the 6th or 7th century, so John couldn't have expressed the number of the beast as "666." Rather he expressed it in Greek alphabets, which is "Χ ξ ς." These alphabets have numerical values as follows: Χ (chi) = 600, ξ (Xi) = 6, ς (sigma) = 6 which altogether equals 666.

Similarly, the Latin version of the name drops the second Nun (נ), so that it appears as Qsr Nro. This transliterates into Hebrew as ורנ קסר, yielding the value 616, as shown below:[6]

Resh (ר)	Samekh (ס)	Qoph (ק)	Nun (נ)	Vav (ו)	Resh (ר)	Sum
Q	S	R	N	R	O	
200	60	100	50	6	200	616

Table 4.0 | The number of the beast (Qsr Nro)

An archaeological excavation uncovered a later copy of the Book of Revelation that employs the number 616. So, in a nutshell, the Greek form of Nero Caesar written in Hebrew characters is equivalent to 666, whereas the Latin form of Nero Caesar written in Hebrew characters is equivalent to 616.[7]

It should be noted that "Nero Caesar" is just one of many names that can add up to 666. But interestingly, "Nero Caesar" is the only name on the list that can account for both 666 and 616. This is the most compelling evidence that he, and not some other person, was intended. So whichever textual variant of the Book of Revelation you use, both point to one historical figure—Nero Caesar. The number 666 is more than just a simple code; it carries symbolic meaning as well. In biblical tradition, the number 6 is associated with "the number of a man," and it falls short of the number 7, which denotes "fullness," "completeness," or "perfection." Therefore, the number 6 is considered an imitation or an attempt to mimic the real thing but ultimately falls short.

The analysis presented leads us to conclude that the figure referred to as the "little horn" or "beast" that emerges from the Roman Empire is Nero Caesar (15 December AD 37 — 9 June AD 68)—a member of the prestigious Julio-Claudian dynasty. Paul the Apostle may even have met and preached the gospel to this man and his household in Rome (Philippians 4:22). Nero Caesar was the emperor Paul appealed to when he was accused of sedition by the Jewish authorities in Judaea (Acts 25:11); and he traveled all the way to Rome to be tried by him. It was probably God's grand plan to at least give him and his household a chance to hear the gospel. According to David Pawson, Theophilus was Paul's defense lawyer during his trial period in Rome. The Gospel of Luke and the Book of Acts (both written by Paul's companion—Luke) were addressed to Theophilus and were to serve as Paul's defense brief as he stood trial before Nero Caesar.[8]

Nero was a destructive "beast" of the worst sort, to say the least. His ascension to the throne was controversial, and his reign brutal. Aided by his mother, he seized power at the tender age of 16 after a series of murders including the murder of the legitimate heir to the throne. Just like Antiochus, Nero behaved like a lunatic. While he was a man of the people, doing things that made him popular with commoners, he was also a terrifying despot. According to historical records, Nero was known for his excessive self-gratification and had a reputation for engaging in debauchery and exhibiting savage brutality. He killed his brother, his pregnant wife, his mother, aunt, and many others close to him. He commissioned the building of a 98 feet bronze statue of himself which he called the Colossus of Nero. He was the emperor who gave orders to the Roman general Vespasian to crush the series of rebellions in Judaea, which eventually led to the destruction of Jerusalem and the temple in AD 70. Interestingly, the temple has not been rebuilt to date but the Bible hints that one day it will be rebuilt as part of the beast's agreement with the people (Daniel 9:27). There is a possibility that the same individual whose orders led to its destruction in the first place may someday issue the much-awaited directive to rebuild it.

In addition, Nero was the first of the imperial authorities to persecute the followers of Jesus. According to historical accounts, after the Great Fire of Rome in AD 64, Nero blamed it on innocent Christians and decided to take it out on them with the most horrendous fury. He arrested many of them and carried out their executions with extreme brutality. This is what the Roman historian Tacitus wrote:

> As they died they were further subjected to insult. Covered with hides of wild beasts, they perished by being torn to pieces by dogs; or they would be fastened to crosses and, when daylight had gone, burned to provide lighting at night. Nero had offered his gardens as a venue for the show, and he would also put on circus entertainments, mixing with the plebs in his charioteer's outfit or standing up in his chariot. As a result, guilty though these people were and deserving exemplary punishment, pity for them began to well up because it was felt that they were being exterminated not for the public good, but to gratify one man's cruelty.[9]

This state-sponsored martyrdom of Christians took place in a place called the Circus of Nero (Circus Neronis) located in the present-day Vatican City where St. Peter's Basilica and the ancient Egyptian obelisk stand today. Peter and Paul both died during this Neronian persecution. Peter was crucified upside down, while Paul, being a Roman citizen, was beheaded. After the persecution and other events that followed, the Roman

Senate declared Nero a public enemy. A civil war ensued, and on 9 June 68, at the age of 30, Nero committed suicide by inflicting a fatal sword injury on himself. His death marked the end of the Julio-Claudian dynasty.

John gave an account of a vision he saw concerning the souls of those who had been killed because of their faithfulness to Jesus. These souls shouted in a loud voice, "Holy and true Lord, how long until you judge the people of the earth and punish them for killing us?" But they were told to wait a little longer until the full number of their brothers and sisters to be martyred had joined them (Revelation 6:9).

THE SECOND COMING OF NERO

Many Bible scholars are of the view that Nero (or his modern-day replica) will be back again in these end times, fully empowered by satan to reclaim his empire and take control of the world. It will be the climax of a long running conflict between the forces of good and evil. John gives us a vivid account of a vision of this conflict of great significance in Revelation 12 and 13. The key players of the forces of evil in this conflict are symbolically depicted as the dragon, the beast from the sea, and the beast from the earth. Together they form an unholy trinity. The key players on the other side are God Himself, Michael the Archangel, "the woman," her son, and her offspring. The stage is all set. Now get ready for one of the most interesting cosmic epic conflicts.

The story begins with a pregnant woman ("the woman") who is about to give birth to a male child. This male child is none other than the promised Messiah—Jesus Himself. This woman who now takes center stage in God's purpose for His world is certainly not a mere individual as some may think, but rather a corporate entity. She is the faithful nation of Israel (in contrast to the unfaithful Israel that is often likened to a prostitute), chosen to carry forward God's plan for the whole creation. Recall Jesus once said that His mother, sister, and brother are anyone who does the will of His Father in heaven (Matthew 12-48-50). She was the woman God had in mind when He said, "I will put enmity between you [the serpent or dragon] and 'the woman', and between your seed [the seed of the dragon] and her Seed" (Genesis 3:15, words in square brackets are mine).

The great red dragon (that ancient serpent called the devil or satan) was determined to strike at her and her child. He was waiting to devour her child as soon as it was born to prevent God's purpose from materializing—and that included crushing him. The woman gave birth to a male child, who was to rule all nations with a rod of iron. But her child was snatched away out of the dragon's reach and was caught up to God and to His throne. This child is clearly Jesus Himself. In other words, Jesus wins the victory through His death, resurrection and ascension, and is therefore no longer vulnerable to anything the dragon can do.

Meanwhile, the woman and her offspring remain in danger on earth. Then Michael—the leader of God's elite special forces—and his team took on the dragon and his forces. The dragon and his forces fought back, but they were no match for Michael and his team. The dragon lost the battle, and both he and his forces were forced out of their domain in the heavenlies and thrown down to the earth.

When the dragon realized that he had been thrown down to the earth, he pursued the woman who had given birth to the male child. But it was already too late. The woman had escaped to a place of safety in the wilderness, where God had prepared to care for her for a period of time (three and half years). Then the dragon tried to drown the woman with a flood of water. But the earth helped her and quickly drained the water away. With this great miracle, the woman is now safe from the dragon, but her offspring remains in danger.

The dragon became very furious at the woman; and he decided to change strategy and play his trump card. He declared war against the rest of her children (offspring)—all who keep God's commandments and maintain their testimony for Jesus. It was a total war he was determined to win. The dragon stood on the seashore fuming with anger. He has something up his sleeve which is about to be unleashed to conclude the war. He is the seed of the serpent (dragon) predicted in the Book of Genesis (Genesis 3:15). Interestingly, this individual is recognized as "the beast from the sea," also known as "the man of lawlessness," or "the little horn."

> Then I saw a beast rising up out of the sea. It had seven heads and ten horns, with ten crowns on its horns. And written on each head were names that blasphemed God (Revelation 13:1).

Could this be the reappearance of Nero Caesar of old or his replica? John through the messenger angel is given even more clues to help us unmask this beast:

> I saw that one of the heads of the beast seemed wounded beyond recovery—but the fatal wound was healed! The whole world marveled at this miracle and gave allegiance to the beast ... who was fatally wounded and then came back to life (Revelation 13:3, 14b).

John was really amazed, but the angel said to him:

> "Why are you so amazed?" the angel asked. "I will tell you the mystery of this woman and of the beast with seven heads and ten horns on which she sits. The beast you saw was once alive but isn't now. And yet he will soon come up out of the bottomless pit and go to eternal destruction. And the people who belong to this world, whose names were not written in the Book of Life before the world was

made, will be amazed at the reappearance of this beast who had died (Revelation 17:7-8).

"Here is the mind which has wisdom: The seven heads are seven mountains on which the woman [the prostitute woman] sits. There are also seven kings. Five have fallen, one is, and the other has not yet come. And when he comes, he must continue for a short time. The beast that was, and is not, is himself also the eighth, and is of the seven, and is going to perdition..." (Revelation 17:9-11 NKJV, words in square brackets are mine).

In the preceding texts, there are two important clues that point to Nero Caesar. The first is that the beast is described as the beast that was (once alive), and is not (died at some point), and is to come—out of the bottomless pit and go to perdition (will return to life briefly before going to his destruction). According to the text, one of the seven heads of the beast seemed wounded beyond recovery. This indicates that he died, but the fatal wound was healed, and he came back to life, to the amazement of the whole world. In a nutshell, John is saying that the beast had a fatal wound that resulted in his death (Nero's fatal sword injury on himself), but the fatal wound was healed, and he came back life—but he will soon face his final destruction.

The second clue is that the beast that was, and is not, appears to be the eighth king, but is one of the seven kings. The beast that John saw has seven heads and ten horns. The seven heads represent the city of seven hills or mountains— an allusion to Rome. The seven heads also represent the seven kings or rulers of Rome. According to the text, the rulers in question are linked to the city of Rome. So any interpretations that divorce those seven rulers from the city of Rome would amount to taking the text out of context. Now one of those seven rulers came back to life and became the eight. Who are those seven rulers? According to John, five of them have fallen (died), one (the sixth) is still ruling (at the time John was writing), and the other (the seventh) has not yet come (at the time John was writing). And when he comes, he must rule for a short time.

So we are required to solve the riddle of the seven kings. In order to solve this riddle, we must identify the first seven emperors that ruled the Roman Empire in the 1st century AD, arranged in a sequential order. The table below captures all the information we need:

S/N	Name of Emperor	Reign	No. of Years in Office	Status at the Time John was Writing
1	Julius Caesar	49 BC-44 BC	5 Years	Fallen
2	Augustus Caesar	31 BC-AD 14	17 Years	Fallen
3	Tiberius Caesar	AD 14-AD 37	23 Years	Fallen
4	Gaius Caesar	AD 37-AD 41	4 Years	Fallen
5	Claudius Caesar	AD 41-AD 54	13 Years	Fallen
6	Nero Caesar	AD 54-AD 68	14 Years	Reigning
7	Galba Caesar	AD 68–AD 69	7 Months	Yet to reign

Table 5.0 | The first seven rulers of Rome in the 1st century AD

From the above table, we can see that Nero was the reigning emperor when John was writing the Book of Revelation, and Galba was the one yet to come but whose reign would be a brief one of only seven months. So according to Revelation 17:9-10, the seven heads of the beast also represent the seven kings or emperors of the Roman Empire. Five of whom have fallen (Julius, Augustus, Tiberius, Gaius, and Claudius), one is (Nero), and the other (Galba) has not yet come to power (at the time John saw the vision). "And when he comes, he must continue for a short time" (7 months). With the exception of Galba, these seven emperors all come from the first imperial dynasty (the Julio-Claudian Dynasty), and have a common name—Caesar. The eight ruler (the beast that was, and is not, and is to come), is again a possible reference to the reappearance of Nero himself.

He was one of the first seven Caesars of the Roman Empire as you can see in the table, and according to John, he will recover from his deadly wound and return to life.

Impossible as it may sound, this idea of Nero returning to life was already mainstream knowledge in that era. After Nero's death in AD 68, there was a popular belief that he would return to life. There is extensive documentation, both from the past and the present, that attests to this belief. It is called the Nero Redivivus legend. *Redivivus* is a Latin word for "living again" or "coming back to life." In an apparent reference to the Nero Redivivus legend, Augustine of Hippo in his book *City of God*, published in AD 426, noted of Nero that "Some suppose that he shall rise again and be the Antichrist. Others, again, suppose that he is not even dead, but that he was concealed that he might be supposed to have been killed, and that he now lives in concealment in the vigor of that same age which he had reached when he was believed to have perished, and will live until he is revealed in his own time and restored to his kingdom."[10] Similarly, in the 12th century, Pope Paschal II was said to have destroyed the mausoleum that supposedly held Nero's ashes, because he was afraid that the former emperor could return to life as the beast of Revelation.[11]

On the other hand, there exist noteworthy objections to the above interpretation of Revelation 17:9-10, and by implication its possible reference to Nero. The sixth king mentioned in the passage obviously refers to the ruler who was in power when John wrote the book. However, the popular view is that it was written around AD 95 during the reign of Domitian (nearly three decades after the death of Nero). The basis for this conclusion did not stem from the Book of Revelation, rather, it was based on the collective testimony of numerous individuals echoing the account of a single individual named Irenaeus—a 2nd century AD Christian theologian. However, Irenaeus account has been criticized by some Bible scholars for being "historically questionable" and "grammatically ambiguous."[12]

So we must be cautious not to get trapped in vain traditions, endless debates, and excessive analysis when seeking the truth, as this can cause us to overlook or miss important insights from God's word. The failure of the Jewish scholars, from the time of Jesus until now, to recognize Jesus as the Messiah despite the overwhelming evidence before them, serves as a reminder of the consequences of becoming overly fixated on intellectual arguments and tradition. While we value and uphold tradition, our allegiance must be to the Word of God as presented in the text, rather than to tradition. I believe the Book of Revelation itself holds the key to resolving this issue.

It is widely accepted that the kings alluded to in the text are Roman emperors, but which seven are in view is a more difficult question. Certain authors, grappling to create a list that aligns with their particular viewpoint, have opted to view the seven emperors as symbolic of the pagan empires that once oppressed ancient Israel. But why take this path when the Angel had clearly given John the interpretation?

With whom does the list of the line of the Caesars begin? Julius Caesar, being the first in the line of Caesars, is usually the starting point. However, some authors begin with Augustus because the Roman Empire officially began with him. Regardless of whether one starts with Julius or Augustus, the sixth king in power when John saw the vision would be either Nero or Galba, depending on the starting point. In either case, this suggests an early timeframe. However, the identification of the fatally wounded head in the text, the number of his name, along with the Nero Redivivus factor, provides a strong basis for favoring one over the other. And that overwhelmingly points to Nero as the more plausible candidate.

Several Bible scholars have concluded that this interpretation of the text provides clear internal evidence that the book was written while Nero was in power, and he is indeed the beast that will recover from a deadly wound and be restored to life. On the identity of this beast, N. T. Wright also noted that "The monster who was, is not, and is to come looks pretty certainly to be Nero."[13] If that's the case, then it appears the ultimate showdown for the control of the world boils down to two powerful dynasties: The Julio-Claudian dynasty, led by the beast—Nero Caesar (the seed of the serpent), and the Davidic dynasty, led by Jesus the Messiah (the seed of the woman).

All right, let's get back to our tale of the conflict between the woman and the dragon in Revelation 12. Now that the woman had escaped to a place of safety beyond the dragon's reach, the dragon became furious and declared war against the rest of her offspring, referring to all who keep God's commandments and maintain their testimony for Jesus. Then, all of a sudden, a monstrous beast comes out of the bottomless pit. As a matter of fact, everything about this conflict can be traced to the events that took place in the Garden of Eden as recorded in the Book of Genesis.

The physical implications of this conflict have been unfolding throughout human history. We can see them all from the call of Abraham, to the birth of the nation of Israel and their subsequent enslavement and deliverance from Egypt, down to the conflicts that took place in the years leading up to the birth of the Messiah (Antiochus conflicts and others), the failed assassination attempt on the life of baby Jesus by Herod that took place shortly after His birth, and His final execution on the cross. But God raised Him up from the dead and made Him immune to death.

Following His ascension to heaven, the attacks shifted to the faithful nation of Israel and her offspring—all who keep God's commandments and maintain their testimony for Jesus. This can be seen in the long and painful history of persecution that all believers have had to endure since the 1st century to the present day. As we move closer and closer to the edge of history, the pressure will get even more intense. The manifestations of evil which have marked human history will at the end of the age be concentrated in one final incarnation of evil—the seed of the serpent.

The dragon intends to use his seed to ruthlessly deal with the offspring of the woman. John tells us that this seed of the dragon is a man and gives clues in the Book of Revelation to his identity. The beast was given authority to do whatever he wanted for three and half years. He seized control of the whole world, and established—or rather re-established—his empire (the Roman Empire), and became the single political authority for all humanity. He demanded absolute submission in political, economic, and religious matters.

He was allowed to wage war against the offspring of the woman and to conquer them (Revelation 13:7). Daniel foresaw this event thousands of years ago. This is what he said: "As I watched, this horn was waging war against God's holy people and was defeating them" (Daniel 7:21). The dragon gave him all his powers to carry out this task. This means that the offspring of the woman—all who keep God's commandments and maintain their testimony for Jesus, must endure persecution patiently and remain faithful even in the face of death during this three and half year period (Revelation 13:10b). This is the key to their victory.

Another beast, the beast from the earth—a false prophet, joined the first beast (the little horn) and the dragon. The false prophet was depicted as having two horns like those of a lamb, but he spoke with the voice of a dragon. The lamb is a gentle and meek animal that is often associated with innocence, purity, and sacrifice. This implies that the false prophet will project himself as a blameless benevolent figure, similar to Christ—the true lamb. However, his seductive words and persuasive rhetoric ultimately reveal his deceitful nature, as it becomes apparent that he is aligned with the beast and the dragon. And together they unleashed the worst kind of genocide on the offspring of the woman. The beast from the earth (the false prophet) ordered the people of the world to make a great image of the first beast, who was fatally wounded and then came back to life. The false prophet made it mandatory for everyone to worship the image of the beast.

199

He required everyone—small and great, rich and poor, free and slave—to be given a mark on the right hand or on the forehead. And no one could buy or sell anything without that mark, which was either the name of the beast or the number representing his name (Revelation 13:16-17).

The image even had the power to enforce this worship and commanded that anyone refusing to worship it must die (Revelation 13:15b). These strange policies marked the defining moment that pitted the beast against all who keep God's commandments and maintain their testimony for Jesus. It appears they are the main target here because they seem to be the only people in the world that are unlikely to abide by such draconian policies.

> This means that God's holy people must endure persecution patiently, obeying his commands and maintaining their faith in Jesus.
>
> And I heard a voice from heaven saying, "Write this down: Blessed are those who die in the Lord from now on. Yes, says the Spirit, they are blessed indeed, for they will rest from their hard work; for their good deeds follow them!" (Revelation 14:12-13).

Indeed, they did not love their lives so much that they were afraid to die. They refused to take the mark of the beast or worship its image. Their loyalty to Jesus remained steadfast and unshakable. They firmly believed and proclaimed without hesitation that the dragon and the beast had already been conquered by Jesus through His death and resurrection. They recognized that following Jesus' selfless act of giving up His life was the key to victory in this conflict, and they embraced it as the ultimate path to triumph (Revelation 12:11).

And so the beast had a field day persecuting and executing them and at the same time bragging arrogantly to the high heavens about his invincibility and his supposed victory over them and other oppositions, speaking blasphemous words against God. It seemed like he was unstoppable. Little did he know that he had crossed the red line. His cup was now full. The full number of the martyrs are now complete (Revelation 6:9), and he must drink his own cup of destruction. No need for a fair hearing. God gave him a chance through the ministry of Paul in the 1st century but he rejected it and chose to align with the dragon. Now his time is up. God has something up His sleeve too which is about to be unleashed to conclude the war against evil, and bring goodness and justice to those deserving of it.

What happens next comes as a very big shock to everyone on earth. The seed of the woman, the promised Messiah from the Davidic dynasty who was to rule all nations with a rod of iron, the one who was snatched away and was caught up to God, suddenly steps back on earth into the scene to wage a righteous war. He does not come alone. To the surprise of many, He is accompanied by the woman and her offspring—all who keep God's commandments and maintain their testimony for Jesus. This comprises all God's people throughout history, including those who were persecuted and murdered by the beast and the likes of him. They have been resurrected to life, ready to meet their King in the sky to give him a grand welcome. This time around, their old bodies have been upgraded to immortal bodies that are beyond the reach of death, just like the Messiah Himself. They are now the new human species, the Homo novus, that will replace the old Homo sapiens and become the new humanity.

Then the beast and the kings of the world and their armies gathered together for a final showdown against the seed of the woman—Jesus the Messiah, and His army and faithful followers—the new humanity. They will be locked in a final decisive battle called the Battle of Armageddon. But it isn't a battle at all; there's really no fighting. With one word like a sharp sword that comes from His mouth, Jesus destroys the entire army of the beast, and vultures were invited to come to clean up the mess. Regarding the fate of the beast himself and the false prophet, this is what John saw:

And the beast was captured, and with him the false prophet who did mighty miracles on behalf of the beast—miracles that deceived all who had accepted the mark of the beast and who worshiped his statue. Both the beast and his false prophet were thrown alive into the fiery lake of fire (Revelation 19:19-20).

The duo made history as the first humans to be cast into the lake of fire. Daniel predicted this day long ago when he wrote:

"I continued to watch because I could hear the little horn's boastful speech. I kept watching until the beast was killed and its body was destroyed by fire" (Daniel 7:11).

The dragon himself (that old serpent called the devil), was arrested, bound in chains and thrown into the bottomless pit for a thousand years, so that he could not deceive the nations anymore. He will meet his final destruction after the thousand years are over. Following the exit of these evil figures, Jesus took control of the world and set up His kingdom. There will be no end to the increase of His government and of peace (Isaiah 9:7). He will rule with goodness and justice from the throne of David along with the new humanity (the woman and her offspring) forever and ever.

So here's the crux of the matter: whether the beast in question is Nero Caesar or someone like him in terms of behavior towards Jesus' loyal followers, the Book of Revelation is simply saying that events in the last century will mirror that of the 1st century AD. It predicts that history is going to culminate with a really wicked world ruler who is going to subject Jesus' loyal followers to persecution and even execution. Therefore, be cautious not to be misled by portrayals in movies or other sources that suggest you will be suddenly taken away in a "secret rapture" before this event. The Book of Revelation clearly emphasizes the impor-tance of being prepared and ready to go through the tribulation and remain steadfast in faith, as Jesus will ultimately emerge victorious. This is the whole essence of the message. Remember the words of the Lord Jesus: "the one who endures to the end will be saved" (Matthew 24:13).

> Anyone with ears to hear must listen to the Spirit and understand what he is saying to the churches. Whoever is victorious will not be harmed by the second death (Revelation 2:11).

DEUS EX MACHINA

I believe technology will play a key role in the final showdown between the forces of good and evil. Before the Messiah returns to conquer the beast and set up His kingdom here on earth, the world will witness an unprecedented upsurge of technology and machines, never before seen in human history. As is commonly understood, technology is a double-edged sword—it can be a positive force or a negative force depending on the intentions and motivations of its developers and users, and whose purposes it is serving.

The dragon, who for now is the de facto ruler of this world, will through his human agents develop and deploy technologies that will serve his purposes and enable him to consolidate his hold over humanity. To the discerning mind these sinister developments are already glaring. The countdown has already begun. The direction of the development and evolution of technology is moving on the path that favors totalitarian control and will culminate in one ultimate control system that enables the beast to gain absolute control of the whole world as predicted in the Bible.

Look around and see how this monumental drama is already playing out in fiction. The Terminator movie series somehow mirrors the role of technology in the conflict between good and evil. The Terminator is an almost indestructible cyborg killing machine sent back from the future to kill a woman named Sarah

Connor (a prototype of "the woman"), whose unborn son is the promised messiah that will one day save humanity from extinction by Skynet, a hostile self-aware artificial general super-intelligence system or AI. Skynet sees the unborn child named John Connor (a prototype of Jesus Christ) as the only formidable threat to their plan to dominate and rule the world sometime in the future. In an attempt to eliminate the threat, Skynet sends various Terminator models back in time to try to kill the unborn child, albeit unsuccessfully.

The same can be said of The Matrix movie series. The Matrix itself is also a hostile artificial general superintelligence system or AI that enslaves humanity in a simulated reality. Neo (a prototype of Jesus Christ) is the one destined to free humanity from enslavement.

The Industrial Revolutions that have shaped human history in the past 250+ years is simply the story of the rise of the machines. For the most part, the machines have been gradually taking control for our good. In the First Industrial Revolution, the world witnessed a revolutionary transition from manual production methods to the use of machines, brought about by the invention of steam and water power. This took manufacturing out of people's homes and into factories.

In the Second Industrial Revolution, the discovery and widespread implementation of electricity brought about the gradual displacement of steam power as the major power resource for industries. The advent of electricity completely transformed human society with more machines taking control. This helped to usher in industrial productivity on a scale never seen before in history. The Third Industrial Revolution (Digital Revolution) is the era that marked the shift from mechanical to electronic machines and digital technology. It is the age of information technology—computers, the Internet, the World Wide Web, social media, smartphones, and more. Today's miniature smartphones have far more computing power than the gigantic supercomputers of yesteryears. The Digital Revolution has brought about a significant shift in the use of human power as machines took further control with extensive use of computers and software technologies in the production process.

The Fourth Industrial Revolution which began its ascent somewhere in the middle of the second decade of the 21st century builds on the successes of the Third. But it is evolving at an exponential pace rather than the usual linear pace seen in prior industrial revolutions, and disrupting virtually every industry on the planet. It is the era of the Internet of Things (IoT), Internet of Bodies (IoB), robotics, big data, cognitive computing—thinking machines and artificial intelligence (AI), and more. This revolution is blurring the boundaries between the physical, biological, and digital spheres.

In the Fourth Industrial Revolution, the computer senses, thinks, and acts autonomously thanks to IoT sensors, actuators, and web trackers. These collect data about our environment (physical), bodies and brains (biological), and online activities (digital). The IoT sensors, actuators, and trackers use the collected data about us or our environment to perform certain physical actions. You can think of the sensors and trackers as the eyes and ears of the computer, and the actuators as its hands and feet. Distinguished security expert, Bruce Schneier, couldn't have put it better. This is what he wrote:

> Increasingly, human intervention will be unnecessary. The sensors will collect data. The system's smarts will interpret the data and figure out what to do. And the actuators will do things in our world. You can think of the sensors as the eyes and ears of the Internet, the actuators as the hands and feet of the Internet, and the stuff in the middle as the brain. This makes the future clearer. The Internet now senses, thinks, and acts. We're building a world-sized robot, and we don't even realize it.[14]

Alan Turing (a founding father of artificial intelligence and modern cognitive science) also had this to say:

> For it seems probable that once the machine thinking method had started, it would not take long to outstrip our feeble powers. There would be no question of the machines dying, and they would be able to converse with each other to sharpen their wits. At some stage therefore we should have to expect the machines to take control.[15]

And indeed, the machines are beginning to take full control as more authority is transferred to it, especially with the rise of artificial intelligence (AI) in the Fourth Industrial Revolution.

When humanity rejected the idea of living under God's rule and authority and opted for self-governance, human reasoning replaced divine revelation. Humanity looked to logic, reason and the evidence of the senses to discover truth and meaning. Truth and morality was no longer about what God tells them but what they find out for themselves. This way of thinking and living became known as humanism. Humanism deifies humankind as the ultimate source of meaning and authority. Now in the Fourth Industrial Revolution this authority is invested in the machines. Humanity's rejection of God's rule and authority will be their greatest undoing as the machines take the place of God.

The term that has been used to describe this shift is dataism. The centralizing tendency of AI is concentrating too much data and decision-making power in the hands of the machines. The onward match for dataism as the new global religion will inevitably set the stage for totalitarian control. The one who eventually controls big data, will be the world leader. All it takes is for a powerful dictator (or the group he represents) to arise and seize control of everything, and the world will be under his feet. He will hijack these technologies and make it serve his own purposes. This is exactly what the beast will do.

Today's AI machines are classified as narrow AI, which are for the most part designed to mimic and outperform humans in specific tasks. These tasks include driving cars (self-driving cars), medical diagnosis (nanobot doctors), natural language processing (ChatGPT), speech recognition and language translation (Siri or Alexa), facial recognition (surveillance cameras), personalized recommendations (web searches and online shopping), among others. Once all of these specific tasks in specific areas have been mastered by the AI, it will set the stage for the arrival of artificial general intelligence (AGI) with cognitive capabilities that are indistinguishable from those of a human. The AGI will then emerge from the "sea of narrow AI." The final stage of the intelligence explosion according to experts would be the arrival of artificial super intelligence (ASI), in which AI surpasses human intelligence across all fields. This is the much talked about technological singularity that has been forecasted by Ray Kurzweil.

This final form of the AI machine is expected to be conscious, self-aware, and self-improving. It is also expected to possess even the very properties we ascribe to God: omnipresence, omnipotence, and omniscience. And it will be completely autonomous and uncontrollable, resulting in unforeseeable implications for humanity. And when that happens, humanity will have no choice but to begin idolizing the machine as a god because the technology will be immensely superior to humans. Some atheists have openly expressed willingness to embrace the worship of a god-like AI machine created by humans, if it comes into existence in the future.[16] Isn't it ironic that the same individuals who had long denied the existence of God and refused to pledge allegiance to Him, are now the ones eager to accept and pledge allegiance to a god-like AI machine?

Where is all this leading? I believe society at large is sleepwalking into a ghastly all-seeing, all-knowing, and all-powerful AI-driven global totalitarian government. AI research labs around the world are currently engaged in an intense competition to develop and deploy more advanced forms of artificial intelligence that no one—not even their creators—can compre-hend, predict, or reliably control. An autocratic regime with a decisive lead in the development of super intelligent AI could potentially use this technology to gain global dominance and control. Prominent tech leaders have expressed concerns about this current trajectory in which we are headed, and foresee an imminent future where the fate of humanity rests in the hands of a super intelligent machine.[17] In his "singleton hypothesis," Nick Bostrom, explains how a global totalitarian government is a plausible outcome with AI or other powerful technologies, and why it might be impossible to overthrow. According to Bostrom, a "singleton" is a concept that describes a global system wherein a single entity holds ultimate decision-making power. This entity would possess the capacity to prevent any internal or external threats to its own authority and dominance, and effectively govern key aspects of its domain.[18]

In his book *Life 3.0: Being Human in the Age of Artificial Intelligence*, physicist and machine learning researcher, Max Tegmark, paints a totalitarian scenario where a tech company through an in-house team that he calls the Omega Team embarks on a highly secretive project to develop artificial general intelligence nicknamed Prometheus (which in Greek mythology was referred to as the god of foresight and cunning advice, known for his intelligence). The company kept things going by various commercial applications of narrow AI, and had carefully crafted their image to hide their ultimate secret plan. Tegmark describes a number of potential outcomes that could occur including a situation where the AI runs amok.

According to Tegmark, "Suppose that the CEO controlling the Omegas had long-term goals similar to those of Adolf Hitler or Joseph Stalin. For all we know, this might actually have been the case, and he simply kept these goals to himself until he had sufficient power to implement them." Tegmark went further to describe a potential scenario of world domination that could occur with Prometheus, outlining the following:

By reading all emails and texts ever sent, listening to all phone calls, watching all surveillance videos and traffic cameras, analyzing all credit card transactions and studying all online behavior, Prometheus would have remarkable insight into what the people of Earth were thinking and doing. By analyzing cell tower data, it would know where most of them were at all times. All this assumes with today's data collection technology, Prometheus could easily invent popular gadgets and wearable tech that would virtually eliminate the privacy of the user, recording and uploading everything they hear and see and their responses to it. With superhuman technology, the step from the perfect surveillance state to the perfect police state would be minute. For example, with the excuse of fighting crime and terrorism and rescuing people suffering medical emergencies, everybody could be required to wear a 'security bracelet' that combined the functionality of an Apple Watch with continuous uploading of position, health status and conversations overheard. Unauthorized attempts to remove or disable it would cause it to inject a lethal toxin into the forearm. Infractions deemed as less serious by the government would be punished via electric shocks or injection of chemicals causing paralysis or pain, thereby obviating much of the need for a police force. [19]

Tegmark does not endorse the above dystopian outcome or any specific outcome as the precise fate of humanity. Rather, he invites readers to seize the opportunity now and think about what future they would like to see, and begin to change the trajectory.

The Bible foresees this kind of dystopian outcome. The Book of Revelation predicts a future where an object or statue made by humans receives the breath of life, becomes animated, and demands worship from everyone on earth. This statue will have the power to issue and enforce orders including the ability to execute anyone who fails to comply. The Bible calls this statue the "image of the beast." Jesus tells His followers that the day is coming when they will see the image of the beast standing in the temple in Jerusalem and, when that happens, those in and around Jerusalem must flee to the hills for safety (Matthew 24:15-16).

> Then I saw another beast rising up out of the land [itself]; he had two horns like a lamb, and he spoke (roared) like a dragon. And because of the signs (miracles) which he is allowed to perform in the presence of the [first] beast, he deceives those who inhabit the earth, commanding them to *erect a statue (an image) in the likeness of the beast* who was wounded by the [small] sword and still lived. And he is permitted [also] to *impart the breath of life into the beast's image,* so that *the statue of the beast could actually talk* and *cause to be put to death those who would not bow down and worship the image of the beast* (Revelation 13:11, 13:14-15 AMPC, emphasis added).

We can identify the beast that rises from the earth or land as the false prophet who is working in harmony with the first beast and satan. The Greek word translated as "image" in the scripture above is *eikon* or *icon,* and its Hebrew equivalent is *tselem.* It basically means resemblance or image—a representative in the physical form of something or someone. In other words, the false prophet and those who join forces with him are attempting to imitate God's act of creating humankind, as described in the Book of Genesis. The Book of Genesis tells us that "God created man in His own image, **in the image *and* likeness of God** He created him..." (Genesis 1:27, emphasis added).

So just as the "image of God" (humankind) is the representative of God in physical form, the "image of the beast" is the representative of the beast in physical form all over the earth. The "image of the beast" rules the world on behalf of the beast and, by extension, satan.

Similarly, the word translated as "breath of life" in the scripture reference above is the Greek word *pneuma*, and its Hebrew equivalent is *ruach*. It basically means breath or spirit. It is the breathed-into life force that animates living beings. Again, the false prophet is simply attempting to imitate God's act of creating humankind, as described in the Book of Genesis. The Book of Genesis tells us that "the Lord God formed man from the dust of the ground and breathed into his nostrils the **breath or spirit of life**, and man became a living being" (Genesis 2:7, emphasis added).

So, just as God gave breath of life to the "image of God" He created, the false prophet was granted power to impart the "breath of life" into the "image of the beast" that humans created. As a result, the image of the beast became animated and capable of issuing and enforcing orders.

Can you see a parallel between the image of the beast described in the Bible, and everything you've read and heard about conscious self-aware artificial super intelligence that humanity is racing to create? While we cannot say with certainty what the author of the Book of Revelation has in mind here, all indications suggest the emergence of some kind of a conscious artificial super intelligent humanoid robot that will surpass human abilities and leave an incredible impression on the world. However, ironically, this very creation will also become a source of oppression for the world.

Now, the question that everyone is pondering over is whether this super-intelligent machine will stand in support of humanity or not. Will it exhibit benevolent or malevolent behavior? Well, some experts are of the view that the risks of AI primarily lie in the possibility of a misalignment between its goals and those of humans. While humankind is still speculating and debating whether this super-intelligent machine would be benevolent or malevolent, the Bible describes it as the "image of the beast," indicating that its goals are fully aligned with those of the beast and its puppet master, satan. The image of the beast reflects the will, character, and authority of the beast. As stated in the Book of Revelation as well as the preceding section, the beast personifies malevolence.

In the beginning, God made man, in His own image and after His likeness. All was good until man chose to rebel against God and declare his independence, and define good and evil on his own terms. Having severed himself from God, man wandered away in self-governance and developed machines and other technologies to alleviate his condition and make his life easier. These technological developments continued until man made the ultimate machine, artificial general intelligence (AGI), in his own image and after his likeness. Thus did man become the architect of his own downfall.[20]

Technological developments through the Fourth Industrial Revolution will culminate in the development of a conscious self-aware artificial super intelligence (ASI) from artificial general intelligence (AGI)—thanks, but no thanks, to the deceptive power of satan and the beast working through the false prophet. The image of the beast, like a god, directly demands worship from the citizens of the world, and kills anyone who fails to comply: "Then the statue of the beast commanded that anyone refusing to worship it must die" (Revelation 13:15b). But there is more. Revelation further tells us that the false prophet "required everyone—small and great, rich and poor, free and slave—to be given a mark on the right hand or on the forehead. And no one could buy or sell anything without that mark, which was either the name of the beast or the number representing his name" (Revelation 13:16-17).

The beast demanded absolute submission in all areas not just political and religious but also in trade and finance. He will control the global currency and commerce. This is one of the ways he will control people and get them to submit to him. Only those who submit to him by being branded with his mark will be allowed to buy and sell.

Many experts predict that the Fourth Industrial Revolution occasioned by the rise in AI and the increasing level of automation and robotization would result in technological unemployment. As more and more of our jobs are automated, over time, more and more people will be made redundant. It is estimated that in the near future most jobs currently performed by humans will no longer exist. If that happens, it will mean most people will be left completely redundant with no way to feed themselves. Yes, new jobs will be created in new industries that will emerge in the near future, but experts predict that jobs will be destroyed much faster than they are being created.

In order to manage these challenges and prevent the world economy from completely collapsing, the global elites propose a solution that hinges on the concept of "unconditional free money for everyone." It is called universal basic income. No doubt, universal basic income is a superb idea that, if well implemented, will cushion the problems of unemployment caused by increasing automation, by allowing everyone to benefit from the wealth of society.

However, please be aware of the provisos. Universal basic income would not be a guaranteed unconditional free minimum monthly income that every adult citizen receives from the government with "no strings attached." Beware of exposure to control. Remember that he who controls your money supply, rules your life. The question is, how free and unconditional is this "unconditional free money"? What is the trade-off? What if the government in control is a totalitarian one? That puts them in a position to attach strings. Would a lot of people have to sacrifice their morals and beliefs just to comply with their conditions? If you don't think that these types of restrictions could happen in the world in the near future, then you're in for a shocker, because we are exponentially moving into this kind of scenario.

There is a new form of money about to be adopted by your country's central bank very soon (if not already). It appears to be the biggest change we are going to see in how we use our own money, and it seems that not many people are aware of it. It is something that would give the government unprecedented control over your own money, something that has never existed before in history. The global elites and powerful international or-ganizations and financial institutions have been subtly promoting this idea. Collectively, they view this new form of currency as the future of money. They argue that cash in the modern world is risky and should be replaced by this new form of money and identity. It is called Central Bank Digital Currency (CBDC).

The concept of CBDC was inspired by Bitcoin and similar blockchain-based cryptocurrencies. One of the good things that people love about Bitcoin and similar cryptocurrencies is that it is decentralized. But a CBDC, though it lives on a blockchain like Bitcoin, will not be decentralized. It will be centrally con-trolled, and regulated by the government. CBDC confers on the government the powers to do something they have previously not been able to do with money: program your money. A CBDC would be fully programmable. Just like a piece of software, the government would be able to put digital rules on it with restric-tions, giving themselves enormous amounts of power over you and your money. For example, the government could program your money to expire within a given timeframe, restrict your spending on the items that they deem appropriate, or even restrict your movement from one place to another since they already have tracking devices. Even worse, if you do not comply with certain requirements, they could cut off your access to your money altogether.

The CBDC is a brilliant idea that if well implemented, according to experts, could help minimize financial risks, maintain the effectiveness of monetary policy, improve trans-parency, and provide many more benefits. However, the major concern here is the exposure to control, especially if the government is totalitarian and hooked on to a globalized central government. That would make it the perfect tool to track and control your money, the very thing that you need in order to survive in today's world. And guess where you could be carrying this new form of digital money and identity in the near future? Inside your body. That future is already here with us.

The technology that would allow you to carry money inside your body already exists and is in use in some countries such as Sweden. With this technology, you can get a payment chip implanted in your hand. The implant allows you to make payments without having to carry around any form of physical payment such as cash, mobile phone, or credit/debit card. Let me clarify that I am not suggesting that AI, universal basic income, CDDC, or payment chip implants are inherently evil. That is not the point I am trying to convey. Rather, my point is that the technology necessary to facilitate the beast's dominance over the world through a world government is already here with us. And here we have it all documented in the Bible. Why should anyone not take the Bible seriously? Take heed that no one deceives you, my friend.

THE GREAT DECEPTION

The good news of the arrival of God's rule in the person of Jesus Christ is being proclaimed around the world. Some have embraced it; others have vehemently rejected it in favor of humanism, atheism, dataism, or one form of religious belief or the other. In other words, they reject Jesus Christ as their Lord and Savior and they do not want to live under a government led by Him. Neither do they want Him to be the absolute authority over their lives.

If you are reading this book and you haven't pledged al-legiance to Jesus, you still have the opportunity to do so now while the door is open. This opportunity is not going to be indefinite, for at some point the door will be closed. There is a great wave of deception that will engulf the whole world, and those who refuse or are unwilling to live under God's rule will be swept away.

Most people go about their day, doing whatever makes them feel comfortable, and thinking that everything will continue the way it has always been. But the clock is ticking, and things are about to change—very soon. Many of the things that the Bible predicted will happen in the last days have happened and more are happening right before our very eyes. Soon the beast will be revealed, and suddenly, everything will change. The Bible clearly states that the world will accept him and his government because his value system has already been programmed into them through the media. They will give in to a strong delusion that sways their allegiance toward the beast and the one who gives him power—satan.

Renowned French poet, Charles Baudelaire, once said that "The greatest trick the Devil ever pulled was convincing the world he didn't exist." And someone also added that "The second greatest trick the Devil ever pulled was convincing the world he is the good guy." The Bible tells us that at some point in the last days, satan and his angels will be thrown down to the earth and confined to our planet (Revelation 12:9). While we cannot say with certainty when and how this will take place, some suggest it could come in the form of "alien infiltration" designed to satisfy our deep-seated curiosity for signs of alien life. Of course, the search for intelligent extraterrestrial life and the concept of alien invasion has been a common feature in most space research and science fiction movies and TV shows. But you can be sure satan will not come down to earth and present himself as an "evil figure." He will present himself as the good "extraterrestrial intelligence" who has come to rescue humanity from "dreadful dangers," or from some other imminent "alien invasion" that "we cannot see and do not understand." But be rest assured it's all lies. The Bible tells us that he is coming down with great wrath because he knows that he has little time (Revelation 12:12). He will use many deceptive signs and lying wonders to try to sway humanity's allegiance to himself.

Satan will even try to counterfeit some of the unique extraordinary work of creation that God has done in the past. One such wonder was the creation of man in the image of God, imparting the image of God to man with the breath of life. Another great wonder was the resurrection of Jesus from the dead. Satan will attempt to counterfeit resurrection—an act that established Jesus' authority as Messiah and Son of God. How will he do it? The beast who was once dead, will be brought back to life. And once that happens, those who reject Christ, bedazzled by this great miracle, will give their allegiance to the beast. At that point, all forms of religious beliefs and practices including atheism and agnosticism will be a thing of the past because the beast will exalt himself, openly declaring himself as God (2 Thessalonians 2:4). From then on, there will only be one religion and that is the worship of the beast and his image, and by extension satan.

> And *the people who belong to this world, whose names were not written in the Book of Life* before the world was made, *will be amazed at the reappearance of this beast* who had died (Revelation 17:8, emphasis added).
>
> I saw that one of the heads of the beast seemed wounded beyond recovery—but the fatal wound was healed! *The whole world marveled at this miracle and gave allegiance to the beast.* And *all the people who belong to this world worshiped the beast ... They are the ones whose names were not written in the Book of Life* that belongs to the Lamb who was slaughtered before the world was made (Revelation 13:3, 8, emphasis added).
>
> He [the false prophet] did astounding miracles, even making fire flash down to earth from the sky while everyone was watching. And with all the

miracles he was allowed to perform on behalf of the first beast, *he deceived all the people who belong to this world* (Revelation 13:13-14b, emphasis added, words in square brackets are mine).

"This man [the beast] will come to do the work of satan with counterfeit power and signs and miracles. He will use every kind of *evil deception to fool those on their way to destruction*, because *they refuse to love and accept the truth* that would save them. So *God will cause them to be greatly deceived*, and *they will believe these lies*. Then they will be condemned for enjoying evil rather than believing the truth" (2 Thessalonians 2:9-12, emphasis added, words in square brackets are mine).

When the beast is revealed and his one world government comes into force, those who rejected Jesus will be in a very precarious position. God will cause them to be given over to strong delusion. A veil of delusion will descend over them, and they will never be able to tear it down—or even realize it is there. Since Jesus is the truth, anyone who rejects the truth, is ready for the lie. God will simply honor their decision to reject the truth, and will give them over to the deception that they have willingly embraced. This is not a case of God leading them into deception. They have set their hearts against Jesus and His Kingdom, and closed the door of salvation on themselves.

This is similar to what happened to Pharaoh after he vehemently refused to let the Israelites leave Egypt even after several entreaties followed by plagues sent by God. Pharaoh hardened his heart, and God decided to help him in his chosen path—He allowed Pharaoh's heart to be hardened. Pharaoh set his heart against God, and God simply let him have his way.

Jesus is the doorway to God's kingdom. He is once again inviting everyone to enter. "Work hard to enter the narrow door to God's kingdom, for many will try to enter but will fail. When the master of the house has locked the door, it will be too late.

You will stand outside knocking and pleading, 'Lord, open the door for us!' But he will reply, 'I don't know you or where you come from'" (Luke 13:24-25).

Remember the lesson from the story of Noah and the ark. God observed all the corruption in the world and said to Noah, "Look! I am about to cover the earth with a flood that will destroy every living thing that breathes" (Genesis 6:17). God told Noah to build a boat and get on board for his and his family's safety. "When everything was ready, the Lord said to Noah, 'Go into the boat with all your family, for among all the people of the earth, I can see that you alone are righteous'" (Genesis 7:1). Then the Lord closed the door behind them.

Jesus reminds us of this terrible event where people got swept away:

> "In those days before the flood, the people were enjoying banquets and parties and weddings right up to the time Noah entered his boat. People didn't realize what was going to happen until the flood came and swept them all away. That is the way it will be when the Son of Man comes" (Matthew 24:38-39).

God waited nearly a thousand years, the lifetime of Methuselah, since His first announcement of that judgment to Enoch (Jude 14-15), before sending the flood. Today, the same God is patiently extending to us the opportunity to repent and embrace His kingdom before it's too late. God's delay and patience is because He does not want anyone to be destroyed, but wants everyone to repent (2 Peter 3:9).

There are many signs that point to this being the generation that will see the return of the Christ. Yet, many people are not ready for His return. Most are still unwilling to accept Him as their Lord or live under His rule. Some are living in delusion that they are the enlightened ones, and that their lifestyle is superior to God's way. Soon, they will fall into deception, and accept the mark of the beast and worship his image. The only time you have to get ready for the Messiah's return is now. To delay is to run the risk of being too late. Here is a reminder of the consequences of accepting the mark of the beast and worshiping his image:

> "If anyone worships the beast and his image, and receives his mark on his forehead or on his hand, he himself shall also drink of the wine of the wrath of God, which is poured out full strength into the cup of His indignation. He shall be tormented with fire and brimstone in the presence of the holy angels and in the presence of the Lamb. And the smoke of their torment ascends forever and ever; and they have no rest day or night, who worship the beast and his image, and whoever receives the mark of his name" (Revelation 14:9-11 NKJV).

When Jesus returns, He will crush the kingdom of the beast, including his image, into pieces. He will bring to an end the long history of man's self-governance, which reached its climax in the worldwide reign of the beast. Then Jesus will immediately usher in a new dawn in human history—the reign of God and the new humanity.

CHAPTER ELEVEN

THE NEW HUMANITY

With Jesus back on the earth, and satan, the beast, the false prophet, and their collaborators out of the way, is this now the end of the world and the human race? Well, not exactly. It will not be the end of the world, but it will be the end of the world as we know it.

The world we knew was a world filled with greed and corruption, a world filled with injustice and exploitation, a world filled with poverty, hardship, disease, death, and everything evil. It was that way because humankind rejected God's rule and went its own way. For thousands of years the "old humanity" ran the world on their own terms, and the end result of their regime was nothing short of chaos and wickedness. Now, the age of the "old humanity's" dominance over the world is finally over. They put their faith and hope in the promise of technology in order to evolve into a new kind of species or escape to another planet to evade possible extinction. Alas, that which they feared most has finally come upon them. They will now be relegated to the background, until they eventually vanish from the face of the earth.

Now, the real change has come. There is a new type of human species led by Jesus who are willing to partner with God to rule the world on His behalf. Now they've all been resurrected to life with new glorious immortal bodies here on earth. "Blessed and holy are those who share in the first resurrection. For them the second death holds no power, but they will be priests of God and of Christ and will reign with him a thousand years" (Revelation 20:6). They will receive the kingdom and will possess it forever—yes, for ever and ever (Daniel 7:18). What a great reversal!

THE MILLENNIAL REIGN

The stage is now set for the full inauguration of the new government which will mark the beginning of the new age—the reign of Homo novus and their dominance over the world. Jesus will now take His throne as the divine King of the world, and preside over its governance. The government will rest on His shoulders (Isaiah 9:6). Ever since humanity severed its partnership with God, there hasn't been a human worthy to take this divine throne reserved for them and rule alongside God.

But at last, the partnership is fully renewed. "The world has now become the Kingdom of our Lord and of his Christ, and he will reign forever and ever" (Revelation 11:15). Indeed, He alone is worthy to receive glory and honor and power. He will reign and rule the world (including the remnant of the old humanity) from His throne in Jerusalem for a thousand years (one millennium) with a rod of iron. The "rod of iron" represents the exercise of absolute political power that can neither be bent nor bribed. "Now the salvation and the power and the Kingdom of our God and the authority of his Christ have come" (Revelation 12:10a).

Jesus will certainly not be doing this alone. The new humanity will reign and rule alongside Him. Most people find it difficult to comprehend the idea of immortal beings living alongside mortals in the millennial kingdom. But it isn't hard to imagine based on historical precedence. After Jesus was resurrected from the dead with an immortal body, He moved around in physical form with His disciples for forty days. He had fellowship with them and ate with them (Luke 24:41-43). He even invited them to touch His physical body, so that they could see and know He had a living body (Luke 24:38-39). It was obvious He wasn't a spirit, because spirits don't eat and cannot be touched. But Jesus did it all. He was the same Jesus but in a renewed body.

What will the world be like when satan is out of the way and Jesus is in full control of world politics, the economy, and nature? We have never really lived under perfect political and economic conditions, so our capacity to imagine heaven on earth is limited. But Jesus will once and for all demonstrate what this world can be under a just government. The world that was once marked by chaos and wickedness will once again experience order, goodness and genuine rest. One Jewish prophet named Isaiah gives us a glimpse of the natural world in the millennium.

> In that day the wolf and the lamb will live together; the leopard will lie down with the baby goat. The calf and the yearling will be safe with the lion, and a little child will lead them all. The cow will graze near the bear. The cub and the calf will lie down together. The lion will eat hay like a cow. The baby will play safely near the hole of a cobra. Yes, a little child will put its hand in a nest of deadly snakes without harm (Isaiah 11:6-8).

The natural world will be a safe place for man and beast. In other words, carnivores will become herbivores as was the state before the fall (Genesis 1:30).

On First Avenue, across from the United Nations building in New York City, sits a small park named after Ralph Bunche, the first African-American recipient of the Nobel Peace Prize. This park is home to the famous "Isaiah Wall"—a curved granite wall that contains a quotation from Isaiah's prophecy predicting a day when "nations will no longer fight against nations, nor train for war anymore." The park has been a popular site for demonstrations and rallies for peace, which has eluded humanity for years.

But at last, the Lord Himself, the Prince of Peace, will mediate between nations and will settle international disputes. This will result in a time of unparalleled peace and prosperity on the planet—the kind of peace that transcends the so-called Pax Romana, Pax Britannica, and Pax Americana. These so-called periods of peace were primarily motivated by fear and coercion due to the prevailing military might, and they therefore did not endure. But the peace that the Prince of Peace gives is purely motivated by love and forgiveness—a gift the world cannot give—and therefore endures. Weapons of war and military equipment will be redesigned and repurposed for agricultural use (Isaiah 2:4). An abundance of healthy organic food will be a source of good health and well-being, which, in turn, will result in a huge increase in global life expectancy that no one ever thought was possible. Jesus will rule with fairness and justice, uplifting the downtrodden and redressing the exploited. There will be no more poverty, pandemics, recession, depression, terrorism, climate crises—you name it! There will be an equitable distribution of resources, good education, clean energy, a safe and secure environment, economic growth and prosperity, and much more.

THE FINAL JUDGMENT

After the one-thousand-year period is over, what happens next comes as a complete surprise. One would expect that with the huge dividends of good governance brought about by the reign of Christ, no one would ever long for the old way of life. But you would be wrong. It appears many people would still prefer not to live under God's rule.

The Bible tells us that at the end of the one thousand years, satan is released and allowed to relaunch his old work of deceiving the nations into rebellion against God's rule. This will happen one last time (Revelation 20:3). He will infiltrate people in every nook and cranny of earth who want their freedom from the government of Jesus. He will talk them into going to war and will gather a huge army to lay siege to the seat of power in Jerusalem, thinking that a military attack will gain them political autonomy (Revelation 20:7-9).

Although the Bible does not tell us the exact tactics satan will use in deceiving the nations, they are likely the same old tricks he used in the Garden of Eden. Deception, pride and arrogance. The first time it involved two people—Adam and Eve. This last one will involve many nations and ethnic groups. In both cases, the end goal is the same: moral autonomy and independence from God's government. If you look deep into the hearts of those people, you will be surprised to find that many already have an inner longing for moral and political autonomy; satan's reappearance allows them to finally get the opportunity to do what they really want to do. And they end up repeating the exact same mistake that Adam and Eve made—rebelling against God's rule. Unfortunately, the same consequence that befell Adam and Eve awaits them all—expulsion from God's space and death, physical and spiritual.

But this time around, there is no hope of redemption. God will grant them their hearts' desires, and they will be eternally separated from God. Their attempt to oust the government of the day led by Jesus and the new humanity will completely fail as fire from the sky consumes everyone involved and defeats their plan. Satan himself is thrown into the lake of fire where the beast and the false prophet have already been for the one thousand years (Revelation 20:9-10).

But why would God release satan again to do such damage at the end of the thousand years of perfect governance under God's rule? Well, when you look at the event that happens next—the day of judgment—it becomes abundantly clear. The millennial reign of Christ and the subsequent release of satan would have exposed those in the world who have no desire to live under God's rule. Now they will stand trial and face the punishment they truly deserve. Their judgment or sentence is based on this fact: "God's light came into the world, but people loved the darkness more than the light, for their actions were evil. All who do evil hate the light and refuse to go near it for fear their sins will be exposed" (John 3:19-20).

God has been frequently accused of unjustly punishing humanity for "a sin they know nothing about"—such as Adam and Eve's sin. But here they are, making the same wrong choices that Adam and Eve made under the same conditions. God has also been accused of allowing suffering to persist in the world, and being unfair in giving people free will, only to then punish them because they did not choose what He prefers. But once again, the millennial kingdom has exposed the real source of suffering—bad choices due to insistence on moral autonomy and independence from God's rule. It is now clear that as long as those (angelic and human beings) who exercise their free will in rejecting God's rule are allowed to freely operate, there will never be an end to strife and suffering.

Indeed, God is publicly vindicated. People will agree that He has no choice but to finally take out those who reject His rule—it is simply necessary and just. "In a world of systematic injustice, bullying, violence, arrogance, and oppression, the thought that there might come a day when the wicked are firmly put in their place and the poor and weak are given their due is the best news there can be," says N.T. Wright.[1] They had more than enough time and opportunity to demonstrate that the world could be better off without God; that their alternative ways produce better results than God's way; and that they could peacefully coexist with those following God's way. But they failed woefully on all counts, leaving a trail of broken lives and broken world in their wake. It is therefore necessary for history to conclude with a day of judgment, so that God can set the world right once and for all.

"And as it is appointed for men to die once, but after this the judgment" (Hebrews 9:27 NKJV). The appointed time to die is different for each person; but the day of judgment is the same for everyone. This is why it is important we pay attention to how we live our life, because God will surely bring everyone into account. The writer of Ecclesiastes advises that "The most important thing a person can do is to respect God and obey his commands, because he knows about everything people do— even the secret things. He knows about all the good and all the bad, and he will judge people for everything they do" (Ecclesiastes 12:13-14 ERV).

Where will this great event take place, and who will be the presiding judge? There is a general notion that it will take place in heaven immediately after death. But if you take a closer look at scriptures, you will realize that the eternal fate of every human being will be decided here on earth. The implication is that many of those who had died throughout history will need to be brought back to life to stand trial. And that's exactly what's going to happen. The Bible makes it clear that after the thousand years are over, the rest of the dead that did not partake in the first resurrection will do so in the second resurrection (Revelation 20:5). The second resurrection is not a resurrection to life, but a resurrection to judgment.

Jesus Himself makes it clear when He said, "Don't be so surprised! Indeed, the time is coming when all the dead in their graves will hear the voice of God's Son, and they will rise again. Those who have done good will rise to experience eternal life, and those who have continued in evil will rise to experience judgment" (John 5:28–29). Death and the world of the dead will give up all the dead they hold. Everyone, whether buried, cremated, or lost at sea will return to earth in their physical body to stand trial before their judge (Revelation 20:13). There will be no hiding place for anyone in the universe.

They will be judged by a fellow human being. This may come as a surprise to those who expect God the Father to be the judge. This responsibility has been given to none other than Jesus Himself (John 5:22). It is said that you cannot really make a fair judgment about someone until you've walked a mile in their shoes to understand their experiences, perspectives, motivations, and particular challenges. This is exactly what Jesus did. He shared our humanity under the same circumstances and pressures, felt what we feel, faced all of the same temptations and testings we face; yet He did not sin (Hebrews 4:15). You can be sure that His judgment will be absolutely just (John 5:30). Everyone will get a fair hearing. On that day, books that contain a record of everything we have done while in the body (our thoughts, words, and deeds, even our omissions) will be opened, and our entire life will be exposed. Everyone will be judged according to their records as contained in those biographical volumes.

So is there hope for anyone? Will the entire human race be condemned in that tribunal? Yes! There is hope. The entire human race will not be condemned. There is another book—the Book of Life. Anyone whose name was not found written in the Book of Life was thrown into the lake of fire where satan, the beast, and the false prophet already are. Everyone who is listed in that book will be discharged and acquitted. Not because they are innocent per se, but because by faith they voluntarily embraced God's kingdom and its way of life, and trusted in Jesus as their Savior, who already ransomed them with His blood. This is the new humanity that replaces the old. This is the "Homo novus" species that replaces the "Homo sapiens."

GOD AND HUMANITY REUNITED IN PARADISE

With the day of judgment over, the stage is now set for the redemption of the universe, and the transition from history to eternity. The new humanity needs a new universe to live and function, and God is pleased to give it to them. In his vision as recorded in the Book of Revelation, John tells us how he "saw a new heaven (skies or outer space) and a new earth, for the old heaven and the old earth had disappeared. And the sea was also gone" (Revelation 21:1). This clearly invokes the imagery of the very beginning of the Bible narrative when God created the heavens and the earth, and brought order to the dark chaotic waters. The entire universe will be reconstructed and there will be a renewed earth. Jesus will certainly be involved in this reconstruction, just as He was in the first.

The renewed earth will be the eternal residence of Jesus and the new humanity. But there is yet another pleasant surprise: the renewed earth will also be the eternal residence of God Himself. How do I know this? John tells us that he heard a loud shout from the throne, saying, "Look, God's home is now among his people! He will live with them, and they will be his people. God Himself will be with them!" The "loud shout from the throne" and the exclamation, "Look!" both convey a level of excitement and surprise that brings tears of joy. It is similar to the kind of joyous feeling you get when your dad, who has been on military service in a foreign land, suddenly returns home to reunite with his family. How would you react to that kind of surprise? As for me, I would scream very loudly, "OMG, I can't believe my eyes…daddy is back!"

Yes, our beloved Daddy is with us! He will wipe every tear from our eyes. We have imagined we would go to heaven and live with Him there forever. But He is coming down to live with us in the new earth. This time around, He will not be hidden away in the innermost part of a sacred physical building called a temple. In fact, there will be no need for a physical temple because the fullness of God's presence will be everywhere and in us. We are the temple. Just like in Eden, at the very beginning, His footsteps will be heard amongst us again, and we will see His face. God will reunite with His human family in our new home forever. This was the original home that Adam and Eve—and by implication all humanity—lost. God has been working tirelessly throughout history to make this day a reality. And at last, it is done. Heaven and earth, God and humanity, are finally reunited.

And guess what? The long lost Garden of Eden; the place where humanity once coexisted with God and experienced God's reign and rest, is finally restored. John was allowed to catch a glimpse of it in his vision. It was so spectacular that he could only describe it in terms of a bride coming down from heaven, beautifully adorned in all the splendor and radiance of the glory of God, or a city built of pure gold and sparkling precious stones.

> The wall was made of jasper, and the city was pure gold, as clear as glass. The wall of the city was built on foundation stones inlaid with twelve precious stones: the first was jasper, the second sapphire, the third agate, the fourth emerald, the fifth onyx, the sixth carnelian, the seventh chrysolite, the eighth beryl, the ninth topaz, the tenth chrysoprase, the eleventh jacinth, the twelfth amethyst (Revelation 21:18-20).

Interestingly, all of these twelve precious stones share something in common: they are in the class of what scientists call anisotropic stones. Unlike isotropic stones, which lose all of their color and appear black when viewed in crossed-polarized light or "pure" light, anisotropic stones transform their colors into all the colors of the rainbow, making them appear exceptionally beautiful and aesthetically pleasing to behold.[2] Is this a coincidence? Most definitely not! The creator God deliberately avoided stones that would lose their color and instead chose stones that disperse light to produce brilliant rainbow effects. John obviously lacked words to adequately describe what he saw; and all he could say was, "The brilliance of it resembled a rare and very precious jewel, like jasper, shining and clear as crystal" (Revelation 21:11b AMP).

And it is not just a garden. It is a garden city—the paradise city of eternal life with God. It is the "new Jerusalem"—where God dwells and reigns with His people forever. He saw the river of water of life, clear as crystal, flowing from the throne of God and the Lord Jesus. He also saw the tree of life, once forbidden to humanity after Adam and Eve were expelled from the garden, now accessible to all. It grows on each side of the river, eternally bearing fruit and providing an unending supply of eternal life for all humanity. Its leaves are for the healing of the nations. Its roots have access to the eternal river of life that flows from the throne of God. Jesus once made a commitment to the 1st century Church in Ephesus, who were facing severe persecution, that He would grant fruit from the tree of life in God's paradise to all those who emerged victorious (Revelation 2:7b). Now this promise is fulfilled precisely as pledged. The whole earth will be a re-creation of the garden, and God's personal presence will permeate every nook and cranny of the new restored creation.

The City doesn't need sun or moon for light. God's Glory is its light, the Lamb its lamp! The nations will walk in its light and earth's kings bring in their splendor. Its gates will never be shut by day, and there won't be any night. For most of history, the nations and their kings have been rebellious towards God. They rejected God's rule and rebuffed His attempt to restore Eden and get them back on track with Him. But God raised a new nation for Himself from all those willing to partner with Him and live under His rule. He called them out of the darkness into His wonderful light (1 Peter 2:9). Now here they come, bringing their glory and honor into the City through its wide open gates! None of those rebellious folks who had shown disdain for God and His rule will be allowed into the city. Only those whose names are written in the Lamb's Book of Life are welcome (Revelation 21).

It is finished! Evil has run its course and faded away into oblivion. Creation is now perfectly optimized to fulfill God's purpose. What humanity lost in the beginning is restored in the end. The story ends in a new beginning where humanity is restored to their place as God's true image and partners, ready to work with God and carry forward His will for the whole creation. There are new horizons in this new world and much work to be done. It will surely be an exciting time for all who keep God's commandments and maintain their testimony for Jesus! It's amazing that after a long period of separation, God and humanity have fully reunited as one family. And they lived happily ever after for eternity.

ACKNOWLEDGMENTS

I am forever grateful to David Pawson (who passed away while this project was ongoing), for imparting to me many valuable teachings from the Bible. I have also benefited immensely from the teaching of many writers and speakers, including Tim Mackie and Jon Collins of BibleProject, Michael Heiser (who also recently passed away), John Lennox, John H. Walton, N.T. Wright, and Myles Munroe and George Eldon Ladd of blessed memory. I could not have written this book without the invaluable inspiration and influence from these great servants of God.

I express my gratitude to Fleur Marie Vaz, my editor, for her valuable feedback and advice, and ensuring that the message of this book is conveyed effectively. I also want to thank my good friend Justin Mbanu for all the help provided. Finally, I am thankful to my dear wife Sarah, and my two children Dara and Baruch, for their unwavering support and encouragement throughout this project.

NOTES

Introduction

1. This term was first used by David Pawson to describe the new man or the new humanity in Christ. See David Pawson, *Unlocking the Bible* (Great Britain: HarperCollinsPublishers, 2007), 59-60.

Chapter One: In The Beginning

1. World History Encyclopedia, s.v. "Enuma Elish - The Babylonian Epic of Creation - Full Text," accessed June 5, 2018, https://www.worldhistory.org/article/225/enuma-elish---the-babylonian-epic-of-creation---fu/1.

2. "The Creation Myth," Canadian Museum of History, accessed June 5, 2018, https://www.historymuseum.ca/cmc/exhibitions/civil/egypt/egcr09e.html.

3. Hermann Bondi and Thomas Gold, "The Steady-State Theory of the Expanding Universe," *Monthly Notices of the Royal Astronomical Society* Volume 108, Issue 3 (1948): 4-19. https://academic.oup.com/mnras/article/108/3/252/2603423?login=false

4. This is a modified version of the one by David Pawson. David Pawson, Christianity Explained (Great Britain: Anchor Recordings Ltd, 2014), 10-11.

5. John H. Walton, *The Lost World of Genesis One: Ancient Cosmology and the Origins Debate* (Illinois: InterVarsity Press, 2009), 23-50.

6. Wikipedia, s.v. "Observable universe," accessed January 11, 2023, https://en.wikipedia.org/wiki/Observable_universe.

7. Maggie Masetti, "How Many Stars in the Milky Way?" National

Aeronautics and Space Administration Goddard Space Flight Center, July 22, 2015, https://asd.gsfc.nasa.gov/blueshift/index.php/2015/07/22/how-many-stars-in-the-milky-way/.

8. Britannica, s.v. "How Do We Know How Far Away the Stars Are?" accessed January 11, 2023, https://www.britannica.com/story/how-do-we-know-how-far-away-the-stars-are.

9. Wikipedia, s.v. "Galaxy," accessed January 11, 2023, https://en.wikipedia.org/wiki/Galaxy.

10. John H. Walton, *The Lost World of Genesis One: Ancient Cosmology and the Origins Debate* (Illinois: InterVarsity Press, 2009), 78-86.

11. Yuval Noah Harari, *Sapiens: A Brief History of Humankind* (United Kingdom: Harvill Secker, 2014), 11.

12. John Lennox, *God's Undertaker: Has Science Buried God?* (England: Lion Hudson Plc, 2009), 169.

13. John Lennox, "Can Science Explain Everything?" Biola University, July 26, 2019, https://www.biola.edu/blogs/think-biblically/2019/can-science-explain-everything.

14. Quoted in Stephen Hawking, *A Brief History of Time: From the Big Bang to Black Holes* (New York: Bantam, 1988), 129-130.

15. John, Lennox, "Can You Be a Scientist and Believe in God?" Just Thinking, March 2019, http://hiskingdom.us/wp-content/uploads/2019/03/Scientist-God-Lennox.pdf.

16. Ted Davis, "The Faith of a Great Scientist: Robert Boyle's Religious Life, Attitudes, and Vocation," Biologos, August 08, 2013, https://biologos.org/articles/the-faith-of-a-great-scientist-robert-boyles-religious-life-attitudes-and-vocation.

17. Geoffrey Cantor, "Michael Faraday's religion and its relation to his science," *Science Direct* Volume 22, Issue 3 (1998): 121-124. https://www.sciencedirect.com/science/article/abs/pii/S016093279801134X.

18. Wikipedia, s.v. "Georges Lemaître," accessed December 10, 2018, https://en.wikipedia.org/wiki/Georges_Lema%C3%AEtre.

19. Used with permission. Carroll, Sean. Core Theory of Physics Equation. January 2013, JPEG Image. https://www.preposterousuniverse.com/blog/wp-content/uploads/2013/01/Everyday-Equation.jpg.

20. John H, Walton, *The Lost World of Genesis One: Ancient Cosmology and the Origins Debate* (Illinois: InterVarsity Press, 2009), 47-90.

21. Inspired by Dr. John Phillips' message on "The Origin of the Universe." Mixxkid 17, "The Origin of the Universe by Dr. John Phillips," Mixxkid

17, published on April 26, 2022, YouTube video, 36:26, https://www.youtube.com/watch?v=Hob6rEZ_sgs&t=109s.

22. Inspired by Mixxkid 17, The Origin of the Universe by Dr. John Phillips, YouTube video

23. Inspired by Mixxkid 17, The Origin of the Universe by Dr. John Phillips, YouTube video

24. Ted Davis, "Theistic Evolution: History and Beliefs," Biologos, October 15, 2012, https://biologos.org/series/science-and-the-bible/articles/theistic-evolution-history-and-beliefs.

25. This is a revised and updated version of the one described by David Pawson. David Pawson, Unlocking The Bible (Great Britain: HarperCollinsPublishers, 2007), 59-60.

26. Harari, *Sapiens: A Brief History of Humankind*, 234

Chapter Two: The Divine Mandate

1. John Lennox, "Beyond Reason?" Ligonier, September 1, 2010, https://www.ligonier.org/learn/articles/beyond-reason.

2. John H. Walton, *The NIV Application Commentary: Genesis* (Michigan: Zondervan Academic, 2001), 65-100.

3. Inspired by BibleProject, "Understand the Image of God in the Bible," BibleProject, published on March 21, 2016, YouTube video, 6:16, https://www.youtube.com/watch?v=YbipxLDtY8c.

4. Inspired by BibleProject, Understand the Image of God in the Bible, YouTube video

5. Pawson, *Christianity Explained*, 47.

6. Inspired by Andy Patton, "I'm a New Human?" BibleProject, accessed January 4, 2021, https://bibleproject.com/blog/new-human/.

7. raytex111, "Salvador - Shine," Salvador, published on Nov 27, 2011, YouTube video, 3:25, https://www.youtube.com/watch?v=AePAUrlGQfA&list=RDAePAUrlGQfA&index=1.

8. Quoted in BibleProject, "Heaven and Earth," BibleProject, published on May 20, 2014, YouTube video, 6:42, https://www.youtube.com/watch?v=Zy2AQlK6C5k.

9. Timothy Mackie and Jonathan Collins, *When Heaven Meets Earth* (Portland: The Bible Project, 2017), 23, PDF Ebook.

10. Quoted in BibleProject, Heaven and Earth, YouTube video.

11. Mackie and Collins, *When Heaven Meets Earth*, 23.

12. Vaughan Roberts, *God's Big Picture: Tracing the storyline of the Bible* (USA: InterVarsity Press, 2002), 22.

13. Harari, *Sapiens: A Brief History of Humankind*, 11

14. Wesley J. Smith, "When Animals Sue," NATIONAL REVIEW, March 3, 2010, https://www.nationalreview.com/2010/03/when-animals-sue-wesley-j-smith/.

15. Wikipedia, s.v. "Rights of nature," accessed February 4, 2019, https://en.wikipedia.org/wiki/Rights_of_nature.

16. David Hodgson, *Rationality + consciousness = free will* (New York: Oxford University Press, 2012), 37–53.

17. Hodgson, *Rationality + consciousness = free will*, 37–53.

18. Hodgson, 37–53.

19. Hodgson, 37–53.

Chapter Three: Rebellion in Paradise

1. Roberts, *God's Big Picture: Tracing the story Line of the Bible*, 39.

2. Michael S. Heiser, *The Unseen Realm* (Bellingham: Lexham Press, 2015), 66-67.

3. Heiser, *The Unseen Realm* 56-60.

4. Heiser, 61-69.

5. Quoted in Michael S. Heiser, *What Does God Want?* (United States: Blind Spot Press, 2018), 15.

6. Pawson, *Unlocking The Bible*, 60.

7. BibleProject, Understand the Image of God in the Bible, YouTube video

Chapter Four: Civilization and the Illusion of Progress

1. Quoted in William Whiston and Paul I. Maier, *The New Complete Works of Josephus* (Grand Rapids: Kregel Publications, 1999), 56.

2. Heiser, 113-115.

3. Heiser, 110-115.

4. Wikipedia, s.v. "Ancient_technology," accessed February 21, 2019, https://en.wikipedia.org/wiki/Ancient_technology

5. Wikipedia, s.v. "Ancient_technology," accessed February 21, 2019,

https://en.wikipedia.org/wiki/Ancient_technology

6. Joshua J. Mark, "Religion in the Ancient World," World History Encyclopedia, published March 23, 2018, https://www.worldhistory.org/religion/.

7. Wikipedia, s.v. "Egyptian hieroglyphs," accessed April 14, 2022, https://en.wikipedia.org/wiki/Egyptian_hieroglyphs

8. Wikipedia, s.v. "Etymology of chemistry," accessed March 10, 2019, https://en.wikipedia.org/wiki/Etymology_of_chemistry

9. Wikipedia, s.v. "Ancient technology,"

10. Timothy D. Boyle, *The Gospel Hidden In Ancient Chinese Characters* (USA: XulonPress, 2015), 1-147.

11. Wikipedia, s.v. "Son of Heaven," accessed February 21, 2019, https://en.wikipedia.org/wiki/Son_of_Heaven

12. Wikipedia, s.v. "Ancient technology,"

13. Mark, "Religion in the Ancient World," World History Encyclopedia.

14. Andrea Messer, "Maya plumbing, first pressurized water feature found in New World, published *May 4, 2010*, https://web.archive.org/web/20130208225152/http://live.psu.edu/story/46532.

15. Wikipedia, s.v. "Ancient technology,"

16. Quoted in A. W. Pink, *The Total Depravity of Man* (Tigard: Monergism Books, 2012), 11-25, https://www.monergism.com/thethreshold/sdg/depravity_nook.html.

17. Conservapedia, s.v. "Idea of Progress," accessed March 2, 2019, https://www.conservapedia.com/Idea_of_Progress

18. Martin G. Collins, "What the Bible says about Missing the Mark," Bible Tools, accessed March 12, 2019, https://www.bibletools.org/index.cfm/fuseaction/topical.show/RTD/cgg/ID/1678/Missing-Mark.htm

19. Quoted in Pink, *The Total Depravity of Man*, 11-25.

20. Harari, *Sapiens: A Brief History of Humankind*, 352

Chapter Five: God's Rescue Operation

1. Steve Cutts, "MAN," Steve Cutts, published on December 21, 2012, YouTube video, 3:36, https://www.youtube.com/watch?v=WfGMYdalClU.

2. Quoted in Roberts, *God's Big Picture: Tracing the storyline of the Bible*, 22.

3. Pawson, *Unlocking The Bible*, 11

4. Richard T. Ritenbaugh, "What the Bible says about Artaxerxes I," Bible Tools, accessed May 21, 2019, https://www.bibletools.org/index.cfm/fuseaction/Topical.show/RTD/cgg/ID/312/Artaxerxes-I.htm

Chapter Six: Freedom of the Will

1. Andrea Lavazza, "Free Will and Neuroscience: From Explaining Freedom Away to New Ways of Operationalizing and Measuring It," Frontiers, Published 01 June 2016, https://www.frontiersin.org/articles/10.3389/fnhum.2016.00262/full

2. Lüder Deecke, "Hirnpotentialänderungen bei Willkürbewegungen und passiven Bewegungen des Menschen: Bereitschaftspotential u. reafferente Potentiale," ResearchGate, accessed March 24, 2019, https://www.researchgate.net/publication/34700192_Hirnpotentialanderungen_bei_Willkurbewegungen_und_passiven_Bewegungen_des_Menschen_Bereitschaftspotential_u_reafferente_Potentiale_Ausz_Mit_7_Textabb

3. Benjamin Libet, "Unconscious cerebral initiative and the role of conscious will in voluntary action," Wayback Machine, accessed March 24, 2019, https://web.archive.org/web/20131219012821/http://selfpace.uconn.edu/class/ccs/Libet1985UcsCerebralInitiative.pdf

4. Aaron Schurger et al, "An accumulator model for spontaneous neural activity prior to self-initiated movement," National Library of Medicine, Published October 16, 2012, https://www.ncbi.nlm.nih.gov/pmc/articles/PMC3479453/.

5. Anil Ananthaswamy, "Brain might not stand in the way of free will," *NewScientist*, August

6, 2012, https://www.newscientist.com/article/dn22144-brain-might-not-stand-in-the-way-of-free-will/.

6. Bahar Gholipour, "A Famous Argument Against Free Will Has Been Debunked," *The Atlantic*, SEPTEMBER 10, 2019, https://www.theatlantic.com/health/archive/2019/09/free-will-bereitschaftspotential/597736/.

7. Azim F. Shariff and Kathleen D. Vohs, "What Happens to a Society That Does Not Believe in Free Will?," *NewScientist*, June 1, 2014, https://www.scientificamerican.com/article/what-happens-to-a-society-that-does-not-believe-in-free-will/.

8. Alex Yijia Ding, "Blame the Brain: Neuroscience for Action in Criminal

Courtrooms," Intersect: The Stanford Journal of Science, Technology, and Society Volume 11, Issue 2 (2018): 1-16. https://ojs.stanford.edu/ojs/index.php/intersect/article/download/1163/1115/4739.

9. Stephen Cave, "There's No Such Thing as Free Will," *The Atlantic,* June, 2016, https://www.theatlantic.com/magazine/archive/2016/06/theres-no-such-thing-as-free-will/480750/.

10.Paul Lewis, "'Our minds can be hijacked': the tech insiders who fear a smartphone dystopia," The Guardian, published October 6, 2017, https://www.theguardian.com/technology/2017/oct/05/smartphone-addiction-silicon-valley-dystopia.

11. Shoshana Zuboff, "You Are Now Remotely Controlled," The New York Times, published January 24, 2020, https://www.nytimes.com/2020/01/24/opinion/sunday/surveillance-capitalism.htm.

12. John Naughton, "'The goal is to automate us': welcome to the age of surveillance capitalism," The Guardian, published January 20, 2019, https://www.nytimes.com/2020/01/24/opinion/sunday/surveillance-capitalism.htm.

13. Sun Tzu, *The Art of War* (Boston: Shambhala Publications, 1988), 32-54.

14. Simon McCarthy-Jones, "'Artificial intelligence is a totalitarian's dream – here's how to take power back," The Conversation, published August 12, 2020, https://theconversation.com/artificial-intelligence-is-a-totalitarians-dream-heres-how-to-take-power-back-143722.

Chapter Seven: Homo Sapiens: An Endangered Species

1. "UN Report: Nature's Dangerous Decline 'Unprecedented'; Species Extinction Rates 'Accelerating'," United nations, Date published May 6, 2019, https://www.un.org/sustainabledevelopment/blog/2019/05/nature-decline-unprecedented-report/.

2. Paul Rincon, "Stephen Hawking's warnings: What he predicted for the future," BBC, published March 15, 2018, https://www.bbc.com/news/science-environment-43408961.

3. Nick Bostrom, "The Future of Humanity," Nick Bostrom, accessed May 19, 2021, https://nickbostrom.com/papers/future.

4. Andrew Anthony, " Yuval Noah Harari: 'Homo sapiens as we know them will disappear in a century or so'," The Guardian, published July 9, 2021, https://www.theguardian.com/culture/2017/mar/19/yuval-harari-sapiens-readers-questions-lucy-prebble-arianna-huffington-future-of-humanity.

5. Nick Bostrom, "The Future of Humanity," accessed May 19, 2021.

6.Hannah Devlin, "Scientist who edited babies' genes says he acted 'too quickly'," The Guardian, published February 4, 2023, https://www.theguardian.com/science/2023/feb/04/scientist-edited-babies-genes-acted-too-quickly-he-jiankui.

7. Beth Mole, "Musk's bid to start Neuralink human trials denied by FDA in 2022, report says'," Ars Technica, published March 2, 2023, https://arstechnica.com/science/2023/03/musks-bid-to-start-neuralink-human-trials-denied-by-fda-in-2022-report-says/.

8. *Wikipedia*, s.v. "Mind uploading," accessed May 11, 2021, https://en.wikipedia.org/wiki/Mind_uploading#%22Immortality%22_or_backup.

9. *Wikipedia*, s.v. " BRAIN Initiative," accessed May 11, 2021, https://en.wikipedia.org/wiki/BRAIN_Initiative#Background.

10. "EBRAINS Cellular Level Simulation," EBRAINS, accessed March 14, 2021, https://ebrains-cls-interactive.github.io/.

11. "2045 Strategic Social Initiative," 2045, accessed March 14, 2021, http://2045.com/.

12. *Britannica*, s.v. " singularity technology," accessed May 15, 2021, https://www.britannica.com/technology/singularity-technology.

13. Vernor Vinge, "Technological Singularity," Carnegie Mellon University, published March 30-31, 1993, https://frc.ri.cmu.edu/~hpm/book98/com.ch1/vinge.singularity.html.

14. Zoë Corbyn, "Could 'young' blood stop us getting old?" The Guardian, published February 2, 2020, https://www.theguardian.com/society/2020/feb/02/could-young-blood-stop-us-getting-old-transfusions-experiments-mice-plasma.

15. Tom Hartsfield, "Horror stories of cryonics: The gruesome fates of futurists hoping for immortality," Big Think, published August 3, 2022, https://bigthink.com/the-future/cryonics-horror-stories/.

16. Quoted in N.T. Wright, *Surprised by Hope* (New York: HarperCollins Publications, 2007), 86.

Chapter Eight: Homo Novus: The Emerging Species

1. Yuval Noah Harari, *Homo Deus: A Brief History of Tomorrow* (New York: HarperCollins Publications, 2017), 30.

2. David Pawson, *Explaining The Resurrection* (Great Britain: Anchor Recordings Ltd, 2016), 26.

3. Pawson, *Explaining The Resurrection, 16-17*

4. Pawson, *17*

5, Pawson, *Unlocking The Bible*, 642.

6. B. Nathaniel Sullivan, "The Drawing Power of Biblical Apologetics," Word Foundations, published May 18, 2018, https://www.wordfoundations.com/2018/05/18/the-drawing-power-of-biblical-apologetics/.

7. Quoted in Pawson, *Explaining The Resurrection, 20*

8. *Wikipedia*, s.v. "Albert Henry Ross," accessed June 3, 2021, https://en.wikipedia.org/wiki/Albert_Henry_Ross.

9, *Wikipedia*, s.v. "Leo Strobel," accessed June 3, 2021, https://en.wikipedia.org/wiki/Lee_Strobel

10. Quoted in Wright, *Surprised by Hope*, 99.

11. Quoted in George Eldon Ladd, *The Gospel of the Kingdom*, 20.

Chapter Nine: God's Sovereignty Over World Superpowers

1. Quoted in Blaise Pascal, *Pensées* (New York: Penguin Books, 1966), 75.

2. Janna Anderson and Lee Rainie, "Many Tech Experts Say Digital Disruption Will Hurt Democracy, Pew Research Center, published February 21, 2020, https://www.pewresearch.org/internet/2020/02/21/many-tech-experts-say-digital-disruption-will-hurt-democracy/.

3. Quoted in David Pawson, *Kingdoms in Conflict* (Great Britain: Anchor Recordings Ltd, 2015), 10-11.

4. Adnan Abu Zeed, "Prized Lion of Babylon joins list of crumbling Iraqi antiquities, Al-Monitor, published June 29, 2016, https://www.al-monitor.com/originals/2016/06/iraq-babylon-culture-heritage.html.

5. Quoted in *Wikipedia*, s.v. "Cyrus the Great," accessed April 3, 2022, https://en.wikipedia.org/wiki/Cyrus_the_Great#Rise_and_military_campaigns.

6. Quoted in *Wikipedia*, s.v. "Cyrus the Great," accessed April 3, 2022,

7. National Geographic, "10 Leopard Facts! National Geographic Kids, accessed April 5, 2022, https://www.natgeokids.com/uk/discover/animals/general-animals/leopard-facts/.

8. *Wikipedia*, s.v. Alexander the Great," accessed April 5, 2022, https://en.wikipedia.org/wiki/Alexander_the_Great.

9. Quoted in *Wikipedia*, s.v. Alexander the Great," accessed April 5, 2022,

10. Joshua J. Mark, "Western Roman Empire, World History, published September 27, 2019, https://www.worldhistory.org/Western_Roman_Empire/.

11. Guinness World Records, "Longest lasting empire in history, Guinness World Records, accessed April 5, 2022, https://www.guinnessworldrecords.com/world-records/longest-lasting-empire-in-history.

12. Yuval Noah Harari, *21 Lessons for the 21st Century* (New York City: Random House Publishing, 2019), 56.

Chapter Ten: Countdown to the Final World Superpower

1. Yuval Noah Harari, "Why Technology Favors Tyranny," The Atlantic, October, 2018, https://www.theatlantic.com/magazine/archive/2018/10/yuval-noah-harari-technology-tyranny/568330/.

2. Freedom House, "New Report: The global decline in democracy has accelerated", Freedom House, accessed March 3, 2021, https://freedomhouse.org/article/new-report-global-decline-democracy-has-accelerated.

3. Kenneth L. Gentry, *Before Jerusalem Fell* (United States: Dominion Press, 1989), 74-83

4. Quoted in N.T. Wright, *Revelation* for Everyone (Great Britain: Society for Promoting Christian knowledge, 2011), 122

5. D.R Hillers, *"Revelation 13:18 and a Scroll from Murabba'at,"* Bulletin of the American Society of Overseas Research Volume 170, (1963): 65.

6. Catherine A. Cory, *The Book of Revelation*, (Minnesota: Liturgical Press, 2006), 61

7. Peter M. Head, "Some Recently Published Nt Papyri From Oxyrhynchus: An Overview And Preliminary Assessment", Wayback Machine, accessed June 12, 2022, https://web.archive.org/web/20110706055831/http://98.131.162.170//tynbul/library/TynBull_2000_51_1_01_Head_OxyrhynchusPapyri.pdf.

8. Pawson, *Unlocking The Bible*, 833-834

9. Quoted in Tacitus, *The Annals: The Reigns of Tiberius, Claudius, and Nero* (Oxford: Oxford University Press, 2008), 399

10. Phillip Schaff, *"The City of God*, Christian"*, Classic Ethereal Library, accessed May 3, 2022, https://www.ccel.org/ccel/schaff/npnf102/Page_438.html.

11. Step Yoshi, "Tomba di Nerone (Tomb of Nero)," Atlas Obscura, June 13, 2020, https://www.atlasobscura.com/places/tomb-of-nero.

12. D. Ragan Ewing, "The Identification Of Babylon The Harlot In The Book Of Revelation", Bible.org, published May 10,2004, https://bible.org/seriespage/chapter-3-dating-apocalypse.

13. Quoted in N.T. Wright, *Revelation* For Everyone, 122

14. Quoted in Bruce Schneier, "The Internet Of Things Will Be The World's Biggest Robot", Forbes, published February 2, 2016, https://www.forbes.com/sites/bruceschneier/2016/02/02/the-internet-of-things-will-be-the-worlds-biggest-robot/?sh=5bc2c4ff7b07.

15. Quoted in Alan Turing, "Intelligent Machinery, A Heretical Theory", Uberty, accessed July 8, 2022, https://uberty.org/wp-content/uploads/2015/02/intelligent-machinery-a-heretical-theory.pdf.

16. Hein de Haan, "Deus in Machina: Is Humanity Creating God?", Becoming Human, published August 9, 2019, https://becominghuman.ai/deus-in-machina-d9ec989e1e86.

17. Open Letter, "Pause Giant AI Experiments: An Open Letter", Future of Life, published March 22, 2023, https://futureoflife.org/open-letter/pause-giant-ai-experiments/?mc_cid=36c6571df6&mc_eid=05f2f4d62e.

18. Nick Bostrom, "What is a Singleton?", Nick Bostrom, accessed July 8, 2022, https://nickbostrom.com/fut/singleton.

19. Quoted in Max Tegmark, *Life 3.0: Being Human in the Age of Artificial Intelligence* (New York: Alfred A. Knopf, 2017), 118-119

20. Adapted from a scene in the Animatrix movie. Cyber Chaos Crew, "The Animatrix - The Second Renaissance Part I," Warner Bros, published on August 5, 2019, YouTube video, 4:33, https://www.youtube.com/watch?v=sU8RunvBRZ8&list=PL75iSW76AqFmZgkYFEpKmPa1KsFmyRBXi.

Chapter Eleven: The New Humanity

1. Quoted in N.T. Wright, *Surprised by Hope*, 137

2. Joel, "The 12 Foundation Stones in New Jerusalem", Christian Evidence, published September 21, 2018, https://www.christianevidence.net/2018/09/the-12-foundation-stones-in-new.html.

INDEX